BACKLASH

Backlash

Libel, Impeachment, and Populism in the Reign of Queen Anne

RACHEL CARNELL

University of Virginia Press • *Charlottesville and London*

University of Virginia Press

Printed in the United States of America on acid-free paper

First published 2020

9 8 7 6 5 4 3 2 1

Library of Congress Cataloging-in-Publication Data

Names: Carnell, Rachel, author.
Title: Backlash : libel, impeachment, and populism in the reign of Queen Anne / Rachel Carnell.
Description: Charlottesville ; London : University of Virginia Press, 2020. | Includes bibliographical references and index.
Identifiers: LCCN 2020024990 (print) | LCCN 2020024991 (ebook) | ISBN 9780813944425 (hardcover) | ISBN 9780813944449 (ebook)
Subjects: LCSH: Great Britain—History—Anne, 1702–1714. | Great Britain—Politics and government—1702–1714. | Anne, Queen of Great Britain, 1665–1714. | Great Britain. Parliament—History—18th century. | Political parties—Great Britain—History. | Great Britain—Court and courtiers—Biography.
Classification: LCC DA495 .C37 2020 (print) | LCC DA495 (ebook) | DDC 941.06/9—dc23
LC record available at https://lccn.loc.gov/2020024990
LC ebook record available at https://lccn.loc.gov/2020024991

Cover art: Portrait of Queen Anne, Michael Dahl, oil on canvas, ca. 1702. (© National Portrait Gallery, London)

In memory of my mother,
Sue Powel Carnell (1937–2017)

CONTENTS

Acknowledgments ix

A Note about Texts, Dates, and Terminology xi

Introduction: Backlash Then and Now 1

1 A "Very Murdering" Battle and a Salacious Court Memoir 7

2 Secret History and Seditious Libel 32

3 A Provocative Tory Sermon 57

4 The General Who Would Be King 85

5 A Female Satirist in Court 112

6 Impeachment and Public Opinion 134

7 Impeached but Triumphant 164

8 A Tory Victory Lap and Parliamentary Elections 192

Epilogue: Why the Backlash of 1710 Matters Today 221

Notes 235

Bibliography 263

Index 273

Illustrations follow page 124.

ACKNOWLEDGMENTS

I AM GRATEFUL to everyone who supported this book in its early stages, including my parents, John and Sue Carnell, neither of whom, unfortunately, lived to see it come to fruition. Ruth Herman and Bob Owens deserve credit for introducing me to the life and works of Delarivier Manley. Chris Mounsey has provided invigorating intellectual conversations for over two decades, and delicious meals whenever I am in London. Paula Bloch attentively read through each chapter in sequence, over the course of the year I was writing. Carole Sargent saw value in this project from our first conversation about it. She also generously provided images from *The New Atalantis* and *Memoirs of Europe* from her own Manley collection. At Cleveland State University, Jeff Karem and Jerzy Sawicki have been enthusiastic supporters of my research as long as I have known them. This book could not have been completed without Faculty Scholarship Initiative grants from Cleveland State University's Office of Research for the summers of 2018 and 2019. Will Dube has been a savvy marketer and invaluable in bringing my op-eds based on this research to newspaper readers around the globe. Jane Dugan, Lori O'Laughlin, and Mark Wirtz have provided daily support and friendship in the English Department.

I appreciate the assistance of the staff at the British Library, the National Archive (UK), and Cleveland State University's Ohiolink and Interlibrary Loan departments. Alexa Frost at the Blenheim Archive and Emma Stuart at the Royal Collections Trust, Windsor, were both extremely helpful during my visits. I am grateful to the Fellows of Magdalen College, Oxford University, for permission to reproduce a portrait of Henry Sacheverell and to Rachel Mehta for assistance with the image transfer. Chatham Ewing, at the Cleveland Public Library, was generous with his time and expertise in digital imaging. John Ball, at the University of Akron Library, Archival Services, was incredibly helpful, as was William Claspy, head of Special Collections at Kelvin Smith Library, Case Western Reserve University.

Angie Hogan and Ellen Satrom, at the University of Virginia Press, have been a terrific team during the publishing process. Two anonymous peer reviewers offered comments that greatly improved the manuscript, and Marjorie Panell provided thoughtful suggestions for developing the epilogue. Writing this book would not have been so pleasurable without the daily companionship of my husband and daughter, Gregory and Alison Lupton. My mother, to whom I dedicate this book, was a kindred spirit and my best friend.

A NOTE ABOUT TEXTS, DATES, AND TERMINOLOGY

DURING THE ERA encompassed by the events described in this book, there was a ten-day difference between dates in continental Europe, where New Style (Gregorian) dating was used, and in Britain, where Old Style (Julian) dates were still in use until 1752. Most events in this narrative, with the exception of battles on the Continent (given with the New Style dates used in military histories about them), are referred to with Old Style dating. Letters written on the Continent (e.g., from the Duke of Marlborough to family and colleagues in England) are cited with their NS dates, while letters written in Britain are cited OS. Thus I refer to the Battle of Malplaquet as taking place on 11 September 1709 (NS), but the letters his wife and Sidney Godolphin write to Marlborough about it (in OS) may appear to predate it. In this era, the civil or legal year in England did not begin until 25 March, but I follow the standard modern convention of dating, with the year starting on 1 January.

Citations are from primary sources whenever feasible, and I have retained the original spelling, capitalization, and italicization. In the case of materials available only through secondary sources, the formating has in some cases been modernized. When the letter writer uses a cipher (usually a coded numbering system in which Queen Anne was, for example, sometimes 42, and the Duke of Marlborough 39), I have replaced the number with the person's name.

In this era, the term "ministry" was often used to refer to the government ministers or members of a monarch's cabinet. Thus there was a "change of ministry" when Queen Anne overhauled her cabinet, as she did in February 1708 and again in the summer of 1710. Because of the mix of politics and religion in this work, potential confusion arises for modern readers more accustomed to the religious than the political meaning of the term "ministry," and I have attempted (outside of citations) to use the term "cabinet" to refer to her group of cabinet ministers.

BACKLASH

INTRODUCTION

Backlash Then and Now

In the early years of the twenty-first century, there seemed reason for Americans and Britons to celebrate their respective nations' progress in upholding democracy, equality, and international cooperation. The United States elected its first African American president in 2008, and by 2013 the United Kingdom had reached its fourth decade as a member of the European Union, a union that was guaranteeing peace among a group of nations that in previous centuries had regularly been convulsed by war—from the Hundred Years' War in the thirteenth century to the world wars of the twentieth. By 2016, however, signs of a backlash had started appearing. A real estate magnate known for anti-immigrant race baiting was elected president of the United States, and British voters, in a referendum, chose to exit the EU. Calls to impeach President Trump in the United States in the first thousand days of his term were countered by concerns that impeachment would ignite populist support for him. Yet even as impeachment hearings began in Congress in the autumn of 2019, Trump bragged about his disregard for presidential conventions and congressional oversight. He repeatedly suggested that he was above the rule of law; he even falsely asserted in July 2019 that Article II of the US Constitution gave him the right to do whatever he wanted as president. He ordered members of his own staffs to defy congressional subpoenas in the impeachment proceedings. Brexit produced a simultaneous political crisis in the UK, with Parliament and Prime Minister Boris Johnson still struggling in 2020 to reach consensus on the details of Britain's departure from Europe. In September 2019 the UK Supreme Court was obliged to intervene to reverse Johnson's prorogation of Parliament in the middle of critical debates about Brexit.

While these contemporary political situations may feel unprecedented, three centuries ago, in the winter of 1709, Great Britain experienced a similar backlash and similar partisan battles following three decades of political liberalization. This period of liberalization began during the Glorious Revolution of 1688–89 when Parliament authorized a political coup against James II, a Catholic, by declaring his Protestant son-in-law and daughter, William (of Orange) and Mary, the new monarchs of England. In 1689, William and Mary signed into law the Bill of Rights, establishing Parliament and the rule of law as more powerful than the monarch and ensuring basic liberties to individual citizens. Parliament also passed the Toleration Act, which allowed Dissenting Protestants—including Presbyterians, Quakers, and other Protestants who did not take communion in the Church of England—to practice their religion freely. In 1695 a new era of press freedom commenced, without the censoring constraints of a government licensor. In 1707 England passed the Act of Union with Scotland, joining the two nations into Great Britain. Meanwhile, the British commander John, Duke of Marlborough, was scoring military victories over the absolute monarch Louis XIV, helping to establish a European balance of power between Protestant and Catholic nations. By 1709 the Whigs in Britain were proud of the political progress they had made in defending their Protestant parliamentary monarchy and the rule of law against the threat of Catholic absolutism.

Every year since 1689 there had been sermons on Guy Fawkes Day, 5 November, celebrating Britain's double victory against Catholicism—first in foiling the Gunpowder Plot of 1605 and second in William of Orange's landing on English soil on 5 November 1688. Every November, sermons celebrated the "Revolution principles" that had underpinned the government since 1689. However, on 5 November 1709, a Tory clergyman preached a sermon praising passive obedience to the monarch, implicitly repudiating those principles. That same week a Whig government official arrested a best-selling Tory satirist for libel, contradicting prior Whig support for a free press. A few weeks later, Parliament voted to impeach the Tory preacher, a clergyman in the Church of England, for publishing his sermon. Convulsed by anger over the prosecution of a provocative but popular clergyman, many citizens took to the streets in protest and mob riots, often destroying churches where Dissenting Protestants worshiped. These riots were exacerbated by populist anger stemming from a bad harvest, the increasing costs of a foreign war, and an influx of German-speaking immigrants from Europe. The backlash against three decades of "progress" since the Glorious Revolution had begun.

Queen Anne, the ruler of Great Britain from 1702 to 1714 (second daughter of James II, who inherited the throne after the deaths of William and Mary), did her best to navigate the populist uprisings in the spring of 1710. (That crisis is the backdrop to the events of the 2018 film, *The Favourite.*)[1] Queen Anne, while not adept at witty court conversation, was not the dim, impulsive figure depicted in the film. She had a profound respect for the rule of law and for parliamentary procedure, even if she differed with the Whigs about military policy. Although the Marlboroughs and the Whigs did lose their grip on power that year, it was not because of a lesbian love triangle at court but because of disagreements over when to negotiate a peace treaty with France in the War of Spanish Succession, which saw the Grand Alliance of Protestant nations fighting against France and Spain to curb French power and preserve a balance of power between Protestant and Catholics countries in Europe after Louis XIV supported his Catholic grandson, Philip, in claiming the throne of Spain in 1702, joining an already powerful France with an extensive Spanish empire.

The conflict in Britain that winter, then, was at least in part over the extent of Britain's engagement in the affairs of European nations, to some of which British monarchs were linked by birth or marriage. Sentiment in Britain was divided between the Tories, who wanted to reach a swift, separate peace agreement with France, and the Whigs, who wanted to continue the war until there was what they considered an "honorable" peace satisfactory for all of Protestant Europe. Queen Anne had sided with the Whigs about military policy since she ascended to the throne in 1702, but her patience with the costs of and sacrifices required by the war was wearing thin by 1709, and she was being persuaded toward the Tory point of view by Robert Harley. The Tories wanted to pull back from Europe, negotiate a separate peace with France, and leave the Protestant Allies to their separate negotiations, while the Whigs saw Britain as an integral part of a Protestant Europe and felt morally obliged to continue the war until the demands of all the Allies were met.

The two leading political parties were also divided in their response to immigration. In the summer of 1709, the Whigs welcomed waves of impoverished German-speaking Protestant refugees from the Palatine region of Germany, believing these "poor Palatines" would become industrious workers whose labor would help expand the domestic economy. Tories viewed these new arrivals as indolent "gypsies" or "vermin" who would sap the charitable resources needed by more deserving native Britons. The needs of both Britons and migrant laborers had soared after a bad winter, a poor harvest, and rising grain prices. Queen Anne was initially sympathetic to the plight of the immigrants but later became concerned about the unrest their presence was sparking in London.

At the same time as the immigrant issues were unfolding and questions about involvement in the affairs of the Continent were heating up, Britain was also experiencing a backlash against religious minorities. Many high church clergymen and their parishioners viewed the Toleration Act of 1689 as placing the nation's "true" church in danger. The Whigs, the party supporting toleration, made a tactical error in the winter of 1709 when they began impeachment proceedings against Dr. Henry Sacheverell for his provocative Guy Fawkes Day sermon against toleration and the Glorious Revolution. Sacheverell's impeachment trial in the spring of 1710 brought mobs of angry, often violent protesters out into the streets. Queen Anne, although a loyal member of the Church of England, nevertheless respected the law of religious toleration and prosecuted the protestors, who mistakenly felt they were supporting her and the national church.

In broader terms, Britain was convulsively reacting to several decades of what could be called the progress of liberalism. When Parliament asserted its authority and placed constraints on monarchical power in the 1689 Bill of Rights, it also set the stage for liberal notions of individual liberty to prevail and for the establishment of a social contract between citizens and their rulers that would eventually inspire American colonists in 1776 and French revolutionaries in 1789.[2] Nevertheless, many Tories in Britain were uncomfortable with this ideological break from traditional ideas of monarchical power and religious tradition. Meanwhile, the Whigs in Parliament were not entirely committed to the liberal ideals that emerged after the Glorious Revolution. They reversed their prior policy of favoring a free press by launching a libel suit against the Tory satirist Delarivier Manley and an impeachment trial against Henry Sacheverell for his incendiary sermon.

The culture wars that exploded in 1709–10 between Whigs and Tories anticipated the culture wars transpiring in many Western countries today: between groups that prefer national traditions and a strong authority figure and those that prefer a government of checks and balances with a global perspective on world problems. The cultural divide between those who supported Sacheverell's impeachment and those who opposed it was every bit as intractable as the divide in the United States in 2020 between those who favored impeaching President Trump and those who opposed it, or as the divide in the United Kingdom between those for and against Brexit.

The winter of 1709–10 marked a turning point in political history, but one often overlooked by historians. Traditional Whig versions of Britain's history treat the Glorious Revolution as "restorative and brief" rather than "transformative and chronologically open-ended."[3] These versions of history point to the political stability of the subsequent century, starting with Anne's death in 1714, when the Whigs regained control of national government and held it for more than a century. The four years of Toryism inaugurated by the political backlash of 1710 would come to seem a footnote to history. Only now, as we face a new moment of political backlash around the globe, does the story speak to us across the centuries. As we again face protests by traditionalists skeptical of liberalism and globalism, we again see the powerful impulse to defend local loyalties, local traditions, and local hierarchies against abstract principles such as governmental checks and balances or religious toleration.[4] Ultimately, Britain's governmental balance between Parliament and the monarchy survived the crisis of 1710 because the monarch, the members of Parliament, the lords, and the judges respected the procedures and precedents of their unwritten constitution and did not reverse the fundamental achievements of the Glorious Revolution. It remains to be seen today whether the democratic and international institutions that have arisen across the world since 1688 will survive the current political challenges to them.

This tale of Queen Anne's court in 1709–10 is not merely a history of clashing political ideologies, however. It is also the story of Princess Anne, King Charles II's shy, nearsighted younger niece, who never expected to become queen. Nevertheless, she took the throne of England in 1702 and helped transform the nation into Great Britain, a power that would help counterbalance the military might of Louis XIV's France. A Tory who became monarch because of the Whig Glorious Revolution, Anne demonstrated the skill of a quiet diplomat in upholding the laws that limited her own power. This is also the story of Anne's oldest and most trusted friends, the Duke and Duchess of Marlborough, who gradually fell from her favor. And it is the story of a vain and attention-seeking clergyman and a best-selling female satirist, Delarivier Manley, whom the Marlboroughs' descendant, Sir Winston Churchill, would describe as "notorious" and a woman of "disreputable character."[5] The central figures in this story—the satirist, the clergyman, the captain-general, the royal favorite, and the queen—were each shaping history as they decided when to adhere to laws and traditions and when to break from them. Their actions, during a time of ferocious partisan strife at home and continued war abroad, would help to establish precedents for power sharing between different branches of government, precedents that would help shape modern structures of shared governance in nations around the world.

1

A "Very Murdering" Battle and a Salacious Court Memoir

On the morning of 10 September 1709, John, Duke of Marlborough, captain-general of the Grand Alliance, sat in a military tent in the woods outside the village of Malplaquet, on the contested northern border of France, writing a letter to his wife.[1] The tent was not the ordinary white canvas tent of the era but was constructed of Turkish cotton with silk appliqué designs, probably a military prize or a gift from another military commander.[2] The duke had begun the letter to his wife, Sarah, the day before by thanking her for sending news about Blenheim, where their mansion was slowly rising out of the mud of the construction site; he also tried to allay her concerns that Queen Anne was snubbing her. This morning he added to the letter to let her know that he had received intelligence that the French were about to attack. The French had been avoiding battle all summer, in the eighth year of this War of Spanish Succession. They were reluctant to engage directly against the Protestant Allies (Britain, the Dutch Republic, the Holy Roman Empire, and other smaller nations), whose forces had beaten them soundly in previous summers. But now Allied spies had confirmed that the French commander Claude-Louis-Hector, Duke of Villars, was nearby and preparing for battle. Before going to bed that night, Marlborough added a few more lines to the letter to his wife: "Tho' the fate of Europe if these armies engage may depend upon the good or bad success, yet your uneasiness gives me much greater trouble."[3]

Although presenting himself as a confident leader and gallant husband to his wife, Marlborough understood what hung in the balance. If the Allies did not win a direct battle this summer, political support for the expensive war, already fading in Britain after eight years of conflict, could give the French the advantage. As captain-general of all the Allies, Marlborough knew what was at stake: no less than the autonomy of European Protestant nations against the military power of the Catholic monarch, Louis XIV. While Britain prized its independent Church of England over the authority of the pope, this war was not about religion so much as it was about freedom from an authoritarian leader trying to take control of Europe.

With one of the most powerful armies on the Continent at his command, Louis XIV had encroached on the Dutch United Provinces to the north and the Holy Roman Empire to the west. He had supported his own grandson's claim to the throne of Spain over the claim of Archduke Charles, son of Leopold I, Holy Roman emperor. Even the Vatican, often allied with Catholic France, had become wary of the ambitions of the French king. In 1701, Louis had acknowledged James Francis Edward Stuart—heir to the Catholic line of Stuart monarchs, which had been forced from the English throne in the Glorious Revolution—as the rightful king of England, after the death of his father, James II (who had lived in exile in France since 1688). By recognizing the Catholic pretender to the English crown rather than the reigning Protestant monarch, William III, France was directly interfering in English national politics. After France invaded the Spanish Netherlands, England joined with the Dutch Republic and the Holy Roman Empire and other Protesant Allies to fight against France and Spain, in what became known as the War of Spanish Succession. Eight years later, Louis XIV had not admitted defeat.

Despite its name, this was never a war merely about who should be on the throne of Spain. As Marlborough reminded his wife on the eve of what would be the bloodiest battle in the war, it was about the fate of Europe itself, and whether the Protestant nations could constrain the expanding power of the Catholic tyrant, Louis XIV. The Duchess of Marlborough did not need to be reminded of what was at stake. Her concern about Queen Anne's increasingly disrespectful treatment of her was not just about her own feelings. Sarah was troubled that she was losing the influence she once had over the queen, influence she needed to persuade the queen to stay resolute in backing the war for which her husband was daily risking his life. When the queen gave rooms at Kensington Palace that Sarah had requested for herself to the sister of her favorite bedchamber woman, Abigail Masham, Sarah knew she had been outmaneuvered. It was not that she needed those rooms. Sarah spent little time at Kensington, even when the queen was in residence there, and she had ample accommodations in the other royal palaces. What troubled Sarah was that the queen now valued Abigail's requests for favors more than her own.

Abigail Masham, Sarah's first cousin, held her position at court only because of Sarah's influence. Sarah had taken a penniless Abigail Hill into her household two decades earlier and had found her a position as one of the queen's bedchamber women. In 1707, Abigail married Samuel Masham, an army officer and groom of the bedchamber to Prince George, in a ceremony that Anne attended but that was not disclosed to Sarah until some months later. It was galling to Sarah that Abigail had replaced her in the queen's affections and confidence. Sarah's larger concern was to try to stop Mrs. Masham from carrying backstairs messages to the queen from one of Masham's second cousins, Tory member of Parliament Sir Robert Harley, who was actively working behind the scenes to persuade the queen to negotiate a secret British peace with France, leaving Britain's European allies in the lurch.

Although Marlborough assured Sarah that there was no point in his writing to Queen Anne about their court squabble, Sarah was trying to decide what she would write in her own next letter to the queen. The previous summer Sarah had tried satirical insinuation, suggesting to the queen that it would be difficult for her to maintain her reputation if the world learned about her affection for Abigail: "nor can I think the having noe inclination for any but one's own sex is enough to maintain such a character as I wish may still be yours."[4] It seems unimaginable to write such a letter to an employer, especially if that employer happened to be the queen of England. Yet Sarah, who had been encouraged in her satirical tone by the pamphleteer Arthur Maynwaring, knew that the queen still needed the Duke of Marlborough to bring to a conclusion the ongoing war with France. In the summer of 1708, the queen did not dare dismiss Sarah from court because she felt it would cause Marlborough to resign his command.

When she accused Queen Anne of this inclination, Sarah knew of what she wrote. Sarah had drawers full of passionate letters that the queen had written to her over the previous three decades. Although Sarah subsequently admitted that the accusation of physical lesbian intimacy ("the dark deeds of the night," as a ballad phrased it) was a "lye," she nevertheless recognized the passionate intensity of Anne's feelings, which ran like a current through the letters in her possession.[5] Sarah also knew that she could make those letters public. Every time the queen asked her to return them, the duchess ignored the request. Anne, for her part, had felt no obligation to answer Sarah's impertinent letter of July 1708. And when Marlborough won a victory at Oudenarde the next month, in a battle in which the French and Spanish lost 13,000 troops to the Allies' 3,000 dead, the queen had sent a more public signal to the general and his wife, in her preparations for the service of thanksgiving for the victory at St. Paul's Cathedral.

Sarah, as groom of the stole, the head of the highest-ranking group of women providing personal service to the queen, had laid out for Anne an elegant royal robe and jewels suitable for the August 1708 public celebration of Marlborough's victory.[6] Yet when Sarah met Anne to enter the open carriage for the public procession ride from St. James's Palace to St. Paul's Cathedral, the queen wore no jewelry. Sarah immediately understood that Abigail Masham—who, as a bedchamber woman, one of the next-highest-ranking group of personal servants, had helped dress Anne—had persuaded the queen not to wear the jewels. While Sarah might send poisonous letters in private, the queen had one-upped her by going public with her decidedly uncelebratory wardrobe choice.

Although seemingly a minor detail, such a sartorial decision had an international resonance.[7] The lack of sparkle in Queen Anne's attire in an open carriage in August 1708 would have signaled her increasing impatience with the war, despite Marlborough's success on the battlefield. Moreover, it sent a message to foreign diplomats that the queen might not have been as solidly in support of the war as she had been in previous years, thus emboldening France to make more demands in any peace negotiations. Sarah "knew well that those jewels, or no jewels, would be the talk of every Court in Europe," as the twentieth-century statesman Winston Churchill wrote in a biography of the first Duke of Marlborough, his ancestor. He explains, "All the ambassadors who now crowded in the greatest state upon the once-neglected Court of St. James's would write that night the story of Marlboroughs' failing favour."[8]

While the Duke of Marlborough readied for battle outside Malplaquet in September 1709, it was disturbing for him to know that

Sarah was still feeling snubbed by the queen's preference for Abigail, and that Abigail still had the queen's ear. Through Abigail, so did Robert Harley and the faction of Tories that wanted to negotiate a swift peace treaty with France.

In 1709, Britain was divided between the Whigs, who saw the need to support Protestant Europe, and the Tories, who resented paying for the war and wanted a swift and separate peace without the other Allies. Marlborough better understood the European perspective, having spent more than half his time for the previous eight years on the battlefields and in the royal courts of Europe. But he also saw things from the perspective of someone who had come of age at court in the 1670s, when the then English monarch, Charles II, was being bribed by the French king, through payments agreed to in the Secret Treaty of Dover, to return England to Catholicism. In 1688, Marlborough had put his life on the line in the Glorious Revolution, which forced the openly Catholic James II, Charles II's brother and successor, from the throne to ensure that England remained an independent Protestant nation. Two decades later, he was not going to risk England or Europe falling to Catholic control.

Under Marlborough's command, the Allies had won decisive victories at Blenheim in 1704, at Ramillies in 1706, and finally at Oudenarde in 1708. In 1709 the armies did not leave their winter quarters until May. After a frigid winter that caused food shortages across Europe, soldiers on both sides—many pressed into service against their will—hoped they would not fight at all. Peace negotiations were under way in May and June, and Marlborough believed Louis XIV would sign a treaty by early July. The war was emptying the coffers of France, and Louis hesitated for weeks, but he finally refused to sign the treaty the Allies offered him. As an absolute monarch who had declared his control of his nation in 1643 in the memorable phrase *l'état, c'est moi,* Louis, after six decades in power, did not feel limited in his exertion of power by complaints from the French people.

Although he would not sign a peace treaty, neither did Louis want his troops to be drawn into a direct battle, having lost so many troops the year before. In early summer 1709 the Allies laid siege to the fortress at Mons, ten miles north of Malplaquet, slowly bringing the city to its knees. As the siege took its toll, in late summer Louis finally gave the orders to his generals to engage in a direct battle. When they heard intelligence about the planned attack, Marlborough and the other Allied generals hoped to lure the French army into battle on the open fields south of the fortress. But the French commander Villars knew he was outnumbered and would lose on an open battlefield. Instead, he hoped to draw the Allies into battle in a tight gap between the woods of Warquignies and Tanières. Confident of their ability to defeat Villars despite the geographic noose, Marlborough and the Allied commanders, with 110,000 troops ready for battle, hoped to pierce the French lines, just as they had done at the Battle of Blenheim five years before, in August 1704.

■

IN THE HAZY DAWN of 11 September 1709, tens of thousands of soldiers faced off in the gap in the woods. As depicted in a commemorative tapestry hanging in Blenheim Palace, the Duke of Marlborough arrived on horseback in an embroidered red-and-gold waistcoat, wearing a full powdered wig and tricorner hat and brandishing a commander's baton as he directed the troops. Despite the elegant attire of the officers so tapestried, the battle was brutal and bloody. The French resisted with tenacity and then offered a surprise ambush to Allied troops. Marlborough ordered fresh troops, and the Allies finally pierced the French lines. By day's end the French army had retreated, but the woods and fields were covered in the carnage of the battle

Marlborough returned to his tent and finished his letter on the evening after the battle, telling his wife, "I have but strength enough to tel you that we have had this day a very bloody battaile."[9] He wrote another brief letter that same evening to their close friend, Sidney, Earl of Godolphin, Lord Treasurer of Britain, describing the "very murdering battle" that had just concluded. He also told both his wife and his friend that this was likely to be the last battle he would ever fight.[10] He felt the victory was decisive enough to bring the French to the negotiating table and allow the Allies a peace on their own terms. He recommended that Godolphin offer a reward of £500 from the Treasury to the bearer of the good news, Lieutenant-Colonel Metcalf Graham—who would travel at top speed by horse, then by boat across the channel, then take to horseback again to bring news of the victory to Queen Anne at St. James's Palace in London.

Over the course of the next day, Marlborough surveyed the tents of wounded soldiers and the bloody corpses of the slain troops strewn through the woods and fields, and was overcome by a headache and dizziness. As he visited the soldiers mutilated by musket and canon fire, Marlborough felt his own blood heat up and his mind become disordered; he probably suffered a mild stroke. The Allies tallied their slaughter: 24,000 troops were dead or captured, to the enemy's 15,000. As maréchal Villars reported to Louis XIV, "If by the grace of God, we lost another such battle, your Majesty could count on your enemies being destroyed."[11] The queen wrote no letter of congratulations to Marlborough or directed any word of praise for him via Sarah or any of the Marlboroughs' married daughters who served as ladies-in-waiting at her court.

After visiting the wounded men from the different Allied nations, Marlborough took to his tent for a day. Too ill to write, he asked his commander-in-chief, Adam de Cardonnel, to write to the duchess to allay her anxieties about his health. Cardonnel's letter served only to increase her worries and make her want to board the first ship to France and join her husband in the field. Rumors soon circulated that Marlborough himself had died.

■

IN A SMALL apartment over a printing shop on Lambeth Hill in London, a few blocks south of St. Paul's Cathedral and slightly north of the muddy banks of the Thames, Delarivier Manley heard the news of the carnage at Malplaquet, as well as the rumor of Marlborough's death. Manley, the daughter of a royalist military commander knighted by King Charles II, dipped her quill in an inkwell and added a sentence toward the end of a work of satire that she was rushing to get to press: "Much about this time the couragious Marquis fought a decisive Battle with the Enemy, which it was not only his Misfortune to lose, but to perish himself."[12]

In this passage in her *Secret Memoirs and Manners of Several Persons of Quality, of Both Sexes. From the New Atalantis, an Island in the Mediterranean,* Manley not only expresses little sympathy for the rumored death of the most famous military commander in British history but almost suggests that he deserved this end. She describes him as "cover'd with Honour and Wounds! A Fate which generally at the long run attends all *Heroes* who still believe they shall *escape,* because they have so often *escaped*."[13] She dipped her quill again, and explained that such heroes were "unwilling to embrace those Opportunities they may find favourable, towards making an *Honourable* Peace." Here she is expressing the Tory desire to reach a swift peace treaty with the French rather than prolong the war to satisfy all the Allies with the "*Honourable* Peace" the Whigs sought.

Despite the rumors of his death, in early October 1709 the Duke of Marlborough was still on the battlefield facing the French. The French defeat at Malplaquet had not brought Louis XIV back to the negotiating table; the extent of the Allied casualties probably emboldened him to keep fighting. By the time Manley's satirical secret history appeared in booksellers' windows, probably in early October, Marlborough had redoubled his efforts in the siege of Mons. When that citadel fell to the Allies on 20 October, however, Marlborough did not send a military commander to ride with all speed to St. James's Palace. A high-ranking messenger would have expected a reward of several hundred pounds, as had been given to Lieutenant-Colonel Graham after Malplaquet. When Colonel Parke brought news of the victory at Blenheim in 1704, Queen Anne made him governor of the Leeward Islands. This time Marlborough hesitated and sent only an ordinary military messenger with the good news, not trusting that the queen would be in the mood to give his second victory in 1709 the celebration it deserved.

Marlborough also exchanged anxious letters with Sidney Godolphin about securing the queen's approval for his appointments to replace the officers who had died at Malplaquet. The Tories at court, sensing the queen's growing distrust of the Whigs, were hoping to replace the deceased military commanders with their own favorites. But Marlborough was a professional, and he needed soldiers he could absolutely trust on the battlefield. He was relieved to learn from Godolphin that the queen had approved his appointments, but he was not looking forward to his return to court, where, he worried, he would feel the snub of a queen apparently more loyal to her Tory bedchamber woman than to her captain-general winning battles for the Allied cause.

■

THE MARLBOROUGH family motto, *Fiel pero Deschidado,* means "Faithful but Unfortunate." Delarivier Manley satirically inverted this motto in her *New Atalantis* by describing the Duke of Marlborough as a "*Mignion of Fortune*."[14] Indeed, everything about his life's story seemed touched by good luck. Born in 1650 to impoverished royalist gentry in the aftermath of the English civil wars, John Churchill and his family were taken in by his widowed grandmother, a supporter of Cromwell. From his earliest youth, John set about mastering the diplomatic tact necessary for living in tight quarters with extended family members on both sides of a national political divide. When the Stuart monarchy was restored in 1660, John's elder sister, Arabella, became a maid of honor (the third group of personal attendents to royalty, working in the drawing room rather than the bedchamber) to the wife of James, Duke of York, heir to the throne. She soon also became the duke's mistress, reputedly after a fall from a horse revealed the shape of her legs. Through his sister's connections, John Churchill became a page to the Duke of York and a soldier in his armies. John's physical charm, his verbal tact, and his skill on the battlefield soon distinguished him at court.

With intelligent eyes, full lips, and skill in making whomever he was speaking to feel his complete sympathy, John Churchill was described as "handsome as an angel," with an "inimitable sweetness and gentleness" of manner that made him a gifted courtier.[15] Belying his "indolent" air and "delicate" shape, however, was his courage as a soldier, and he advanced swiftly in the Duke of York's battalions, often chosen by King Charles II for special diplomatic missions.[16] He soon caught the eye of Charles II's mistress, Barbara Palmer (née Villiers), Countess of Castlemaine, subsequently Duchess of Cleveland. Known both for her passion and for her temper, Cleveland was skilled at manipulating Charles II into giving her jewels, land, and titles. She was also adept at retaining her position at court despite her infidelities to the king. Political satire from that era depicts Charles as easily duped by Cleveland. One such account describes the king taking his crown and placing it on his mistress's head, thus casually acknowledging her as the de facto monarch of England.[17] Court watchers in the 1670s were not afraid that the Duchess of Cleveland was running the country, but they were concerned about the rumors that Charles II was receiving secret payments from the French monarch Louis XIV—as in fact he was—in exchange for promising to return England to Catholicism. Published anecdotes about a mistress who so easily manipulated the king only reminded English readers of their fear that Louis XIV was likewise manipulating Charles.

The young John Churchill was certainly aware of these rumors about Charles II. Some of the diplomatic missions he was sent on in the mid-1670s involved asking the French king for funds. As a loyal member of the Church of England, Churchill would not have wanted his country returned to Catholicism. But he was not yet in a position to take a stand against a monarch's rumored betrayal of the national religion. He would do so eighteen years later, risking his life and the safety of his wife, children, and fortune. In 1670, however, Churchill was merely trying to find his way in the world: he sought to advance in his military career and find a wife whose dowry would secure his fortune and help pay his parents' debts. His parents were trying to negotiate a match with the wealthy maid of honor Katherine Sedley, but Churchill, while obedient to their wishes, was for the moment following opportunities as they arose.

Whether Barbara, ten years older than John and a distant cousin, first seduced him or he seduced her, Churchill knew that their affair might incur the king's wrath. Playing his hand carefully, as he did in every aspect of his personal and professional life, Churchill managed to bring off the liaison to his own advantage. Cleveland, generous with the fortune granted her by the monarch, endowed Churchill with £5,000, an immense sum of money, equivalent to over $1 million today. He promptly invested £4,500 in annuities that would pay him £600 per year (over $100,000 in modern currency) for the rest of his life.[18] The guarantor of the annuity, Lord Halifax, clearly overestimated the likelihood that the soldier would die young, either on the battlefield or in a duel over a court mistress.

Charles II refused to acknowledge the paternity of the daughter that Cleveland bore in 1672, who was probably fathered by Churchill (and sent to France to be raised in a nunnery). Charles also at first refused to approve Churchill's promotion to gentleman of the bedchamber in the Duke of York's household. However, Charles did not seek further revenge. Known as the Merry Monarch, Charles II was tolerant of his courtiers and his mistresses. He was careful to make few enemies at court or in Parliament, the body that had ordered his father's execution in 1649. By 1670, Charles was losing interest in Barbara, having begun a new liaison with the French aristocratic beauty Louise de Kéroualle, who had been introduced to court by French sympathizers hoping to use her as a conduit of influence. The Duchess of Cleveland left court in 1675 to establish residence in Paris. John Churchill probably saw her while on a diplomatic mission that year, but he soon became preoccupied with a woman who became even more central to his rising fortune, one who had already attracted the interest of others, including the ten-year-old Princess Anne, second daughter of James, Duke of York, and third in line to the throne.

Count Fortunatus, as Delarivier Manley would dub the future Duke of Marlborough in her 1709 *New Atalantis,* returned from Paris in 1675 and became entranced with Sarah Jenyns, a fifteen-year-old maid of honor to James II's second wife, Mary of Modena. She was described by one court watcher at the time as "a young beauty" with "rayes about her head like a sun," a beauty that attracted a crown of followers "wherever she goes."[19] Her first court portrait shows a teenage girl with a direct but innocent gaze and strawberry-blond ringlets, clutching a nosegay of flowers; later portraits make her abundant and silvery ash-brown hair into more elegant natural waves, and her gaze becomes more intelligent and confident. Sarah, like John, had come to court to make her fortune; her family, like his, was in debt after the English civil wars. Even the costs of the clothes she would need to appear at court were stretching the family fortune. Her court position paid £20 per year but cost her "four or five hundred a year" for a personal maid, laundry, travel expenses, and elaborate clothing for events such as royal birthdays, plays, balls, and mourning.[20] Sarah's mother lodged with her at St. James's Palace, in part because Sarah was young when she first became a maid of honor and in part because at court, Frances Jenyns was out of reach of her creditors.

Although Jenyns and Churchill quickly fell in love, Sarah was rightly wary of John's intentions, which were not necessarily honorable. Sarah knew of his illegitimate daughter by the Duchess of Cleveland and that his parents were negotiating a marriage for him with another maid of honor. Her mother had warned her repeatedly about two maids of honor who had left court with "great bellies," insisting that she would not allow her own daughter to "have the third."[21] Sarah was frequently annoyed by her mother's interference, but she also needed every trick of resistance to fend off her persistently charming suitor until she secured him on honorable terms.

Her strategy of choice, a strategy she would use in other relationships over the years whenever she was displeased with anyone, including the queen, was avoidance. Although John was constantly sending notes at court, vowing "to be your slave as long as I live," Sarah knew that these smoothly romantic *billets-doux* could be used to seduce her while his parents arranged a match with Sedley. While Sarah accepted John's love letters and sometimes met him in the duke's or duchess's drawing rooms, she kept him at a careful distance, refusing to meet him in private and often leaving a room when she saw him enter. When he scribbled a note asking "if I may have the happiness of seeing you tonight," Sarah would often refuse the request, once writing back that it was in his power to make himself happy only if he would offer her an honest proposal of marriage.[22] A marriage between them became possible two years later when Sarah's elder brother died, leaving her and her sister co-heirs to a small estate. John and Sarah married quietly at court in 1677 but spent months at a time apart, as John continued to attend the Duke of York in his postings abroad.

In the same year that John and Sarah wed, the politician and poet Andrew Marvell published an ostensible "eye-witness" account of the private negotiations between Charles II and Louis XIV, culminating in the Secret Treaty of Dover; during the negotiations, Charles promised to convert to Catholicism in exchange for generous payments from the French king. The secret treaty was signed in June 1670, six months before a public treaty about the military alliance was approved, a public treaty that made no mention of this promised conversion. Marvell writes in his *Account of the Growth of Popery* as if he were a fly on the wall witnessing both the secret negotiations and the discussion in Parliament about the camouflage treaty designed to serve as a cover for the secret agreement. While there had been whispers at court about Charles II's back-channel discussions with Louis XIV, this published account only served to raise the level of public concern that Charles was indeed trying to return the country to Catholicism, or "Popery." As Marvell suggests in the first sentence of his *Account,* "There has now for diverse Years, a design been carried on, to change the Lawfull Government of *England* into an

Absolute Tyranny, and to convert the established Protestant Religion into downright Popery."[23]

England had been Protestant since Henry VIII broke with Rome in 1534 so that he could marry Anne Boleyn. When Henry's Protestant eldest daughter, Mary I, tried to return England to Catholicism in the 1550s, she burned Protestants at the stake, forever etching in England's collective memory the fear of a Catholic monarch and earning her the epithet "Bloody Mary." To return England to Catholicism was political suicide, something that Charles II—whose own father had been executed by Parliament in 1649 for less extreme policies—knew all too well. Nevertheless, he took the French monarch's bribe, and rumors of his secret agreement with Louis XIV worried the nation.

In the 1670s, many Englishmen and women were deeply troubled about Louis XIV's influence over Charles II.[24] English MPs in 1670, while suspicious of Charles's relationship with the French king, had few options for removing him from office. Although impeachment was a long-standing tradition in English legal history, a method by which Parliament could prosecute government officials "for high treason or other significant crimes and misdemeanors," it was not intended to depose a monarch. As Laurence Tribe and Joshua Matz explain, "The political theory of rule by divine right made it inconceivable that Parliament could lawfully remove the king from power." What Parliament could do was to impeach royal cabinet members and other members of government "not only for personal misconduct, but also to express disapproval of royal policies."[25] In that era, the House of Commons could impeach "almost anyone in the realm" other than the monarch, even a clergyman in the Church of England holding no other government position, although impeachment was most often used in England against royal cabinet ministers to upend unpopular monarchical policies.[26]

At this juncture in English history, the only known way to remove a king was through assassination or execution. Executing a monarch, as Parliament discovered after the execution of Charles I in 1649, might only create a martyr and provoke another civil war. The Englishmen who were concerned that Charles II was acting as an agent of the French king would bide their time and watch carefully for signs that Charles had secretly converted to Catholicism. The English would devise a new way to remove a king in 1688, by inviting a foreign ruler to invade their own country—a method so extreme that American delegates to the Constitutional Convention in 1787 took care to craft language against it.[27]

Even more troubling than Charles's secret promise to convert to Catholicism, however, which in any event he showed no public signs of doing, was that Charles II's brother James, Duke of York, had already converted. James was next in line to the throne, since Charles had sired no legitimate children by his wife, only illegitimate ones by his mistresses. Rather than going through the motions of attending Church of England services, as Charles II did, James attended Catholic mass at court with his Italian Catholic wife and took his religious instruction from Father Edward Petre, a Jesuit priest who aroused much suspicion among Protestant courtiers. In the late 1670s, Parliament would repeatedly attempt to pass legislation known as bills of exclusion that would exclude James from the throne. Each time such legislation was introduced, Charles II would promptly dissolve Parliament to prevent any such bill from being passed.

As concerned as John Churchill was by James's Catholicism, he was not willing to give up a promising military career under the patronage of the king's brother. Because of the Secret Treaty of Dover, England was allied with France against the Dutch in the Third Anglo-Dutch War (1672–74), a war that Charles II had to fund with secret French subsidies and justify by fabricating diplomatic incidents. Thus Churchill found himself in English regiments fighting under the command of French commanders whom he would later face as enemies when England, under a different monarch, formed alliances with Protestant nations against Louis XIV.

Churchill, however, would not tie his fortunes exclusively to the openly Catholic Duke of York. He was also developing his connections to James's Protestant daughters, Princess Mary—married to the Protestant Prince William of Orange—and her younger sister, Princess Anne, whom he and Sarah had known at court since she was a girl. Although Charles II was in secret agreement with Louis XIV on returning England to Catholicism, he saw the strategic need to remain Protestant himself and raise as Protestant his two nieces, Mary and Anne. These Protestant daughters, born to James's first wife, were second and third in line to the throne as long as James's second, Catholic wife did not bear a son. Charles also saw the wisdom in keeping his unpopular Catholic brother, James, out of England, banishing him first to Brussels and then to Edinburgh. In Edinburgh, John and Sarah Churchill joined James's household, which included his youngest daughter; Princess Anne, then in her teens, became further enamored of Sarah, five years her senior, whom she had admired when she was a girl and Sarah a teenager at court.

■

WHEN PRINCESS ANNE married Prince George of Denmark in 1683, she insisted (against her father's wishes) that Sarah be offered positions as lady of the bedchamber and groom of the stole. Once installed in Anne's household, Sarah was frequently torn between spending time with her own family at their estate at St. Albans, just north of London, and attending Princess Anne and her husband at Whitehall Palace. It was during this period that Anne penned some of her most passionate letters to Sarah. Although she genuinely loved her husband, Anne felt particular attachments to some of her female friends. While a teenager at court, she had written romantic love letters to her friend Frances Aspley, using pseudonyms from the popular stage play *Mithridates:* Anne addressed Frances as "Semandra" and signed herself "Ziphares," the male hero of that production. Now she showered those emotions on Sarah, regularly writing to Sarah when she was at home with her family, testifying to her passion for her and begging for a letter in return. This letter from 1684 is typical: "I am sure you cannot write to one that is more sincerely yours than I am and I hope that next to Ld Churchill I may claim the first place in your heart. I know I have a great many rivals." She scribbled on the back, "Pray let nobody see this."[28]

Since Sarah requested all her correspondents—including her husband and the future queen—to destroy her letters after reading them, we have only indirect evidence of how she replied to such effusive expressions of passion. In a letter written on the same day as the letter in which she begged for first place in Sarah's heart, Anne wrote again, after having received Sarah's "dear kind letter," which, she said, she had "kissed a hundred times." Anne added, "I would say more, but if I writ whole volumes I could never express how well I love you nor how much I long to see you."[29] A modern biographer of Anne speculates that Sarah likely answered some of this gushing language with romantic language of her own; this style of phrasing was not unusual in close female friendships among the ranks of gentry and nobility during this era.[30] Sarah, however, was disinclined to attend at court as often as Anne wished, and she often delayed responding to Anne, sometimes prompting her husband, when at court in Sarah's absence, to remind her that Princess Anne would very much appreciate a reply to her most recent letter. Anne was passionately attentive, but Sarah found her company dull; spending afternoons together in "solitary tête-à-têtes" became "something of a strain." As Sarah wrote years afterward, "Nobody can maintain that she was wise or entertaining in conversation."[31] Only when she had lost Anne's confidence and friendship, several decades later, did Sarah begin to understand the value of her monarch's loyalty, friendship, and generosity.

John Churchill, meanwhile, continued to cultivate the confidence and trust of Anne's father, James, Duke of York, who valued his courtier's tact, political savvy, and military prowess. The one matter in which James would not rely on Churchill, however, was religion. James remained adamantly committed to the Catholic faith, while Churchill remained among the cadre of courtiers who insisted on taking communion in the Anglican Church of England.

■

When Charles II died in 1685, without any legitimate heirs, James II was crowned king of England. Shortly thereafter the Duke of Monmouth, the illegitimate but Protestant son of Charles II, encouraged by political supporters, led an attack on the monarchy. John Churchill was one of the commanders of the armies of James II and William of Orange that put down this rebellion. Although neither Churchill nor William wanted a Catholic king on the throne of England, they were upholders of the traditional idea of monarchy and did not wish to rock the established social order by placing a royal bastard on the throne. For the next three years the English people gave James II the benefit of the doubt, hoping he might allow England to remain peacefully Protestant, as his brother Charles had.

Instead of following his brother's example, however, James II soon began replacing Protestant officers in his army with Catholic ones and pressuring his attendants to attend Catholic mass. At the same time, he emulated Louis XIV's French model of creating a modern Catholic "centralizing bureaucratic state" as opposed to the Dutch model of a modern Protestant nation that prioritized religious toleration and "political participation rather than absolutism."[32] John Churchill saw the dangers of both the religious and the administrative policies James II was imposing. And when James II's young Catholic second wife gave birth to a healthy son in June 1688, a Catholic baby boy who would supersede James II's elder Protestant daughters, Mary and Anne, in the line of succession, Marlborough joined with six Whig leaders to commit treason against the king. Churchill pledged his loyalty to William in order to preserve a Protestant royal succession in England. Churchill, a military commander, was not an earl, duke, or bishop—like several of the other letter writers—yet he was the only one to send a letter in plain English rather than in coded cipher.[33]

Churchill placed some of his estates and bank accounts in a trust for his children. On 4 August 1688 he wrote to William of Orange confirming that he was "resolved to die in that religion that it has pleased God to give you both the will and power to protect."[34] William, long an enemy of Louis XIV, had spent his whole career trying to defend the United Provinces of the Netherlands—the Dutch Republic—from the expansionist military power of the French monarch. As the Protestant ruler of a Protestant nation married to the Protestant eldest daughter of England's Catholic monarch, William was also a valiant military commander and defender of Protestant Europe.

Historians long referred the Revolution of 1688 as "Glorious" and considered it relatively bloodless.[35] However, William of Orange was not anticipating a bloodless coup. Borrowing money from sources across Europe, including the Sephardic financier Francisco Lopes Suoasso (who demanded repayment only if the venture was successful), William prepared to transport 40,000 troops in 463 boats.

While James II had been warned of William's preparations, which were too substantial to disguise from intelligence agents, he nevertheless refused to believe that his son-in-law would actually invade England. He also thought, when no invasion had taken place by September, that William would surely wait until the following spring, giving him time to rally his armies to respond. When William's forces were blown back by a gale in mid-October, James II took it as evidence of "divine providence."[36] With God on his side, he did not feel obliged to prepare further. While James persuaded himself that he was safe, several of James's highest-ranked Protestant commanders had already made plans to defect, including Princess Anne's husband, George of Denmark, and John Churchill.

William landed on the coast of Devon on 5 November 1688, which happened to be Guy Fawkes Day, celebrated as the day the government discovered and halted a Catholic conspiracy to blow up Parliament in 1605. Two weeks later, Marlborough and Prince George coordinated their midnight defection from James II's army to William's army with Princess Anne's secret flight from the royal palace in London to a safe haven in York. Sarah would lead Anne out of St. James's Palace down the back stairs to a carriage and thence to a safe house arranged by the Anglican bishop of London. For several days, Sarah and Anne had been waiting for a messenger to proceed with their plan. Before their husbands' message got through to them, however, James II had learned of Churchill's and Prince George's defection and had already sent orders to Whitehall Palace to place Sarah under arrest and seize all the possessions of the traitor John Churchill.

Sarah, the steely courtier who at fifteen had resisted the seduction maneuvers of the most charming young man at court and who took the adoring epistles of a princess as a matter of mere routine, remained unphased by palace guards at Whitehall with orders to arrest her. Although she later admitted to being terrified of what the returning royalist forces might do to her, the future Duchess of Marlborough describes how she took things in stride at the time: "In all this trouble, I got out, for the guards were very easy, & went to a house in Suffolk Street, where I found the Bishop of London. He told me he would go to his friends in the City to advise what would be done, & that he would come to the Cockpit at twelve that night."[37] Sneaking down the back stairs at midnight, Anne and Sarah fled with Henry Compton, Bishop of London, a former military commander under Cromwell. Armed with pistols, he led Princess Anne from one safe house to another until they reached Nottingham on 1 December 1688. Learning of the defection of his own daughter and his most trusted military commander, James II panicked, suffering recurring nosebleeds. Two weeks later he fled for France with his wife and infant son. When he returned to England in mid-December, having been picked up by sailors who had not realized his identity, he was taken prisoner by William's troops, but guarded loosely enough that he was able to escape once again to France, never to return to England.

Without any monarch to convene Parliament, MPs summoned themselves to a parliamentary convention in February 1689 and voted that James II had abdicated and that William and Mary should be joint monarchs of England. The Glorious Revolution of 1688 has been described as the "first modern revolution," one in which England chose a modernized English nation on the model of the Dutch Republic rather than the divine right autocracy of Catholic France. As Steve Pincus explains, "The revolutionaries imagined that England would be most powerful if it encouraged political participation rather than absolutism, if it were religiously tolerant rather than Catholicizing, and if it were devoted to promoting English manufactures rather than maintaining a landed empire."[38] This revolution became a model for the American colonists in 1776 and for the subsequent spread of democracy around the globe.

Most participants at the time, however, would not have understood its long-term political implications. Many, including the Churchills, still thought of their actions in terms of personal loyalty and religion. They put their lives on the line to save England from Catholicism and to sustain the Protestant line through William and Mary. As traditional courtiers, they expected favors and recognition in return. The landed gentry were not looking to turn England into a more participatory democracy with anything like full suffrage. These courtiers and army officers were instead looking for the traditional royal rewards of land, titles, and preferment at court and promotion in the army. They could not have anticipated the increased political power of public opinion, especially as it would come to be expressed in pamphlets, satires, and secret memoirs. Although the term "Whig" came into use in English history to refer to those who supported the Glorious Revolution, many who participated in it, including John Churchill, still thought of themselves as Tory. His father, after all, like Delarivier Manley's father, had remained a loyal royalist during England's civil wars.

William III granted Churchill an earldom in 1689, making him Earl of Marlborough and so a member of the House of Lords. William, however, appeared distrustful of the talented and charming Earl of Marlborough and did not promote him after his brilliant military victory against the ousted King James at the battles of Cork and Kinsale in Ireland in 1690. He did not make Churchill a knight of the garter, nor did he give him the military command of the English forces in Ireland. As Winston Churchill opines in a biography of his ancestor, "John Churchill was then forty-three, in his prime. He possessed all the military knowledge and experience upon which he afterwards acted." Watching others carry out "infirm yet stilted manoeuvres . . . he no doubt felt how surely and how swiftly he could reshape the scene."[39]

Given his frustration with King William's ingratitude, it is not surprising that Marlborough was seen in Hyde Park in discussion with agents of the exiled King James. William accused Marlborough of treason and locked him up in the Tower of London. As the wife of an accused traitor, Sarah tried to resign her court offices. Princess Anne, however, not only refused her resignation but left court herself, rather than obey Queen Mary's orders to dismiss Sarah. Anne and her husband lived in exile for two years, first at Syon House, the Duke of Somerset's estate on the Thames, outside London, then at Berkeley House in Piccadilly. She was ostracized by most courtiers and polite society, yet Anne insisted that "as dull and despicable as some people may think it, I am so far from . . . repenting . . . that, were the year to run over again, I would tread the same steps."[40]

During these years of Princess Anne's and the Marlboroughs' exile from court, William depended on his wife, Queen Mary, to cultivate the affection of the English people. William III, who spent six months of the year fighting in military campaigns against Louis XIV, was disliked at court, where he promoted his Dutch friends and favorites. He needed the pen of Daniel Defoe to bolster his reputation with the jaunty poem *The True-Born Englishman,* in which Defoe celebrated the "True-Born Englishman" as "a Het'rogenous Thing" or "a Mixture of all Kinds" or "a Mongrel half-bred Race" from "eager Rapes and furious Lust begot."[41] At this point in history, Defoe was celebrating England as a melting pot in much the way Americans would celebrate the United States in the late twentieth century. Defoe and other political pamphleteers profited from Parliament's relaxation of censorship laws against the press in the mid-1690s. Despite the rise of Grub Street (a street in an impoverished area of London that served as home to many hack writers, low-end printers, and booksellers during this era), neither William nor courtiers such as the Marlboroughs were yet aware how significant the role of public opinion would become in the sphere of politics.

■

QUEEN MARY died of smallpox in 1696. King William died in 1702, after a fall from a horse. When Anne acceded to the throne at the age of thirty-eight, she was nearsighted, significantly overweight, and unsuccessful in bearing a healthy Protestant heir, though she had been pregnant at least eighteen times. She had endured thirteen miscarriages or stillbirths and the deaths of four children in infancy.[42] Her one child to survive infancy had died at age eleven. Despite these disappointments, Anne was a loyal friend and a grateful monarch, eager to put all her energy into serving the people of England. She showered her closest confidants with titles and salaried positions. Sarah, Countess of Marlborough, became mistress of the robes, groom of the stole, keeper of the privy purse, and ranger of Windsor Park; each position came with an annual salary and other perks. John, Earl of Marlborough, became a member of the Privy Council and captain-general of Anne's military forces. Though William III had spent most of his lifetime battling Louis XIV in wars, it was only after his death, when Marlborough took command of the Allied forces, that the Allies were able to win decisive victories, including the Battle of Blenheim in the summer of 1704.

In recognition of that victory, Queen Anne raised Marlborough to the title of duke and granted him royal lands on which to construct Blenheim Palace, the only nonroyal, non-Episcopal country house in England that holds the title of palace. This royal gift, in lieu of a more visible monument in London, would cause the Marlboroughs difficulty in the press, as the construction project dragged on for more than a decade, incurring great cost overruns. Delarivier Manley would refer to it sardonically in *The New Atalantis* as the "*Superbous* Palace" of the Marquis and Marchioness of Caria—one of her pseudonyms for the Marlboroughs.[43]

Although she owed her throne to the Whigs' orchestration of the Glorious Revolution, Queen Anne was nevertheless a high church Tory and a traditionalist. Her oldest and closest friend, Sarah, Duchess of Marlborough, was a staunch Whig who was frequently asked by Whigs in Parliament to use her influence with the queen. Drawing on her usual tactic of giving the silent treatment to friends and family alike when she was displeased, Sarah was frequently cold and disrespectful to Queen Anne. She would refuse to attend at court, refuse to answer her letters, and insult Anne by suggesting that Anne did not understand the risks of appointing so many Tories to her cabinet. In 1706, when the Whigs pressed Sarah to persuade the queen to appoint Charles Spencer, third Earl of Sunderland (a leading Whig and the Marlboroughs' son-in-law) secretary of state, she began to treat the queen coldly, in response to the latter's reluctance to do so. She then wrote a scathing letter suggesting that her own preference for Sunderland was not because of her family connection to him but because she was so concerned for the queen's "security and the nation[']s" if Sunderland were not appointed to her cabinet. Moreover, she hoped that the queen and Prince George would "see the errors as to this nation before it is too late."[44] The queen was horrified that Sarah would accuse her of error in running the nation. Only when their mutual friend, Anne's Lord Treasurer Sidney Godolphin, intervened to persuade Anne that Sarah had meant to write "notion" rather than "nation" was the quarrel smoothed over. Yet their friendship was irrevocably strained. As one modern biographer has observed, "Though politically she [Sarah] had triumphed, she was no longer loved."[45]

At the same time, Sarah's cousin Abigail saw her opportunity to develop a more sympathetic relationship with her employer. The only known portrait that might be of Abigail Masham shows a slender woman with intelligent eyes and high cheekbones. Abigail was considered plain in her own era, although her features would be deemed attractive according to twenty-first-century standards of beauty. In any case, she seemed to share some of her cousin Sarah's conversational wit and satirical bent. Queen Anne likely had been attracted to Sarah as much for her verbal confidence at court and her ability to speak up for Anne's needs as for her beauty. So was she now drawn to Abigail, who strengthened the monarch's resolve in replying to Sarah's scathing letters. Sarah and John became concerned that the queen was now using vocabulary in her letters not previously typical of her. However, the queen apparently knew her own mind well enough to decide when to borrow a friend's phrasing.

By 1709, Abigail was unofficially carrying out most of Sarah's daily duties as groom of the stole and mistress of the privy purse. She was also encouraging the queen to match Sarah's satirical tone in her replies to her letters and even to use Sarah's old trick of refusing to respond. During her quarrel with the queen about the jewels for the victory ceremony in August 1708, which risked being overheard by bystanders, Sarah had whispered sharply to Anne to "be quiet." Thereafter, whenever Anne chose not to reply to one of Sarah's letters she could refer to "the commands you gave me on the Thanksgiving day of not answering you."[46]

■

DURING THE WEEKS before the Battle of Malplaquet in September 1709, while the Duke of Marlborough was encamped on the battlefield, his wife moved restlessly in her private coach between royal castles and stately homes in England. She spent a few days with her daughter and son-in-law at the elegant Spencer (Sunderland) family estate at Althorp, and then a few days in the village of Woodstock, near Oxford, to inspect the construction of Blenheim Palace, followed by a few days at Windsor Lodge, while Queen Anne was at Windsor Castle. Sarah may have joined the queen for an evening of cards, but she was increasingly reluctant to spend time in the queen's presence. The Duchess of Marlborough retained her court positions, but she knew that she was no longer in the queen's confidence or her most trusted adviser. Rather than increasing her time at court in an attempt to win back the queen's favor, Sarah avoided court, where she often felt slighted by Anne's visible preference for Abigail.

As soon as she heard news of the carnage at Malplaquet and of her husband's weakened physical condition, Sarah repaired to Holywell, her family's manor house near St. Albans, north of London, where she had spent her childhood before going to court at age thirteen. This was the home to which she and her husband often returned in times of conflict at court. When John and Sarah were banned from William and Mary's court in 1692, they returned there, and John designed and planted an apple orchard with his favorite varietals. In September 1709, just as the fall apple harvest was beginning, Sarah became frantic about her husband's physical condition after the Battle of Malplaquet. She sat and wrote letter after letter to John—letters that were delayed by contrary winds that prevented ships from crossing the channel. Finally, on 3 October, he sent a letter in reply thanking Sarah for her letters of 2, 3, 6, 8, and 9 September. John reassured her of his health and addressed her concerns that Queen Anne had never said anything to her by way of acknowledging the Allied forces' victory.

Marlborough also wrote to Sidney Godolphin, expressing his wish to spend the winter in Europe, with the other Allied commanders, but the lord treasurer insisted that Marlborough was needed as soon as possible in London, to use his much-valued diplomatic skills in persuading reluctant Tories in Parliament to vote for the next funding bill and to convince the queen of the importance of his most recent victory. Although Marlborough retained his personal charm, he was pessimistic that he would be able achieve these feats of persuasion. Instead of approaching the queen as a fawning courtier, he would write to her in mid-October as an impatient general, tired of having to persuade his monarch that he was fighting for the good of her country and her religion. Hoping to be allowed merely to finish the war he had begun under William of Orange eight years earlier, he asked the queen to name him captain-general for life.

This ill-conceived request only served to fuel his enemies' perception that he was not fighting for the good of his country but for his own personal gain. Worse yet, in asking for the position for life, he gave the impression that he should not merely be captain-general but that he thought of himself as king of Great Britain. In Tory circles he was known as "King John the Second."[47]

■

By the time Marlborough set sail home from The Hague in early November, all London was gossiping about Delarivier Manley's *New*

Atalantis. Marlborough himself appears many times in different scenes—several focusing on his easy charm and his skill in flattering and putting others at their ease, even when he was refusing them what they asked for. Manley's depictions of the Duchess of Marlborough render her a caricature of greed and arrogance. To make matters worse, the book also flattered a certain new court favorite named Hilaria, who is depicted as a paragon of virtue and loyalty to the queen. Manley describes Hilaria, this "rising Favourite," as "fitted for *Grandeur*" and having "a capacious Repository for the Confidence of *Royal Favour.*"[48] This admirable personage was obviously recognizable as Abigail Masham.

Neither the Duke of Marlborough nor his wife read the book. Their son-in-law, the Earl of Sunderland, however, had read it and was furious. Despite his Whig belief in a free press, he wrote to his mother-in-law: "I shall spoil their writing, at least for some time, for I promise them I will push it, as far as I can by law."[49]

2

Secret History and Seditious Libel

When the Earl of Sunderland charged Delarivier Manley with libel, he did not yet know her first name. He certainly had not guessed that she was female. As secretary of state for the Southern Department, he was one of two secretaries sharing the position equivalent to home secretary in the modern UK, with additional responsibilities for foreign affairs (split between northern and and southern jurisdictions). In his capacity of regulating domestic affairs and keeping the peace, Sunderland signed two arrest warrants on 28 October 1709, one for the printers John Woodward and John Morphew, whose names were on the title page of *The New Atalantis,* and another for "_____ Manley" and the printer John Barber, who financed the work. The charge listed on the warrants was for spreading "many false, malitious and scandalous Reflections upon Several of the Queen's Liege Subjects and highly tending to the Disturbance of the publick Peace and Quiete of her Majesty's Government."[1] Unlike modern charges of civil libel—against a person's individual reputation—this charge was about the destruction of the reputation of a person in service (in liege or allegiance) to the queen. By insulting such persons, the publication had the potential to create uprisings against the government. The charge against Manley and her printers was not libel in the modern sense but *seditious* libel—with the emphasis on sedition. After an initial investigation, this offense would to be tried at the Court of the Queen's Bench in Westminster Hall.

Until the mid-1690s, all publications had been subjected to government censorship. Printing presses had to be registered with the Stationers' Company. Starting in 1642, printed publications required a government license. During Charles II's reign, Roger L'Estrange, as licenser, refused to license publications critical of the government or the Church of England. Works that were critical of the king or government—including secret histories of Charles II—were often printed in Amsterdam rather than London. But during William and Mary's reign, a Whig Parliament in 1695 refused to renew the Licensing Act. The only category under which prosecution could be pursued for publications the government found offensive was that of seditious libel. In 1704, Chief Justice John Holt established the precedent that "seditious libel could bring scandal on the government by reflecting on it as a whole as well as by reflecting on the individuals in it."[2] The Whig cabinet members in charge of Anne's government in 1708 had generally opposed bringing charges of libel, for ideological reasons.[3] Transparency had been fundamental to bringing to light the corrupt practices of Charles II; the Whigs had justified their position before the Glorious Revolution through publications such as Andrew Marvell's *An Account of the Growth of Popery,* which had made the public aware of Charles II's corrupt Secret Treaty of Dover with Louis XIV of France.

The Earl of Sunderland, one of the staunchest defenders of Revolution principles, was brilliant, highly educated, and fluent in many languages. He had studied at the University of Leiden in the Netherlands—a republic, not a monarchy, and a nation with a freer press than Britain's and greater religious tolerance. He was certainly aware of the value of an unfettered press. He was also known for his temper. When he wrote to the Duchess of Marlborough about *The New Atalantis,* his anger was evident in his plan to "spoil their writing, at least for some time." Nevertheless, his promise "to push it, as far as I can by law," signals his Whiggish belief that the law, rather than the monarch, was the foundation of government.[4] His concern about the difficulties of maintaining Whig votes in Parliament for the increasingly bloody War of Spanish Succession meant that he was also worried. Like the Duchess of Marlborough, concerned about the war and writing angry letters to the queen, Sunderland allowed his temper to dictate how he responded to Tory satire in the fall of 1709 when he broke with prior Whig precedent and began harassing the press.

Sunderland presumed that the author of *The New Atalantis* was a Grub Street hack being fed information on behalf of a more powerful figure in court or in Parliament. He thought the writer was in league with the Earl of Peterborough, a controversial military commander who had become an ally of the Tories after being dismissed by Sunderland at the Duke of Marlborough's request. Sunderland also suspected that the writer "had some dealings with Mrs. Masham," who was depicted in the book in glowing terms.[5] Certainly the complimentary depictions of Abigail Masham suggested the author might have been hoping for monetary reward.

But Sunderland did not want simply to suppress this book, he also wanted to learn the sources for the behind-the-scenes gossip Manley was relaying. What he did not suspect was that the writer might be an independent thinker, fully capable of writing satire for her own purposes. Nor would he have had any clue that she was no mere hack from the class of apprentice printers but a lady who began her life in the same social class, the impoverished landed gentry, into which the Duke and Duchess of Marlborough were born. Sunderland certainly would not have known that as the daughter of the royalist military commander and historian Sir Roger Manley, this writer considered herself perfectly capable of passing her own judgment on military strategy.

Sunderland, angry and impatient, interrogated Manley in his office in Whitehall shortly after issuing the arrest warrants for her and the three printers involved in *The New Atalantis*. In her fictional autobiography, *The Adventures of Rivella,* Manley describes how he "us'd several Arguments to make her discover who were the Persons concern'd with her in writing her Books; or at least from whom she had receiv'd Information of some special Facts, which they thought were above her own Intelligence." Manley denied having had any assistance from anyone else, insisting that she was writing "for her own Amusement and Diversion" and that whatever likenesses she drew of public figures must have been prompted by "*Inspiration*." Lord Sunderland, who would not have expected her to defend herself as being poetically inspired, retorted angrily that "*Inspiration* us'd to be upon a good Account, and her Writings were stark naught." Manley replied, no doubt in an upper-crust accent comparable to Sunderland's, "that there were evil Angels as well as good; so that nevertheless what she had wrote might still be by *Inspiration*."[6]

Sunderland would not have expected Manley's eloquence and self-confidence in parrying his line of questioning. Her attitude stemmed from pride in what she describes as her "Ancient Family," which had held a coat of arms—a black left hand (showing the origin of their name in the French *main,* or "hand") on a white background—since the thirteenth century. She was also proud of their genteel poverty, occasioned by their having been loyal to "the *Royal Family*" during the civil wars of the 1640s, which left her "Grandfather's Possessions" in "Ruins."[7] Her father had remained loyal to the Stuarts throughout the civil wars, while the Sunderland and Jenyns families had often behaved in a more pragmatic fashion and had been more rewarded for their pragmatism than the Manleys had for their loyalty.

Richard Jenyns, the father of Sarah, the future Duchess of Marlborough, had first supported Cromwell during the civil wars but changed sides in time to curry favor with Charles II when the latter was restored to the throne in 1660, the year Sarah was born. His inherited lands were encumbered by debt, and he needed royal approval for the sale of one parcel, which brought him into contact with James, Duke of York, who also assisted Richard Jenyns in finding a position as maid of honor at court for his eldest daughter, Frances. When James took as his second wife Mary of Modena, a young Italian princess, in 1673, he sought four new maids of honor to attend her, including Frances's younger sister Sarah, then aged thirteen.

Delarivier Manley's family, according to her account, had depleted the value of their estates in rural Wales during the civil wars. So far from London, the Manleys did not have the proximity to court to curry favor easily after the Restoration. Manley's father had left his studies at Oxford to join Charles I's forces in the early 1640s and had been taken prisoner as a royalist soldier at Powys Castle. Following a bold escape, he fled to the Netherlands and found employment in foreign military regiments during much of the next two decades. After the Restoration in 1660, Roger Manley was eventually appointed military commander of the isle of Jersey, and then briefly was commander of the military fort in Portsmouth. His dream during four decades of military service was to be offered a position at court and bring his family to London. He never achieved this dream. Sir Roger Manley's final military post, which he held until his death, was governor (commander) of Landguard Fort, in remote Suffolk, on the east coast of England, sixty miles north of Dover.

Delarivier Manley complains in her fictional autobiography that when Charles II was placed on the throne at the restoration of the monarchy in 1660, he treated long-standing royalists, like her family, less generously than he treated families that had supported Cromwell, like the Jenyns. She blames Charles for taking the "dangerous" advice of a an adviser who encouraged him to "employ his *Enemies,* to try to make them his *Friends,*" and she complains that "the suffering Loyalty of our Family, like Virtue, met little else but itself for a Reward."[8] For Manley, when the beautiful Sarah and Frances Jenyns found positions at court, they were benefiting from preference given to the disloyal rather than the loyal. Sarah was lucky that she was old enough for a place at court in 1673, the year that the Duke of York's new wife arrived from Italy. Delarivier, a decade younger than Sarah, had also been promised a position of maid of honor. Like most teenage girls of her era hoping for such a post, Manley was disappointed. By the time she was of age to take the position in the early 1680s, there was no vacancy for her.

■

Born in the crumbling medieval Mount Orgueil Castle, on the isle of Jersey, in about 1670, when her father was stationed there as lieutenant-governor of the military forts and castles on Jersey, Delarivier was named after the wife of her father's commanding officer—Delariviere (née Chomondeley) Morgan, an heiress from Yorkshire. If Roger Manley had been hoping to curry favor with Delariviere Morgan by naming his daughter after her, there is no record of any future connection between that heiress and his daughter. The Manleys left Jersey while Delarivier was still an infant, when her father took the position as deputy governor of Portsmouth, where he was knighted in 1675 by King Charles II. A few months later Manley's mother, Marie Catherine, a French-speaking noblewoman from the Spanish Netherlands, died of smallpox. Manley herself fell ill with the disease, which left its permanent mark on her complexion. Her father, a learned man who wrote several volumes of military history in Latin, was an indulgent parent who enjoyed good food and drink and had a taste for witty conversation.

Delarivier and her younger siblings were supervised by a governess while living with their father in the governor's residence at Landguard Fort, one hundred miles northeast of London. The fort, on the English Channel across from The Hague, defended Harwich Harbor; it was particularly crucial during seventeenth-century military conflicts with the Dutch. Recognizing the verbal precociousness of his second daughter, Captain Manley sent her for a few months to learn French at the home of an exiled Huguenot minister, thus preparing her better for a court position than either Sarah or Frances Jenyns, neither of whom was taught any foreign languages or given much formal education at all.

Although by her own account she was not as beautiful as her elder or younger sister, Delarivier was apparently witty and physically attractive, despite the facial smallpox scars. There are no known portraits of her, but in *The Adventures of Rivella,* Manley describes (in the voice of a male admirer) her "fine Hands and Arms, a beautiful Neck and Breast, pretty Feet, and . . . Limbs that make up the Symmetry of the whole." Like the Duchess of Marlborough, she had "Hair of a pale Ash-colour, fine, and in large Quantity." She acknowledges that she "was inclin'd to Fat," but insists that her admirers viewed her as "the *Grecian Venus.*"[9] With these charms and her conversational talents, Manley would have flourished at court. However, since the promised position as maid of honor never materialized, she never had the opportunity to make connections or secure an advantageous marriage, as had the radiant Sarah Jenyns, or even to secure the financial security of becoming a royal mistress, as had John Churchill's sister, Arabella. Instead, Manley remained with her younger siblings in remote Suffolk, where she occasionally flirted with officers in her father's regiment. In the winter each year they stayed several months with relatives in Kew, just south of London, so the girls would have had some taste of London society.

Although Manley claims that her royalist father died of disappointment after the Glorious Revolution, in fact he died in March 1687, eighteen months before William invaded England. The sixteen-year-old Delarivier and her younger sister were sent to live with an elderly relation, probably in rural Wales. Manley and Cornelia found themselves stuck in a remote location with little company or entertainment other than her elderly relation's store of French romances. Their dowries of £200 each would not have been enough to entice the type of suitor Delarivier must have dreamed of meeting at court, or enough to compensate for the damage smallpox had done to her face.

When their elderly relation died two years later, their cousin and guardian, John Manley, sixteen years Delarivier's senior, visited the girls and claimed (falsely) that his wife in Cornwall had recently died. He declared his passion for Delarivier, whose time reading French romances made her "fancy every Stranger" as "some disguis'd Prince or Lover." When she fell ill, her cousin attended her devotedly. She claimed later that she married him out of "Gratitude" and because he seemed so "excessively" in love with her. She insisted that she was "not in love with him," nor did she find him "handsome" in "his Person, his Face" or "his Shape."[10] Nevertheless, the cousins were married, not by a Church of England clergyman but by someone who had married a relation of hers, likely by a Dissenting minister—in a ceremony that she either thought or hoped was legal.[11]

Thus Delarivier found herself at a young age "marry'd, posssess'd and ruin'd."[12] Within a short time, her cousin-husband had squandered her small dowry—not surprising for a man who had already mortgaged most of the estates his Cornish wife had brought to their marriage.[13] Delarivier's chances of honorable marriage were now over; she would spend the rest of her life on the margin of polite society. She did have the opportunity, though, to meet men of rank—including courtiers and MPs—at social gatherings where they were not accompanied by their wives, including the soirées of the Duchess of Cleveland and other society mistresses.

The twentieth-century statesman Winston Churchill would refer to Manley as "a woman of disreputable character" when defending his ancestor the Duke of Marlborough against her satire of him.[14] But Manley insisted that she ought to be judged by no harsher standard than that applied to the older cousin who had seduced her. Resisting the double standard applied to female versus male virtue, she insists in *The Adventures of Rivella:* "*If She had been a Man, she had been without a Fault.*"[15] In an another brief account of herself, as Delia in *The New Atalantis,* she blames herself not for having been seduced by her older cousin but for not publicizing his treatment of her sooner. By 1709, Manley had learned the value of public opinion and spin. She expresses regret that she had not immediately "proclaim'd him through all the Streets of *Angela* [London]! For the betrayer of my Glory! The destroyer of an ancient, worthy Family!" so that she could have secured herself "from the reproach of being a conscious Partner to" her own "undoing."[16]

Three hundred years before the #MeToo movement, Manley includes several accounts in *The New Atalantis* of powerful political men taking advantage of innocent teenage girls. Most of these men were powerful Whigs, but she is quick to call out her cousin, a Tory, as a "Traitor to that Trust" her father had placed in him when making him her guardian.[17] This disloyalty and his destruction of her teenage innocence put him on par with the Whigs she mocks for their disloyalty to Queen Anne. As a Tory, Manley did not object to traditional ideals of paternalistic chivalry, but she was quick to call out men who shirked their paternal responsibilities or abused their male privilege, whether Whigs or Tories.

■

DELARIVIER MANLEY accompanied her bigamous cousin-husband to London in 1690. Living in Westminster, pregnant with their son, she was shut out of polite society. When not forbidden to leave their apartment by her jealous cousin, she moved in the circles of court and society mistresses. Eventually she left her cousin, and for six months in 1694 she lived in the household of Barbara, Duchess of Cleveland, former mistress to Charles II—the same Duchess of Cleveland who had seduced the young John Churchill two decades earlier, and then granted him the gift of £5,000. While Manley found Cleveland "*Querilous, Fierce, Loquacious,* excessively fond, or infamously rude," she listened attentively to Cleveland's court gossip from the 1670s.[18] It was from Cleveland that Manley heard the court anecdotes and rumors about the Duke of Marlborough, including "the first ill Impressions of Count *Fortunatus,* touching on his Ingratitude, Immorality, and Avarice."[19]

During the months she spent with the Duchess of Cleveland, Manley seems to have lifted herself out of her initial despair at her situation of being a "ruined" woman and taken consolation in some of Cleveland's jaded observations about society. Cleveland sympathized with Manley about the "Ill-nature of the World, that wou'd never restore a Woman's Reputation, how innocent soever she really were." The duchess also advised Manley to "make her self as happy as she could without valuing or regretting those, by whom it was impossible to be valu'd," advice which Manley apparently took to heart.[20]

Manley managed to stay in Cleveland's good graces for about six months, which Manley describes as "an Age to one of her inconstant Temper."[21] She was peremptorily dismissed by the duchess, however, on the suggestion that she was trying to steal Cleveland's lover, the actor

Cardonnell Goodman. Manley, who was thirty years younger than the duchess and interested enough in the theater that she would subsequently write at least six plays, may well have flirted with the forty-five-year-old actor. However, Manley claims that Goodman falsely accused her of having "made Advances to him" so that she would be dismissed from Cleveland's household before she could inform Cleveland of the other mistresses that Goodman was keeping.

The Duchess of Cleveland was concerned that Manley may have been flirting not only with her current lover but with her eldest son, Charles Fitzroy, Duke of Southampton, one of her children fathered by Charles II. Manley insists that she was visiting her sister during the evening that Cleveland accused her of intriguing with her son. Manley, however, does not try to claim that she was entirely innocent in her attempt to capture the interest of the young widowed duke. She observes in *Rivella,* through the voice of her admiring male narrator: "I have heard several Wives and Mistresses accuse her of Fascination: They would neither trust their Husbands, Lovers, Sons, nor Brothers with her Acquaintance upon Terms of the greatest Advantage."[22] In 1694, when she was flirting with the Duchess of Cleveland's son, she was perfectly aware of her own sultry charm. Had she succeeded, she would have been a duchess before the then Earl and Countess of Marlborough were made Duke and Duchess of Marlborough.

■

Before she achieved celebrity and security for herself through her *New Atalantis,* Manley struggled for years on the edge of financial insolvency. She wrote plays for the stage and a short travelogue in 1696 but was not yet able to make a living as a writer. Part of her difficulty might have been her arrogance and condescension toward theater managers and actors. Her behavior made her the object of satire in a comedy for the stage, *The Female Wits,* in which she is featured, as Marsilia, alongside two other female playwrights from the era—Catherine Trotter and Mary Pix. Trotter and Pix, more successful than Manley in writing for the stage, were also less easy targets for satire. Marsilia (Manley) is depicted as arriving late to rehearsals because "idle People of Quality" stopped her sedan chair to make conversation.[23] In this production, probably written by a group of actors who had worked with her on one of her plays earlier that year, Manley is impatient for her first glass of sherry each morning, quick to take offense at the least slight, and always on the lookout for the duke or nobleman who had promised to drop by the rehearsal. Despite the short-term success of her 1696 tragedy *The Royal Mistress,* in which Elizabeth Barry played the heroine Homais, Manley managed to rupture relations with the theater managers of both the Drury Lane and the Lincoln Inn's Fields theaters within six months—and would have to wait a decade for a change in management before bringing another play to stage.

Manley subsequently became mistress to John Tilly, the governor of Fleet Prison, living with him in the governor's residence there, between about 1698 and 1702. As a lawyer who always stayed one step ahead of the law—he allowed prisoners to come and go from prison for a bribe—Tilly joined forces with Manley to try to mediate, for a reward, a famously protracted lawsuit over a disputed inheritance between the Duke of Albemarle and the Earl of Bath. After incurring substantial expenses in their dealings with one of the claimants to the will, they were shut out of the process without any reimbursement or reward. Manley and Tilly ended their relationship in 1702, when Tilly's lawful wife died and he married a wealthy heiress. Their three children were rumored to be begging on the street, under the supervision of a former inmate of the Fleet; there are court records indicating that Manley and Tilly sparred over their maintenance costs. Manley herself fled London to escape creditors on at least one occasion and was arrested in 1705, likely for debt.[24]

Despite her financial struggles, Manley stayed in touch with the writers she knew through the world of theater. She maintained a flirtatious friendship with Richard Steele, the playwright and essay writer who would become influential as the author of *The Tatler* and coauthor, with Joseph Addison, of *The Spectator.* Steele had written her romantic verses during the years she was involved with Tilly, and she listened to him as he pursued reckless financial schemes, investing in alchemical attempts to turn ordinary metals into gold. They were intellectually well matched, but Steele was looking to marry someone with a substantial dowry—as he did in 1705. After that, he and Manley went their separate ways, until she asked him for a loan of £10 to allow her to flee London when pursued by creditors. He explained subsequently that he did not have the money to loan her, but she would add his name to the list of former friends that she mocked in *The New Atalantis*. He became Monsieur Le Ingrate, approximate French for Monsieur the Ungracious, or Sir Ingrate.

While Manley was struggling, with few honorable means of making money as a woman denied the benefits of a good marriage in polite society, Steele, who had fathered a child out of wedlock (and who owed money to the midwife Manley recommended for his lover's lying-in), was making his way as a Whig journalist and a member of the Kit-Cat Club. In 1707 he secured the position of editor of the *London Gazette*, the official government newspaper, at a salary of £300 a year. He owed this position to his friendship with Joseph Addison, who served as undersecretary to the Earl of Sunderland.

Facing financial hardship after her relationship with John Tilly ended in 1702—the year that Queen Anne came to the throne—Manley persisted in writing and pursuing other schemes that might lead to some financial stability. She never showed any doubt in her own wit, talent, or capacity to hold her own in conversation with gentry and peers of the realm. Although she would later flaunt her Tory credentials, in 1707 she was not above seeking patronage from Whigs. When a new manager took over Haymarket Theater and Manley was finally able to stage a new play, she dedicated it to Elizabeth Montagu, Countess of Sandwich, a Whig patron of the arts. Manley also wrote a begging letter at that time to another member of the Whig Montagu family, Ralph, Duke of Montagu (whose son was married to the Marlboroughs' daughter Mary)—whom she had met through the Duchess of Cleveland, and met again when trying to mediate in the Bath-Albemarle lawsuit a few years later—hoping for some assistance so that creditors would not seize "all her goods."[25]

Manley eventually joined forces with a self-made man, the printer John Barber, who had worked his way up from an apprentice to master printer and a liveryman in the Stationers' Company. He would later become the official printer of the government newspaper the *London Gazette* and for the South Sea Company. In 1709 he was beginning to curry favor with Tories at court and was printing pamphlets critical of the Whigs in power. Born into a lower social rank than Manley, Barber would have been drawn to her for her upper-crust Tory credentials, her snobbish air, her seductive wit, and her powers of conversation. A contemporary writer describes Barber's pursuit of Manley in romantic terms, describing a "Transition from Friendship to Affection." After Manley had known Barber for a few months "she found, that what had pleased her Ear, had touched her Heart; and she soon found, that his Person, good Sense, and Address, had made a Captive of her."[26]

She took up residence in "an Apartment fitted up for her" above Barber's printing shop on Lambeth Hill, just south of St. Paul's Cathedral, where she lived until her death in 1724. Although she may have claimed that she lived there "for the Sake, *only,* of being near the Press and more at hand, to see her own Work done *correctly,* and better attended to than it had been," she and Barber lived and socialized together as a couple, at least for the first few years that she lived there.[27] Together they would dine and play cards with Tory writers, including Jonathan Swift, who would recruit Manley to write political pamphlets for the Tories. Long before she met Swift in 1711, Manley was already well connected to other writers and persons of quality in London from her days writing for the stage in the 1690s. With the prosperous printer supplying the food and wine, Manley would have led the guests in conversation "always new, and which never cloys."[28] Even after Barber moved with a new mistress to a fashionable house at Queen Square, Manley maintained her apartment in his printing house, giving her a secure establishment in central London.

Manley's flair for witty conversation and her ability to recount an amusing anecdote explain the success of *The New Atalantis,* a work that spread unflattering gossip not only about the Marlboroughs but about a full range of court and society figures. The gossip was not new, but it served to remind readers of the past peccadillos of those now in power.

The New Atalantis takes the form of a dystopian travelogue, a dark echo of Francis Bacon's *The New Atlantis,* in which English voyagers discover a utopian island of learning and virtue. In Manley's work, Astrea, goddess of justice, returns to Earth to find an island that could not be less like Bacon's vision. Astrea's mother, the goddess Virtue, gives her daughter a tour of the island of Utopia (Great Britain), the country of the New Atalantis (England), and the city of Angela (London). Their tour guide, Intelligence, described as "First Lady of the Bedchamber to the Princess Fame," recounts anecdotes to her mother about the court and society figures they see on their travels, regaling the visitors with stories of greed, hypocrisy, and adulterous sex.[29] The engraved frontispiece to the second volume depicts Astrea aloft in the sky and holding the scales of justice. In the caption Manley beseeches "Sacred Truth" to "inspire" her and mend her "Rage" so that "reforming Satir" may "mend a vicious Age."[30]

These gossipy anecdotes would have been familiar stories to Manley's readers: how John Churchill, now Duke of Marlborough, was seduced three decades earlier by the Duchess of Cleveland; how William Lord Cowper, now Lord Chancellor of Great Britain, had a second family with a mistress; how his brother, the MP Spencer Cowper, had been tried for murder after his lover, the Quaker Sarah Stout, had been found drowned in a stream in Hertfordshire. The gossip was old, but insider political memoirs usually recycle familiar past scandals; that is part of their appeal to readers, who want to hear repeated their worst suspicions about politicians they loath. When the second volume went to press, it became a publishing sensation and the talk of London. The Whig writer Lady Mary Pierrepont (subsequently Lady Mary Wortley Montagu) was having a difficult time getting hold of a copy in late October.[31]

Much of *The New Atalantis* is amusing. As evidenced by handwritten marginal notes in copies surviving from this era, readers enjoyed matching the romantic pseudonyms to the public persons being mocked. Manley's sharp-tongued comment about the military commander who died because he was too much a "hero" to have ended a protracted war sooner, however, was not funny. It was dark, Juvenilian satire, and it summed up the Tory opposition to an expensive and protracted war. Political secret histories since classical times had mocked powerful political figures by recounting sex scandals. Procopius of Caesarea had inaugurated the genre with his unpublished gossipy anecdotes about the Byzantine emperor Justinian, a manuscript later called *Anekdota* (Greek for "unpublished things") and published in seventeenth-century Europe as *The Secret History.* Whig secret historians had used the genre to spread scandal about Charles II and his mistresses, including Barbara, Duches of Cleveland, in the 1670s and 1680s. Such secret histories were important to building public support for the Glorious Revolution and were one of the reaons why Whigs tended to support an unfettered press.

When Manley began to write secret histories as a Tory in 1709, she tweaked the familiar Whig formulas to her own ends. She did not mock the Tory monarch, Queen Anne, but the powerful Whigs running Parliament and the military. As in *Hattige: or the Amours of the King of Tamaran* (1680), in which the young John Churchill is a minor figure in a Whig secret history about Charles II and the duchess of Cleveland, so in *The New Atalantis,* Manley first depicts Churchill as a youth at court who is seduced by the older and more experienced Duchess of Cleveland. This anecdote is one of many satirical anecdotes about prominent Whig politicians, writers, and society figures. Manley's overall point was not to undermine confidence in the monarch but in the most powerful Whigs at court and in Parliament.

Manley and Barber knew they were taking a legal risk with *The New Atalantis.* That is why Barber commissioned two other printers, John Woodward and John Morphew, to do the actual printing and put their names on the title page, as the "trade printers" for the work. Although Barber was arrested along with Manley and these two trade printers, they had attempted to avoid a charge of libel by using pseudonyms for their satirical targets. The Cowpers became the Volpones; John Churchill appears first as Count Fortunatus, then as the Marquis of Caria; Sidney Godolphin is Count Biron; the Whig journalist Richard Steele is Monsieur Le Ingrate. Manley's cousin-husband, John Manley, becomes "This old Stallion of the Senate-House."[32] Keys to identify the names of the real persons corresponding to the pseudonyms were published and distributed separately for the first edition of each volume, a strategy for avoiding prosecution for libel. This strategy sometimes worked, but if the characters were sufficiently easy to recognize, an assiduous government official—like Sunderland—could decide to prosecute anyway. The Court of the Queen's Bench was still establishing precedent for libel charges of this sort. In a 1713 case the Court would rule that merely omitting a few letters from a name and using a dash in their place was not adequate to prevent a charge of libel "if it needs be understood to signify such a particular Person in the plain, obvious and natural Construction of the whole."[33] But in the case of romantic pseudonyms and humorous anecdotes, in 1709 the Queen's Bench had not yet established detailed precedent for when it might allow pseudonyms to definitely "signify such a particular Person."

The success of Manley's *New Atalantis* and its continuing popularity over the next several decades stemmed from how easily readers recognized the real persons behind the pseudonyms. When the visiting deities notice "that graceful Person upon the high Loll in his Chariot and six Horses," readers would guess immediately that it was the Duke of Marlborough, known for his relaxed charm and his ability to put everyone, even his political opponents, at ease. Yet when Manley's Intelligence recounts his story, Manley associates him with feminized terms, imagining a scene in which the youth is set up for his liaison with the Duchess of Cleveland by an aunt at court, who arranges for him to bathe in the duchess's "Bathing-room" and then "scented his fine Linen" and brought him "to the Bedside" of the amorous duchess.[34]

In romantic bath scenes from literature in this era, it is usually a young teenage girl who emerges from the bath, to be seduced by an older man. Here Manley depicts the most brilliant military leader in Europe in 1709 as a handsome youth in 1670, set up by two older women for a liaison that would help kickstart his career with the duchess's cash gift and influence, which helped him rise in the army. As depicted by Manley, he is not the passive object of two women's schemes but canny and ambitious, traits unattractive to Tories. In Manley's telling, "the possession of the charming'st Woman of the Court" was not "the *Zenith* of his Fortune, but rather the first auspicious, ruddy Streaks of any early Morning" in his future career.[35] In emphasizing his ambition as more powerful than his love for Barbara, Manley recounts the Duchess of Cleveland's version of their romance, "touching on his Ingratitude, Immorality, and Avarice" and relating an anecdote in a subsequent decade when the wealthy and successful Duke of Marlborough refused to lend Cleveland, down on her luck, "twenty Guineas" for a game of basset.[36]

Manley reminds readers that the future Duke of Marlborough benefited from his sister's position as mistress to the king's brother, James, Duke of York. In Manley's account it was not John Churchill's previous military and diplomatic talent that brought him to the attention of the Duke of York but the latter's "Passion for the Sister" that explained how "he either found or fancy'd Merit in him superior to all the Court; he gave him a considerable command in the Army."[37] Manley then relates a well-known incident from 1682 in which James's ship crashed on rocks, and many of his soldiers and sailors perished. The incident was often recounted to demonstrate James's poor judgment in not commanding the men to abandon ship quickly enough to save everyone's life. In Manley's version of the story, James allows other soldiers to die so that he might save the life of the young John Churchill, who then vows that he will seek one day to lose his own life in defending James, insisting "I, *more faithful than fortunate,* can only wish, not expect a Destiny so Glorious."[38]

Here Manley is playing directly on the motto in the Marlborough coat of arms, meaning "Faithful but Unfortunate." For readers in 1709, Manley's irony would have been unmistakable, since Marlborough did not remain faithful to James but joined the side of William of Orange during the Glorious Revolution. Nor did Marlborough appear to have sacrificed fortune for loyalty. Although in 1688 he did put his life and fortune at risk, by 1709 he and his wife, as favorites of Queen Anne, had accumulated immense wealth and estates, including the extravagant Blenheim Palace.

By making Marlborough the target of her satire in his disloyalty to James II, Manley presents the events of 1688 as a tale of ingratitude and the self-interested ambition of courtiers rather than as a glorious revolution of Whig Protestantism. She does not go so far as to suggest that the Revolution of 1688 should not have occurred. Without the defections of the Whigs, James II would have retained power; his Catholic son, James Francis Edward Stuart, would have taken the throne in 1701; and Princess Anne, a Tory, would never have become queen. As a Tory satirist, Manley expressed loyalty to Queen Anne and the Church of England in 1709, and she carefully threaded a needle to criticize disloyalty and personal avarice in the Whigs without renouncing the Glorious Revolution.

Instead of depicting the revolution as stemming from a fear of James II's Catholicism and the threat posed by the birth of his Catholic son and heir in June 1688, Manley rewrites history by recasting James II as female, giving him the pseudonym Princess Ormia. Rather than explaining James II's increasing favoritism toward Catholics and the fear that he would return the country to Catholicism, Manley translates the problem of religion into a problem of gender. In her *New Atalantis,* only females may succeed to the throne, so Princess Ormia attempts to change the law to permit a male line of succession. Manley then blames the English people, who "lov'd Opposition," for the uprising that brought Henriquez and his wife (William and Mary) to the throne.[39]

Manley regales her readers with gossip about William III, focusing on his exceptionally close relationship with his favorite courtier, William Bentinck, on whom he showered land and favors, making him Earl of Portland. Anti-William propaganda from his own reign often depicted William as having a sexual preference for men—particularly his court favorites, first the Earl of Portland, later Arnold Joost van Keppel. Manley invented a scene in which William and Bentinck are both young men at court and William is ill. It is believed that the only way to save him would be by someone else lying naked next to him in bed to warm his body. As Manley tells it, it was with "Pleasure and Boldness" that this favorite threw "off his Clothes" and "got into Bed to the Prince, embracing closely his Feverish Body, from whence he never stirr'd, 'till the happy Effects of his kind Endeavours, were visible."[40]

As a Tory satirist, Manley was on safe ground during Anne's reign in recounting homoerotic gossip about King William, whom Queen Anne hated. He and Queen Mary (Anne's older sister) had treated then princess Anne with great disrespect after they took the throne in 1689. Anne came to despise them, particularly William, whose claim to hold the throne of England in his own right, after Mary's death in 1696, she had conceded only reluctantly in order to facilitate the Glorious Revolution (her own right to the throne, as Mary's younger sister, was better than his). She would become queen only after William died in 1702. In the early 1690s, Anne's pseudonym for William in her letters to Sarah from that era was Caliban, the hideous figure from Shakespeare's *The Tempest.*

Manley mocked William's favorite, the Earl of Portland, not only for his extreme closeness to the king but also for his rumored seduction of Stuarta Werburge Howard, an illegitimate granddaughter of Charles II and a maid-in-waiting to Queen Mary in the 1690s. In Manley's account, Portland was a trusted guardian and father figure to "Mademoiselle Charlot," whom he seduced by isolating her at his country estate and having her read Ovid's account of a Myrra falling in love with her father. As she cries for Myrra's fate, he "drunk her Tears with his Kisses, suck'd her Sighs and gave her by that dangerous Commerce . . . new and unfelt Desires."[41] After seducing this "beautiful product of Innocence and Nature," Portland eventually reneges on his promise of marriage, and marries a savvier woman, who knew to insist on marriage before consummating their love affair. In Manley's account, Portland is the classic politician—asserting power over the young and the innocent. He feeds his own ego by recollecting a maxim he ascribes, inaccurately, to Machiavelli: "none but great Souls can be completely Wicked."[42] Manley makes clear that the men in power who imagine themselves "great" are those most likely to take advantage of innocent girls. In Manley's view, those men were often, though not always, powerful Whigs.

Describing the scandals and corruption of William and Mary's reign (from 1689 to 1702), Manley diverted attention from rumors about Anne's emotionally charged (or, in Whig propaganda, erotically charged) relationship with Abigail Masham in 1709. She subtly reminded readers of the land and favors Queen Anne had showered on the Duke and Duchess of Marlborough when they were in favor by describing the lands and favors William had lavished on his favorites. She also mocked the Marlboroughs for their closeness to Sidney Godolphin. Godolphin's role as lord treasurer, in raising funds and borrowing money for the expensive War of Spanish Succession, was facilitating a conflict that, to many readers, had gone on too long and cost too much money and too many lives. Opponents of the Whig government worried that Godolphin was too close to the Marlboroughs politically. Manley does not mention the war directly but instead invents an anecdote about an adulterous affair between Sidney Godolphin and Sarah, Duchess of Marlborough.

John and Sidney had known each other since both were pages at court in the 1660s. Sarah and Anne had known Sidney almost as long. The Marlboroughs' eldest daughter, Henrietta, was married to Godolphin's only son, Francis. Godolphin was short, unassuming, and quiet, yet brilliant, and had been trusted adviser to the four monarchs before Anne—Charles II, James II, William, and Mary. In 1675, he wed one of the most beautiful maids-in-waiting at court; she died shortly after the death of their first child, in 1678. Godolphin had never remarried but had devoted his energies to his duties as lord treasurer, playing a role comparable to that of prime minister in the modern UK, and to his hobby of breeding racehorses at New Market. He was devoted to Sarah, Duchess of Marlborough, and had spent much time and effort smoothing over misunderstandings between her and Queen Anne.

Godolphin had instructed Anne in the workings of government when she acceded to the throne in 1702. Anne fully appreciated Godolphin's intelligence, his patience, and his skill as a mediator. Early in her reign, after the Marlboroughs retreated from court briefly following the death of their son, she wrote to the three of them, begging for their continued service: "We four must never part till death mows us down with his impartial hand."[43] As long as Queen Anne was happy with both the Marlboroughs and Godolphin, she retained the emotional conviction behind this plea. When Anne, a lifelong Tory, began to break with Whig policies, she would need to break not only with the Marlboroughs but also with Godolphin.

Godolphin's closeness to the Marlboroughs and Sunderland, their son-in-law, meant that the Whigs would remain in control of military and budgetary policies as long as the three of them shared power. While the Duke of Marlborough spent six or eight months every year leading troops on the battlefields of Europe, the lord treasurer remained at court, writing regular letters to Marlborough and Sunderland about politics and military strategy—and also staying in constant contact with the Duchess of Marlborough. At court, Godolphin and the duchess would have been sharing their letters from Marlbough with each other, and sometimes showing them to the queen.

Tory satirists, frustrated at the Marlboroughs' and Godolphin's influence over Queen Anne, had long attacked the closeness between the families by depicting a romantic liaison between Sarah and Sidney, ostensibly sanctioned by John. While it is true that during the months of the active military battles the Duchess of Marlborough would have seen Godolphin more regularly than she saw her husband, the closeness between them was emotional, not physical. As a biographer of the duchess observes, he was her "best friend."[44] Devoted friendship does not make for good political satire, so Manley followed the lead of other Tory satirists, including Joseph Browne in *The Secret History of Queen Zarah and the Zarazians,* in writing about an ostensible affair between Godolphin and the duchess.[45]

Manley adds key details to this familiar fiction by crafting a scene whose humor turns on a second detail she wishes to mock, the Duchess of Marlborough's well-known avarice. In Manley's version, the Marchioness de Caria (Sarah) is dressed as a country girl on her way to an assignation with another courtier but is intercepted by Count Biron (Godolphin), who pretends not to recognize the duchess but bribes the pretty country lass with a purse of gold, which was, as Manley admits, "no Sum to bribe Madam *de Caria,* at her own *Lodging* or in the *Circle,* yet it was a very great one for a Country-Girl." Thus, while both are playing at pretending not to recognize each other, Count Biron "found the way of making himself as happy as he desir'd with his Country-Maid."[46]

Manley moves directly from this scene of seduction to her gender-bending retelling of the Revolution of 1688, in which Lady Olympia (Princess Anne) defects from Princess Ormia (James II). In Manley's version, Madame de Caria is busy playing cards with her lover, Count Biron, when the Marquis de Caria (the Duke of Marlborough) enters and declares, "Does not the *Princess* [i.e., James II] totter in the Throne. . . . I so plainly perceive her fall, that I for my part have determin'd with my self this very hour to abandon her . . . and go over [to] the Duke [William of Orange]."[47] Rather than showing the extreme personal risk Marlborough was taking to save his country from a forced return to Catholicism, Manley depicts Marlborough as looking out only for himself.

In this fictional anecdote, Count Biron and the Marquis de Caria then decide that Madame de Caria should defect from the palace with Lady Olympia (Princess Anne), alluding to Sarah leading the princess on a midnight flight from Whitehall Palace in 1688, defecting from James's cause. In Manley's version, their motivation is not a concern for their country or the national church but a sense that Lady Olympia would be the foundation "*Rock*" on which the Marlboroughs would build subsequent "*Fame*" and "Grandeur."[48] Individual ambition is often admired in modern capitalist countries, but in Manley's Tory view in 1709, individual ambition was at odds with true loyalty to monarch and country. By rendering the Revolution of 1688 a cynical act based on a desire for individual fame and grandeur, Manley undermined the Whigs' own view of that conflict as a "Glorious" foundation to a more liberal and enlightened government, with power shared more evenly between monarch and Parliament.

■

DESPITE MANLEY'S scathing depiction of many prominent Whigs, no attempt was made to prosecute Manley after the publication of the first volume of *The New Atalantis* in late spring 1709. The landed gentry and nobility were leaving London to spend the summer at their country estates. The work was read by some over the summer, but it was not until the publication of the second volume in October, as the *beau monde* returned to London, that public interest in it increased.

Lady Sarah Cowper, mother to Lord Chancellor William Cowper, read the first volume in July at her estate in Hertfordshire, not far from the Marlboroughs' estate in St. Albans, north of London. Now celebrated for the many volumes of a daily diary that she kept from 1700 to 1716, Lady Cowper crafted each entry in beautifully clear penmanship, even when describing a bad-tempered husband and a son accused of murder. She copied out some of the passages in Manley's work about her sons—Lord Chancellor William Cowper, accused of bigamy, and his brother, Spencer, involved in a murder trial for a former lover. She notes that Manley had accurately captured Spencer's state of mind about the lover he had grown tired of: "I believe it True." She observes with relief that she herself did not come off too badly in Manley's depiction of the family scandals: "Methinks among all this Clatter, Lady Volpone comes off well." She also reasons in her diary that the old well-known gossip about her family would not hurt them: "the main matter is but Old Dirt grown so dry it may not stick if it be not mixt with new stuff."[49]

The first volume of *The New Atalantis* is full of gossip about the Cowpers and other scandals from William and Mary's reign, as well as anecdotes about the youthful Duke and Duchess of Marlborough at the court of Charles II. It is in the second volume, which probably appeared in early October 1709, that Manley offers the story of Count Biron seducing Madame de Caria. In this second volume, she also describes the reign of Olympia (Queen Anne) and the greed of the Marchioness de Caria (Duchess of Marlborough), who profited from her court offices by requesting bribes for favors and extracting large dowries from the queen for her daughters' marriages. Manley explains that "her Desires were unlimited; she was starving in the midst of Plenty; she enjoy'd not any thing, though she was in Possession of all things." Manley describes the increasing public outrage at this avarice and the growing "*Odium* of the *People*."[50]

Manley also celebrates Olympia's "new rising Favourite," Hilaria (Abigail Masham), as "really *wedded* to all those *Virtues,* which the Marchioness but *Woo'd,* and that too but *superficially.*" Her flattering depiction of Masham, from whom she may have been hoping for a financial reward, continues: she describes Masham as having "a Soul fitted for *Grandeur;* a capacious Repository for the Confidence of *Royal Favour,*" adding, in a scarcely veiled appeal for literary patronage, "She lov'd and understood Letters introduc'd, nay, applauded the Ingenious, an did always her endeavor to make them taste of Royal Bounty."[51]

Manley creates no pseudonym for the Earl of Sunderland in *The New Atalantis,* but she does manage to take a satirical jab at him. He appears only as a member of the "Council of *six,* sitting in *Biron's Cabinet.*" Here "the six" refers to Marlborough and Godolphin plus the four other influential Whigs who had positions in Anne's cabinet: the earls of Sunderland, Orford, and Halifax, plus John, Baron Somers. These four, along with the Earl of Wharton, had long been known as the Whig Junto, the most elite group of Whig leaders, who regularly urged the Duchess of Marlborough to pressure Queen Anne into following their policies. In a direct insult to these Whigs, who envisioned an ideal of government by law and representation, Manley describes how this "Council of *six*" "in effect reduced" Anne's monarchy "to an *Oligarchy,*" an ideological stab at Sunderland that he, as a fervent supporter of Revolutionary principles, would not have taken lightly.[52]

Manley then invented a fictional scene in which Olympia (Queen Anne) dies in childbirth and cedes regents' power to the heroic Don Haro (Robert Harley) and the virtuous Hilaria (Abigail Masham). At this point, Manley predicts the death of the Marquis de Caria, who "fought a decisive Battle with the Enemy, which it was not only his Misfortune to lose, but to perish himself, cover'd with Honour and Wounds!"[53] Imagining or expressing desire for the death of a monarch could be prosecuted as treason—although no such charge would be brought against Manley for the satirical scene in which Olympia dies in childbirth. Predicting the death of the leader of a monarch's army could certainly be considered sedition. Although this scene is set in some future time after the imagined death of Olympia (Queen Anne), the reference is clearly to 1709. The Tories were also accusing Marlborough of continuing the war for his own personal gain. Manley follows this theme, pointing out "the prodigious Opportunities . . . of *Gain*" and suggesting "Peace would indeed be the end of their Power!"[54]

Following the death of the Marquis de Caria (Marlborough), Manley envisions the decreased influence of Count Biron (Godolphin), who "appear'd but as the *Shadow* of himself; the *Ghost* of his own *departed* Genius."[55] Although Marlborough had not died and Godolphin had not been removed from power in 1709, Godolphin's influence with Queen Anne was daily diminishing as the monarch chose more and more to rely on the advice of Robert Harley (brought in for secret late-night meetings by Abigail Masham). Manley's imagined future scene was in reality an unsettling reflection on the present state of affairs at court.

After imagining Count Biron's death, Manley describes the situation that the Marchioness de Caria would confront: the rumors that would spread about "all the Particulars of her *rapacious sordid* Life, running from *Mouth* to *Mouth,* no long in fear of speaking Truth." Manley also foretells how one morning, "the *Rabble* . . . rush'd altogether like an impetious Torrent upon her *Superbous* Palace," that is, Blenheim Palace.[56] Predicting mob violence could be understood as encouraging it. When Sunderland charged Manley and her printers with "many false, malitious and scandalous Reflections upon Several of the Queen's Liege Subjects" that were "highly tending to the Disturbance of the publick Peace," this passage could certainly have provided the evidence for her arrest, with its potential to incite a real uprising against the Marlboroughs.[57]

Manley does not end the scene with the rabble arriving at the Marlboroughs' palace but instead continues with "generous *Hilaria* [Abigail Masham]" sending "a Party of Horse to secure her Return to Court." Making Abigail the heroine of this scene would have only further infuriated the Whigs who wanted her removed from court. The scene concludes with the rabble entering and plundering the Carias' palace and seizing "an incredible Mass of Money found conceal'd in several *Vaults* and *Recesses,*" which Manley justifies as "rendering back to the *Publick* what she [Madame de Caria] had grip'd from *Particulars.*" Hilaria subsequently persuades Madame de Caria "(with much Difficulty) to resign her self a *Votary* to *Religion.*"[58]

Potentially libelous or not, these scenes struck many readers as hilarious. Arthur Maynwaring, a Whig MP and pamphleteer, was the self-appointed political secretary to the Duchess of Marlborough; he gave her regular updates on matters in Parliament and advised her (often rashly) on the drafts of letters she was writing to Queen Anne. At the duchess's request, he read Manley's *New Atalantis* and summarized it for her so she would not have to read it herself. Commenting on the scene in which Hilaria saves Madame de Caria from the mob, he points out that even the duchess herself "could hardly help laughing."[59] Whether or not the duchess would have appreciated the humor in the book she seems never to have read, her son-in-law was not amused.

■

WHEN MANLEY entered Lord Sunderland's office to be interrogated about her *New Atalantis,* after her arrest, she would have met a tall, imposing figure in a powdered wig, silk stockings, and embroidered waistcoat. Manley, ever confident of her own brilliance, could no longer boast of physical charms. When Jonathan Swift met her in 1711, he described her, at about forty, as "very homely and very fat."[60] Yet Manley retained her flair for conversation and wit. Sitting in Lord Sunderland's office during her interrogation in 1709, Manley projected confidence through her snappy retorts about the "Inspiration" that led her to write *The New Atalantis,* but she was aware of the gravity of the situation. In *The Adventures of Rivella,* she admits her fears the Tories would abandon her and she would be "left to perish and starve in Prison."[61]

Nevertheless, Manley was a fighter and a survivor. She was also well versed in the law, having lived first with John Manley and then with John Tilly, both lawyers. When she was arrested, she was held in the custody of a "messenger" (likely a sergeant-at-arms from court) and his wife, "who most tyrannically and barbarously insulted" her and prevented her from "seeing or speaking to any Person." She was not "allow'd Pen, Ink and Paper," making it difficult to write to friends for assistance.[62] Yet Manley knew her right to sue for habeas corpus, which requires a person to be charged with a specific crime before being detained—a traditional practice in England that had been strengthened by an act of Parliament in 1679 as a protection against potential abuses of power by James II, then next in line to the throne and already feared because of his Catholicism. In 1692, when John, then Earl of Marlborough, was suing for release from the Tower of London, Sarah recounts kissing a copy of the Act of Habeas Corpus, which she described as "one of his best friends."[63]

Within a few days after suing for habeas corpus, Manley was formally charged at the Court of the Queen's Bench and then released on bail until her trial, scheduled for the next legal term, in mid-January. Manley was a Tory, not a Whig, but when facing one of the most influential men in the Whig Junto, she was eager to assert the legal rights and the press freedoms that the Whigs had fought for in the previous century.

3

A Provocative Tory Sermon

Delarivier Manley was released from custody on Saturday, 5 November. By chance, the date was Guy Fawkes Day. While Manley was being released to return to her apartment at John Barber's printing house, two blocks south of St. Paul's Cathedral, a large angry man in clerical robes and an ash-colored wig climbed the steps of the wooden pulpit in that same cathedral to preach the Guy Fawkes Day sermon.

An oil painting of Dr. Henry Sacheverell at Magdalen College, Oxford, shows a red-faced man with a clenched jaw, raised eyebrow, and a condescending sneer. Although there is little that is visually appealing in this portrait to modern eyes, in his own day the preacher was thought handsome to women and known for being expensively, even "foppishly," dressed.[1] At St. Paul's that day, however, no one made note of his wardrobe, only of his facial expression. Another clergyman present at the sermon recalls "the *Fiery Red* that overspread his Face," as well as the "the *goggling Wildness* of his Eyes" as he prepared to mount the pulpit.[2]

The pulpit stood under the 365-foot-high dome of St. Paul's, designed by Sir Christopher Wren and completed only a few years earlier, in the rebuilding following the Great Fire of London in 1666. This new dome made the renovated cathedral the tallest building in the world at that time. As Sacheverell mounted the pulpit, however, all eyes would have turned to his red face and wild eyes and away from the architectural feat of the dome, already disliked by some in London for its resemblance to the Catholic basilica St. Peter's in Rome and its "air of Popery."[3] Sacheverell's theme was supposed to be the plot to blow up Parliament during its annual opening ceremony, on 5 November 1605, but he was not going to tell the story usually recounted in sermons on Guy Fawkes Day.

■

One hundred and four years earlier, at midnight of 4 November 1605, Guy Fawkes, a Catholic conspirator (though not the ringleader of the plot), was discovered, with matches in his pocket, in the basement of the House of Lords, surrounded by thirty-six barrels of gunpowder. The intended targets of the plot were the monarch James I and his son Henry, who would be attending the opening of Parliament. The Catholic conspirators, in a rather convoluted scheme, hoped to kill King James I (the Protestant son of Mary Queen of Scots, who took the English throne after the childless Elizabeth I died in 1603) and his eldest son so they could put the country in the hands of Catholic regents on behalf of James I's daughter, Elizabeth, whom they hoped to marry to a Catholic so as to return England to Catholicism. While the members of the House of Lords were not themselves the direct target of the plot, many would have lost their lives in the explosion.

After the plot was discovered and the traitors were executed, then drawn and quartered for treason, Parliament declared 5 November an annual day of thanksgiving for saving the country from regicide and Catholicism. It was celebrated officially with commemorative services by the Church of England. Unofficially, it was also fêted with bonfires at which effigies of the pope or Guy Fawkes (or some other enemy of the moment) were burned.

In the early eighteenth century, the typical sermon preached on Guy Fawkes Day aligned the foiling of the Gunpowder Plot with William of Orange's landing at Torbay on 5 November 1688 to deliver England from the Catholic James II. However, at St. Paul's Cathedral in 1709, Dr. Henry Sacheverell launched into a sermon that took a different turn. Instead of celebrating 1605 as a bloodless delivery from Catholicism, like the relatively bloodless Glorious Revolution of 1688, Sacheverell likened it to the execution of Charles I in 1649 (after Parliament charged him with tyranny and treason). He railed against "the irreconcilable rage and bloodthirstiness of both the popish and fanatick enemies of our Church and Government," linking "these TWO DAYS" as "but One *United Proof*, and visible *Testimonial* of the same *Dangerous*, and *Rebellious Principles* these *Confederates* in *Iniquity* Maintain."[4]

When he turned to the events of 5 November 1688, Sacheverell did not try to draw correspondences between the landing at Torbay and victory against the plotters in 1605 but actually denied any parallels between the two. Rather than asserting, as was usual in Guy Fawkes

Day sermons, that God had authorized the right to resist James II in the Glorious Revolution, Sacheverell instead insisted that there had not been any resistance in 1688. Since James II had finally fled the country (after his country was invaded by his son-in-law at the head of 40,000 troops to depose him), Sacheverell argued that he had abdicated peacefully. Thus God had not condoned an act of resistance in 1688, and so the Whigs' reasons for venerating "resistance" as a central principle of the Glorious Revolution were false.

Sacheverell also lashed out against the Toleration Act of 1689—legislation that removed penalties from Protestant Dissenters for not attending the established (Anglican) Church of England. For Sacheverell, this liberalization resulted in harboring "such *Monsters,* and *Vipers* in our Bosom, that *scatter Their Pestilence at Noon-day,*" putting church and state in danger. These vipers will "*Rend, Distract,* and *Confound,* the firmest and *Best-settl'd Constitution* in the World.[5] Word quickly spread that Sacheverell had "preached against the Revolution."[6]

In a sermon that went on for over an hour and a half, Sacheverell insisted that the real danger facing the nation of Great Britain lay not in Catholics but in Dissenting Protestants and in the members of the Church of England who tolerated them. Dissenters were members of Protestant churches other than the Anglican Church of England and included Baptists, Presbyterians, and Quakers, among others. These Protestants were more likely to be Whigs than Tories, as were the members of Parliament who allowed them to serve in government (through such legal loopholes as the practice of "occasional conformity," or taking communion in the Church of England just once per year). These tolerant MPs Sacheverell labeled "false brethren." His main theme, and the title under which he would publish this sermon, was *The Perils of False Brethren, both in Church, and State.* In his mind, these false brethren posed a threat both to the established national church and to the Kingdom of Great Britain itself, since in his version of conservative Toryism, political stability relied on the foundation of religious strictness rather than toleration. He insisted that he did not intend to give "Offence" but spoke "from a Good Intention, and a Tender Concern for her *Majesty's Person* and *Government,*" as well as from a "hearty Zeal for the *Honour* and *Safety* of our Excellent *Church,* and *Constitution.*"[7]

Although England may have saved itself from Catholicism by expelling James II in the Revolution of 1688, the Church of England was shaken by the process. Since so many English Anglicans were involved "actively or passively, with rebellion against James," the revolution challenged "their cherished principles of divinely-ordained authority in the State, and broke down that special relationship with the monarchy which was their greatest strength."[8] Sacheverell recognized this effect of 1688 and took it as a wedge issue to generate populist anger against the Whigs.

In response to those who believed that "*the* Pulpit *is not a place for* Politicks" or that "*'tis the Business of a* Clergy-man *to* Preach Peace," Sacheverell explains in the dedicatory preface to the printed sermon that the "Peril of Rebellion" had long been understood by the established church as more significant than "any other Sin."[9] For Sacheverell, the virtuous model of political and religious behavior was "passive obedience" to the crown and the church. Although the majority of merchants and alderman in the City of London were Whigs, the Lord Mayor of London, Sir Samuel Garrard, was a Tory. Garrard had known exactly the sort of sermon Sacheverell would deliver, and he had requested it with every intention of snubbing his Whig colleagues in London. The fiery preacher did not disappoint.

Sacheverell's prose style was not subtle. As the historian Geoffrey Holmes observes, "Sacheverell did not seduce his audiences with words; he bludgeoned them with metaphor and epithet."[10] Not only did his imposing physical presence and livid face make an impression, his voice was resonant and mellifluous, as the dean of Peterborough Cathedral observed, "audible without Noise or any *harsh grating Accent* to impress the close of a sentence upon the ears of the congregation." This same clergyman also ominously predicted the outcome of Sacheverell's resonant preaching by observing the irony in preaching passive obedience in a style that potentially incited his listeners to "raise Insurrections." In short, "The Doctrine of Passive Obedience . . . might teach Men other better Expedients . . . than by *lifting their Voice like a Trumpet* . . . before the giddy Vulgar."[11] As it turned out, the sermon would not raise insurrections that day, but mobs incited by Sacheverell's provocative language would begin gathering before the end of November.

■

For all of his high church anti-Dissenting rhetoric, Sacheverell was descended from Dissenters. His grandfather and great-grandfather had been Presbyterian clergymen, and his grandfather had died while imprisoned for preaching at a Dissenting meeting. His ancestor's courage in going to prison for his Dissenting beliefs did not inspire Sacheverell to religious toleration, however, but rather to acute embarrassment about his ancestors and the Dissenters in his extended family, one of whom, his uncle Benjamin, would subsequently rebuke his outspoken nephew in a pamphlet titled *Sacheverell against Sacheverell* (1710).

Sacheverell was descended not merely from ecclesiastical radicals but from political radicals. His mother's father was believed to have been the MP Henry Smith of Leicestershire who signed the execution warrant against Charles I in 1649, after Parliament found him guilty of treason. Henry Sacheverell may even have been given that grandfather's first name. Sacheverell's subsequent "shameful neglect of his widowed mother" during his own years of professional success has been explained by his embarrassment over his own ancestry.[12]

Henry did take pride in his family name, Sacheverell, of French Norman origin—Saute de Chevreuil. He also took pride in the Church of England, which his father had joined while at Cambridge University and in which he was subsequently ordained. His father became rector of St. Peter's church in Marlborough, Wiltshire—a market town of which an ancestor of John Churchill had been earl half a century earlier, before the earldom temporarily became extinct (until it was resurrected for John Churchill in 1689).

In 1674, nine years after the birth of the future Queen Anne and four years after Delarivier Manley was born on the island of Jersey, Henry Sacheverell was born in the rectory of St. Peter's, the third son of a large family. His father died when he was ten, and Henry was adopted by his high church godparents, Edward and Katherine Hearst. As a child, he impressed his adoptive mother with his pious habits, "always retiring to his private *Devotions* before he went to School."[13] His adoptive father was an apothecary and financially comfortable enough to send Henry to university, a requirement for anyone intending to become a clergyman in the Church of England. (Those training to become Presbyterian ministers, as was a young Daniel Defoe, were sent to Dissenting academies.)

In 1689, the same year that Delarivier Manley was seduced into a bigamous marriage by her older cousin, Sacheverell began his studies at Oxford, where he earned his B.A. in 1693 and his M.A. two years later. He did not make a mark at university for any feats of intellectual genius, nor did his general behavior impress his superiors as much as it had impressed his adopted mother. It was rumored that he beat a college cook with a leg of mutton. He was regularly disrespectful to the president and vice-chancellor of Magdalen College.[14] When he sought ordination as deacon in 1697 and was denied because of mistakes in his Latin grammar, his arrogant response to the bishop of Litchfield was that his "'twas better *Latin* than he or any of his Chaplains could make." The bishop who refused to ordain Sacheverell at that time was not only unimpressed with Sacheverell's Latin, he was also concerned about his "very raw and ignorant" answers to fundamental questions about divinity.[15] He instructed the young man to return to his books before applying again. In 1697, Sacheverell was finally ordained, but his personality made it difficult for him to hold down a position as clergyman.

After his first appointment as curate for the parish church of Aston, Sacheverell was refused the appointment as vicar of the parish when the position fell vacant. As the mother-in-law of the former vicar explains, "his Behavior was exceedingly light and foolish, without any of that gravity and seriousness which became one in holy orders"; he was in short, "*fitter to make a player than a clergyman.*"[16] Sacheverell, with the talents of a "player" (i.e., actor), lacked the basic empathy to fulfill the religious needs of a parish. When he finally was made deacon and secured a position as curate in the parish of Cannock, in Staffordshire, he was impatient with his rural parishioners, demonstrating "his overbearing Contempt of the Common People."[17]

Finding he had little interest in or capacity for ordinary parish duties, Sacheverell returned to Oxford to become a fellow at Magdalen College, where he was active as a teacher and administrator, becoming librarian and bursar. He was eventually granted a doctorate in divinity (on the basis of either his "authoritative teaching" or his growing reputation as a provocative preacher, but not because of any remarkable academic scholarship), and in 1708 he became dean of arts.[18] Although hardworking and successful in his academic career, Sacheverell was disliked by his peers, who found him arrogant and disrespectful, as well as a hard drinker in a town and a university where heavy drinking was the norm. A contemporary describes him, in Latin, as "*vir ignarus vinolentus, loquax, audax,*" a "noisy, presumptuous wine-soaker."[19] Known for fastidiousness in his attire, always sporting expensive clerical collars and gloves, he was also known to have mistreated a glover named Riley, to whom he owed money. When the glover found him in his rooms at Magdalen College, he was repulsed without payment. Sacheverell "fell a cursing and a swearing," insisting "that if he sued him to Eternity, he would not pay him."[20]

Continuing his career at Magdalen College, Sacheverell gradually established a name for himself as a firebrand, preaching against the dangers of Dissenting Protestants. His oratorical gifts served him well as he projected the outrage of a high church Tory against Dissenting Protestants. A sermon he preached at Oxford in 1702, in which he had urged Anglicans to "hang out the bloody flag and banner of defiance" against Dissenters, had spurred Daniel Defoe to use his rhetoric as the model for the style of an extreme high church Tory sermon, which Defoe caricatured in *The Shortest Way with the Dissenters.* In Defoe's satire, the high church preacher rails, with increasing threats, against Dissenters. This caricature of a preacher accuses them as having "butchered one King! deposed another King! and made a Mock King of a third!" Defoe's high church clergyman finally ends with a plea to destroy the Dissenters: "Now *let us Crucifie the Thieves.*"[21]

Defoe was charged with seditious libel, placed in the pillory, fined, imprisoned, and plunged into debt for his satirical mockery of the high church position. Only by agreeing to write in support of policies favored by Robert Harley, who cultivated skilled propaganda writers (including Defoe and, later, Jonathan Swift), was Defoe able eventually support his family and gradually discharge his debts. Dr. Sacheverell meanwhile continued developing his firebrand style of preaching and attracted the attention of high church Tories hoping to bring his voice into the mainstream now that Queen Anne, a high church Tory herself, had taken the throne. In May 1709, Sacheverell was named chaplain at St. Saviour's Church in Southwark (now Southwark Cathedral), just south of the city of London. From there it was about a one-mile walk across Old London Bridge and along Canon Street to reach St. Paul's Cathedral, although Sacheverell might have taken a sedan chair (carried by chairmen through the streets) or a hackney coach to visit St. Paul's. When Sacheverell was elected to the position at St. Saviour's, the archbishop of Canterbury, Thomas Tenison, a Whig, was extremely concerned about his proximity to the pulpits of London.[22]

The Tories who had pushed to bring Sacheverell to St. Saviour's wanted to change the laws governing Dissenters, particularly a feature of the law that allowed Dissenters to participate in government. There were plenty of laws on the books restraining the activities of Catholics at this time: they could not attend university; they could not hold public office; they could not even live within a five-mile radius of London (which is why the poet Alexander Pope lived in Twickenham). Dissenters, however, were able to attend Dissenting academies in lieu of Oxford or Cambridge. They were able to enter government through the practice of occasional conformity, a practice fiercely protected in Parliament by the Whigs, who knew that Dissenting Protestants tended to be Whigs rather than Tories. There were some Dissenters so pure in their faith that they refused to take communion in the Church of England even once per year, but many Whig Dissenters found the compromise acceptable.

The Tories opposed occasional conformity for the same reason that most Whigs supported it—the political advantage it gave Whigs. In his Guy Fawkes Day sermon, Sacheverell suggests that the danger of Dissenting Protestants was their tendency to challenge both liturgy and authority; for him this amounted to "*Universal Scepticism,* and *Infidelity,*" which were similar to the dangers to society posed by "*Atheists* or *Catholics.*" Although he was ostensibly speaking only about other Christians, Sacheverell borrowed long-standing European tropes of antisemitism in disparaging supporters of occasional conformity: "Thus Our FALSE BRETHREN, as the *Jews* did our *Blessed Saviour,* Crucify his *Church Betwixt Thieves.*"[23]

The sermon, in no way subtle, organizes his ranting complaints against Dissenters and the Anglicans who tolerate them into three categories of guilt: against the church, against the state, and against individual persons. Sacheverell describes the danger to the Church of England in allowing the practice of occasional conformity, as well as the acceptance of a broad range or latitude of practices within the Church of England, known as latitudinarianism. He specifically derides Gilbert Burnet, Bishop of Salisbury—whom he refers to in his sermon as bishop of Sarum, the medieval name for that cathedral town. Although Sacheverell claims not to doubt Burnet's concern about Catholicism, he asserts that Burnet was putting the church in more danger than was posed by Catholics through his support of the Toleration Act of 1689 and his low church latitudinarian position, allowing variation in official church practices from church to church.

In singling out the "individual persons" who put the church and state in danger, Sacheverell also marked for his censure certain "*Volpones*" in the government. The name of Volpone (suggesting a creature as cunning as a fox) was a pseudonym for Lord Treasurer Sidney Godophin in many anti-Whig pamphlets and secret histories. Godolphin, like Marlborough, was still nominally a Tory, but both men had long allied themselves with the Whigs to ensure enough votes in Parliament to continue funding the War of Spanish Succession. Sacheverell is cruel in his treatment of such nominal Anglican Tories who were cooperating with the Whigs. He complains that "these *Men* . . . *Cover* their *Treachery* with the *Sacred,* and *Plausible Pretences* of FRIENDSHIP, whereby they are capable of doing *much more Mischief,* than a *barefac'd* and *profess'd Enemy.*" He rails against "the *Crafty Insidiousness* of such wilely *Volpones.*"[24]

■

IN THE PULPIT at St. Paul's Cathedral, Sacheverell insulted these "Volpones" more directly than Delarivier Manley had maligned Godolphin in her *New Atalantis.* Manley also informs her readers in her preface that she is writing satire, in the tradition of Varro—deploying "different Subjects, Tales, Stories and Characters of Invention"; her intent, she claims, is the "scourging of Vice" and the "exhortation to Virtue." Her treatment of Godolphin is mocking but drawn with a certain admiration: she acknowledges his charm and finesse in her fictional scene of him seducing the Marchioness of Caria in exchange for a purse of gold. Sacheverell no doubt also believed that he was condemning vice and exhorting virtue, but in his bombastic rant about the enemies to church and state, there was nothing charming, funny, or subtle in his portrait of the "wiley *Volpones*" he lambasts as posing such a threat to the nation.

Sacheverell's sermon was not erudite; it was not intellectually subtle. It was a rabble-rousing outcry clearly intended to prey on his auditors' most primitive tribal instincts against Catholics, Jews, Presbyterians, Quakers, and other Dissenters, as well as those Anglicans who tolerated Dissenters taking communion in their church and holding positions in the national government. It was a performance typical of him, the sort of sermon on which he had built his reputation in high church circles. For all its provocative rhetoric, however, Sacheverell's sermon did not attract overflowing crowds at St. Paul's on 5 November 1709. It was a performance in front of a relatively small crowd: the lord mayor and other city politicians, his supporters from Southwark, as well as some Jacobites (supporters of the Catholic line of succession to the throne through Anne's half-brother).

Queen Anne was attending a separate Guy Fawkes Day service that Saturday a few miles away at the Chapel Royal at St. James's Palace, where the sermon was preached by Dean Stanhope, with many courtiers in attendance. Although those in attendance at St. Paul's knew the sort of sermons for which Sacheverell was famous, "they can hardly have anticipated anything half as extravagant as the event they were to witness that autumn afternoon."[25] Of the thirty clergymen present, three of them left firsthand accounts of the occasion. Even before it was printed and published, word of its rhetoric and its treatment of Godolphin would likely have reached the lord treasurer in his rooms at St. James's Palace by Sunday morning.

After dining with the lord mayor, whom Sacheverell claims encouraged him to print the sermon, Sacheverell then adjourned to a favorite tavern that evening to boast to his admiring high-flying Tory friends that had the Dean of St. Paul's Cathedral been present at the sermon, he "would have thrown my Volpone directly in his face."[26] The dean of St. Paul's Cathedral at this time was none other than Dr. Henry Godolphin, Sidney Godolphin's younger brother.

It would be difficult to imagine two men more different than Henry Sacheverell, the firebrand, and Sidney Godolphin, the patient peacemaker. Even their portraits emphasize the difference in their personalities. The red-cheeked and scowling Sacheverell stands with shoulders back and gaze defiant in the painting owned by Magdalen College. Sidney Godolphin, a shorter man, is seated in a court portrait, holding his long thin wooden staff of office as lord treasurer. He looks straight at the viewer and is neither smiling nor frowning. His gaze resonates authenticity, without arrogance or bluster.

Godolphin was a man of principle: "in an age of flattery and rampant corruption he hated sycophants and jealously guarded the public interest."[27] He was also infinitely loyal to his friends. His contemporary the Earl of Shaftsbury observed of him, "Once he has conceived a good opinion of a man, he will bear anything for him."[28] Godolphin had struggled in 1688, having retained the trust of James II at the same time that he was gaining the trust of William of Orange, whose side he ultimately chose. Loyal to the Marlboroughs as well as to Queen Anne, Godolphin was known for his capacity to mediate between the Duchess of Marlborough and Queen Anne just as readily as he mediated between the Whigs and Tories in Anne's cabinet.

While a young man at court in the 1660s, the understated but brilliant Sidney Godolphin secured the heart of the stunningly attractive Margaret Blagge, so beautiful that when she arrived at court, at sixteen, "every body was in love with, and some allmost dyeing for her."[29] After his engagement to Margaret, he then patiently waited nine years to marry her, while saving up resources to launch their domestic life in London. When she died giving birth to their son Francis, two years after they wed, Sidney remained loyal to her memory, never remarrying—unlike most men of his era, who typically sought a second wife soon after the death of the first.

As first lord of the Treasury under William and Mary, then lord treasurer under Anne, Godolphin was obliged to fund expensive wars against France for more than two decades. His patience and his diligence paid off in improving the efficiency of tax collection and in increasing public confidence in the Bank of England. England was able to triumph so often over the French in battle not just because of Marlborough's brilliance as a military commander but also because of Godolphin's financial acumen, allowing the British government to raise money more effectively than the French.

Quietly confident, Godolphin was disinclined to call attention to himself or seek personal monetary reward for his loyalty to the nation. He had regularly made requests on behalf of the Marlboroughs—reminding Queen Anne of promises of generous gifts for their daughters' dowries or grants of royal land for their houses—but he amassed no great fortune himself while serving Queen Anne. Earning the rank of Earl of Godolphin from his service to the crown through four monarchs, and purchasing Godolphin House in London through his own frugality, Godolphin sought no further advancement in title or property. With his only son married to the Marlboroughs' eldest daughter, Henrietta, he welcomed his son and daughter-in-law into Godolphin House with their children and gently encouraged Henrietta to find her own set of friends beyond her mother's sphere of influence.

Sidney Godolphin was content to spend his leisure time outside London either visiting the Marlboroughs at Windsor or St. Albans or breeding racehorses at Newmarket. His son Francis would become second Earl of Godolphin, after his death, and his daughter-in-law, Henrietta, would inherit the title of Duchess of Marlborogh *suo jure* (in her own right) after her father's death. Although dukedoms almost never descend through the female line, Parliament passed a special act for the Marlborough title to pass to Henrietta and subsequently to her sons (or nephews) after the tragic death of her brother, John, in 1703. While Sidney Godolphin may have asked for little for himself because he knew that his eldest grandson was heir to the Marlboroughs' lands and titles, he was also simply not materialistic: he put all of his energy and effort into his court duties. Rather than seeking to accumulate land or titles, Sidney contented himself with the pleasure of staying connected to his closest friends. In a letter to the duchess in August 1709, he observed, "I begin to take the only satisfaction I have left now, which is writing to you."[30]

The unlikeliest target of satire to those who knew him well, Sidney Godolphin was a lightning rod for those who resented Whig policies. He had been dubbed Volpone in Joseph Browne's *Queen Zarah and the Zarazians,* the 1705 satire in which Sarah, Duchess of Marlborough, is caricatured as Queen Zarah and given the throne of the kingdom by the actual reigning queen. Godolphin had long been capable of gently persuading Queen Anne to agree to government and military policies that he thought best. He was losing his sway at court, however, in the autumn of 1709, as was clear from Delarivier Manley's mention of his appearing "as the *Shadow* of himself; the *Ghost* of his own *departed* Genius."[31]

Manley's acknowledgment of Godolphin's fall from royal favor is poignant, especially after her depiction of him as the savvy Count Biron, managing to seduce the Marchioness de Caria. Overall, Manley's anecdotes about Godolphin were more comic than jabbing, and her joke was more about the Duchess of Marlborough's cupidity than about Godolphin's character. Moreover, Manley did not use the nickname Volpone for Goldolphin. She used it instead for the family of the Lord Chancellor William Cowper, including his mother, Lady Sarah Cowper, relieved at Manley's innocuous depiction of Lady Volpone. Manley's use of the name for a different family of prominent Whigs would lessen the possibility that a charge of libel could be brought against Sacheverell since the name, now overly determined with meanings, could not be said to refer definitively to a particular person.

In writing satirical secret history, Manley was producing works that readers could choose to read or not. Sacheverell used the disparaging nickname of Volpone in a public sermon preached on a national holiday at the invitation of the lord mayor of London. Not only was the public use of this pseudonym insulting, but Sacheverell pronounced a sentence of misery after death on the "*Volpones*" and other "false brethren": they would take their "*Portion with Hypocrites and Unbelievers, with all Lyars, that have their Part in the Lake which Burns with Fire and Brimstone.*"[32] Sachverell would be able to claim that he intended no particular individual here, and his use of *Volpones* in the plural would make it less easy to pin him down—but his target was clear.

Godolphin was already feeling caught between the Duchess of Marlborough, ever lobbying him to pressure the queen with Whig requests, and the queen herself, who was increasingly resisting advice from the Whigs. On the same day that Sacheverell was in St. Paul's insulting such Volpones in the pulpit, Godolphin wrote a letter to the Duchess of Marlborough, expressing his impatience at the pressure being put on him to persuade the queen about new appointments to the Admiralty Board. The Whigs were lobbying for two Whigs to be appointed, yet Queen Anne would put in only one of their choices. Godolphin was clearly doing the best he could in persuading the monarch to a further Whig appointment, but Sarah had insinuated in her last letter that the Whigs in Parliament doubted the force of his lobbying with the queen. "You will have it that I differ from you," he writes, taking umbrage at the suggestion that he was not working hard enough on their behalf: "at the same time I am laboring like a slave in the galleys for what you desire."[33]

Even before he had heard the details of Sacheverell's sermon, in which he was tarred as a false brother, Godolphin was frustrated that the Whigs themselves had complained about him to Sarah behind his back, casting doubt on the sincerity of his efforts on their behalf: "I don't know who those Whiggs are that tell you they don't believe me, but I should bee very glad they would tell mee soe, that I might not give them the trouble of conversing with anybody so unsincere." He wishes they could see that he has no "other views in this affair, but what they give mee" and that he is taking "twice as much pains as all of them together, to bring it to passe." He adds that whoever had misrepresented his aims to her, "is either very ill informed, or had a mind to doe mee an ill office to you." Godolphin adds a dark final sentence in his letter to Sarah: "So many [ill offices] have been done already and with so much success, that the best office anybody can doe mee now is to take mee out of the world."[34]

Godolphin may have felt caught between the Whigs, the duchess, and the queen, but he was persisting in his duties, daily attending meeting after meeting at court with the queen, with other members of the Privy Council and the House of Lords. He also continued patiently to write to the Duke and Duchess of Marlborough almost daily, putting every effort into working with them for what they thought was the good of the nation. Godolphin was greatly relieved when he heard from the Duke of Marlborough in the middle of October that he was preparing to return to England for the winter break in the war; in that era wars were routinely put on hold for four to six months because the roads were impassable from mud and snow. Godolphin assured Marlborough that he would "not bee negligent in your commands about the yachts and the men of warr" for his return.[35] Godolphin also makes clear how important Marlborough's presence will be to helping settle various other political affairs, both domestic, and international. He encourages Marlborough in his intention to return to England as soon as possible: "I beg you to bee perswaded, nothing can bee so material as your hastening to us."[36] Godolphin was pleading with Marlborough to return home as soon as possible even before Sacheverell preached his sermon or before he guessed at the venomous letters the Duchess of Marlborough had recently been sending to Queen Anne.

■

The Duke of Marlborough was as smooth and charming to his enemies as he was to his friends. His skill as a diplomat had impressed monarchs from Charles II to William III just as it had worried them, should such powers of persuasion ever be used against them. Manley, who claims to have seen him at the gaming tables at the Duchess of Cleveland's residence, acknowledges his "gracefulness" and the "solemn joy" in "Face" in her *New Atalantis* even as she satirizes him for his ambition and avarice.[37] Marlborough's presence as a dealmaker in the House of Lords and a voice of persuasive charm in the Privy Council was essential to ensuring the Whig agenda and funding for the War of Spanish Succession. While Marlborough was fighting on the battlefield or negotiating treaties in the courts of Europe for six to eight months out of every year, not only was Godolphin deprived of his assistance in the Privy Council and in the House of Lords, but the Duchess of Marlborough was left to act on her own, taking advice from confidants other than her husband. Sometimes the duchess sent drafts of her letters intended for the queen to Marlborough first for his approval. Sometimes she asked him to write to the queen on her behalf, and sometimes she eschewed her husband's advice altogether.

Lacking the tact of her husband and the patience and diplomacy of Godolphin, the Duchess of Marlborough prided herself on her frankness and honesty. In the early 1690s, during the reign of William and Mary, Princess Anne had initiated the pseudonyms of Mrs. Morley and Mrs. Freeman for her correspondence with Sarah, to put them on equal footing, rather than having Sarah address her in letters as "your Royal Highness" this or "your Royal Highness" that. Sarah had always felt it her duty to inform the queen whenever she appeared to be leading the nation the wrong way. Such outspokenness, however, had become increasingly unwelcome to Anne as she understood that Sarah may have felt she was speaking "truth" but was in fact speaking the "truth" of the Whigs. Anne herself, who had sought unsuccessfully to keep a cabinet and Privy Council balanced between Whigs and

Tories, had often attempted to persuade Sarah that she was "mightily mistaken in [her] notion of a true whig" and that the "character" Sarah ascribed to them "does not in the least belong to them."[38]

As a modern biographer explains, once Anne took the throne, Sarah was denied "direct political involvement" but was "totally unfitted by temperament to exercise the kind of unofficial influence which the Queen's fondness for her might otherwise have permitted. Tact, sensitive persuasion, respect for another person's point of view, were to her simply 'flattery & artifices.'" Sarah considered Anne "ignorant in everything but what the parsons had taught her as a child" and "unable to see that in supporting the Tories, she was being imposed on by knaves and fools," a point that Anne repeatedly refuted.[39] As early as 1703, Queen Anne was observing to Sarah that once Sarah came to know the Whigs better, she would "find they are not what they would be thought to be." Anne herself understood that there were "knaves" in both parties, a point that Sarah would never acknowledge. The queen also recognized that some Whigs were "good reasonable people"; she only wished there were a larger number of such reasonable people "in both partys."[40]

Of course, when the queen had been taking Sarah's advice without question, Sarah did not consider her being imposed on by knaves or fools. Only when the queen was thinking for herself carefully enough to choose between Tory or Whig counsel on a particular policy did Sarah accuse her of being incapable of thinking for herself.

■

BY 1703, LESS THAN two years since she had taken the throne, Anne was so hurt by Sarah's rudeness to her over matters of policy that she complained, when anticipating the difficulties of the ensuing winter, "your Coldness added to it will make it insupportable."[41] In February that year, Sarah was shutting Anne out in part because of her own overwhelming grief at the death of her only surviving son, John Churchill, a promising young man who at age seventeen had contracted smallpox and soon thereafter died. Anne herself had suffered the death of her only son to survive childhood a few years earlier, in addition to having endured numerous other miscarriages or stillbirths, and she wanted to comfort Sarah in her grief. But Sarah asked only her husband and Sidney Godolphin to share her first weeks of mourning, responding to

Anne's concern with coldness. After John left for the military campaign just two weeks later, Sarah was seen wandering in widow's garb, pacing the cloisters at Westminster Abbey, leading some observers to believe her head was "near touched."[42] But still Sarah shut Queen Anne out and refused her attempts at comforting. She also continued to harass Anne for trying to find a balance between Whigs and Tories in her cabinet.

As early as 1705 the queen increasingly ignored Sarah and her outspoken criticism of anything the Tories proposed, and sought the more soothing companionship of Sarah's cousin, her bedchamber woman Abigail Masham. When Sarah did write to the queen out of fear of the policies Abigail was promoting on behalf of Robert Harley and the Tories, she was often imprudent in her phrasing. The more partiality Anne showed toward Abigail, the more Sarah panicked. In her panic, she turned to cruelty, hoping to shame the queen into dismissing Abigail by taunting her about her attachment to her bedchamber woman.

In the summer of 1708, Sarah wrote the reckless letter in which she threatened the queen with a loss of her virtuous reputation if she continued in her closeness with Abigail: "nor can I think the having noe inclination for any but one's own sex is enough to maintain such a character as I wish may still be yours."[43] Sarah's assumption that Anne would be troubled by public opinion is surprising, given Anne's long indifference to precisely that opinion when it ran in opposition to those she loved. In exasperation at Sarah's pestering her about Abigail, Anne finally insisted, "Sure I may love whom I please."[44] Sarah herself, once the recipient of that love, should have recalled Anne's tenacity in it.

She should have remembered how, in 1692, Princess Anne had exiled herself from William and Mary's court rather than dismiss Sarah from her retinue. At the time, she even took pride in this act of resistance. When she and Sarah visited Bath in the summer of 1692, Anne received no reception from the mayor, under orders from Queen Mary, and she told Sarah "tis a thing to be laughed at" if William and Mary thought they could either "vex" or "gaine upon" her "by such sort of usage." Anne was more loyal to those she loved than concerned about what the court or the public thought, even if Sarah found the stress of public resentment gave her the "spleen."[45] Yet by 1709 Sarah seems either to have forgotten Anne's tenacity or to be surprised that it could be exerted against her, rather than in her favor.

In 1709, encouraged by Arthur Maynwaring, Sarah continued to mention Abigail from time to time in her letters to the queen, despite Anne's repeated requests that she cease doing so. The Duke of Marlborough was not pleased with the influence that Maynwaring had over Sarah's correspondence with Anne. The younger man was a staunch Whig MP and a writer of pamphlets and prologues for the stage. He had written some scurrilous ballads about Abigail and the queen, which Sarah enjoyed singing with her Whig friends. Maynwaring was not married but lived openly with his mistress, the talented actress Anne Oldfield. He flattered the Duchess of Marlborough as "more capable of business than any Man," a compliment similar to that that Ralph, Earl of Montagu, extended to Delarivier Manley during their mediation over the Bath-Albemarle lawsuit when he told her he had never met any other woman of "so great Ability as herself."[46]

As much as the Marlboroughs' marriage was a love match, the reality of male privilege in this era meant that the Duchess of Marlborough always had doubts, not about her husband's enduring love but about his monogamy. Having come of age at the court of Charles II, in which both the king and his brother kept multiple mistresses, and having himself had an affair with the Duchess of Cleveland, Marlborough likely considered it acceptable to engage in extramarital relations. He was not merely charming and diplomatic but, as a military commander responsible for espionage operations (among his other leadership duties), perfectly capable of keeping secrets. He was not, however, capable of containing the rumors that circulated about him; nor was he capable of assuaging Sarah's own suspicions about his behavior. Early in their marriage, in 1678, Sarah had worried that her new husband and James, then Duke of York, were womanizing in Edinburgh, while she was left in London pregnant with their first child—a not unreasonable fear, insofar as the Duke of York set the example as a notorious womanizer; it was said that "[he] exhausted himself by his inconstancy."[47]

In the spring of 1708, the Duke of Marlborough complained that Sarah was treating him with "coldness and indifferency," behavior probably prompted by rumors she had heard about an intrigue with the actress Hester Santlow.[48] It would have been little comfort to her that others gossiping in London found that although Sarah, approaching fifty, was "many years older," she was still "ten times handsomer" than the suspected mistress.[49]

Sarah's underlying love for John was especially evident whenever she was concerned about him on the battlefield. And if he ever left for military campaigns on the Continent while she was still angry with him, she would swiftly write him a letter repairing their relationship, as she did later, in the spring of 1708. But having spent many decades likely taking for granted her own stunning beauty, as well as the adoration of her husband, Sidney Godolphin, and Queen Anne, the loss of the queen's favor and her suspicions about her husband's intrigues would have made her welcome the charm and intellectual flattery of Arthur Maynwaring. She also welcomed his advice to add a satirical tone to her correspondence with the queen.

Although Marlborough had specifically advised Sarah to cease speaking or writing to the queen about politics, in 1709 she continued to write to the Queen Anne about Abigail—despite the queen's plea not to do so and her protest that her insinuations did wrong "to Masham and me."[50] She joked with Arthur Maynwaring that this phrase echoed the phrase King James I had often used when referring to his lover, the Duke of Buckingham: "Steenie and I."[51] But she was no doubt genuinely hurt that the passionate devotion from Anne she had taken for granted had disappeared. Not knowing how to rekindle that spark, or perhaps suspecting that it would have been impossible to do so, Sarah instead turned to attacking Anne about Abigail.

Initially, Sarah tried to confront Abigail directly about her treatment of her and for having changed Queen Anne's view of her. Abigail, who had been taken in by the Duchess of Marlborough two decades earlier in charity, agreed to meet with Sarah to discuss their relative positions with the queen. Sarah had hoped Abigail would admit to her efforts in turning the queen against her and mend her behavior. Sarah subsequently described their meeting in October 1707, when Abigail had the audacity to respond that she was "sure the Queen, who had lov'd me so extremely, would always be very kind to her me."[52] This confident, "superior air" put on by a relation she believed she had "raised from the dust" left Sarah stunned.[53] It also explained to her who was responsible for the noticeable increase in sarcasm in the queen's letters to her.

After Abigail's refusal to do anything to ameliorate Sarah's position with the queen, Sarah began her ill-conceived letter-writing campaign to persuade Anne that the world was laughing at her for her relationship with Abigail and to shame her into dismissing Abigail from court. Sarah justified these epistolary attacks by the fact that the Whigs and the Duke of Marlborough felt that removing the queen from Abigail's influence would allow them to pursue their strategy in the War of Spanish Succession. On the one hand, Marlborough had requested her never to write Anne about politics. On the other hand, in August 1708 he had written to her that they must get Anne "out of the hands of" Abigail "or everything will be labour in vain."[54]

Even if Marlborough had warned Sarah to refrain from writing to Anne about politics, she knew that he believed the political situation, as well as the continued Allied participation in the War of Spanish Succession, depended on separating the queen from her bedchamber woman. Sarah still continued to raise the rumors of lesbianism when she felt panicked about the progress of the war. In 1708, after Harley had been forced out of his position as secretary of state (after a power struggle between Marlborough and Godolphin and the queen over Harley's increasing influence), there was talk among the Whigs, particularly by Arthur Maynwaring, of proposing an act of Parliament to dismiss Abigail from her court offices. The Whigs' concern about Abigail's influence was made evident when Harley bragged, once he had been dismissed from Anne's cabinet in February 1708, that he would "play [Masham] against anybody."[55] Although he was no longer in the cabinet, he knew he still exerted influence over the queen.

Sarah saw the danger in asking Parliament to intervene in regard to Abigail, which would give the public perception that she had engineered the ouster out of private spite. So, rather than encouraging Maynwaring to act publicly, she chose again to act through private correspondence.

In late October 1709, in a state that one biographer has described as "bordering on mania," Sarah sent a "voluminous headlong narrative" she had written to the queen describing her years as a royal favorite and citing from the queen's many early affectionate letters to her.[56] She drew on a popular devotional manual, *The Whole Duty of Man,* in instructing the queen about the evil of "forsaking" a "friendship for slight or no cause." In constructing her own version of their decades-long friendship in narrative and referencing the queen's youthful letters to her, Sarah was demonstrating that she could quickly put together a memoir to publish. When she showed some of the queen's early passionate letters to Godolphin, he warned her that "they should not bee seen but by very few."[57] The duchess made clear in her reply to Godolphin that although the queen had asked her to return the originals of those letters in her possession, she was "resolved" that she would "not part with whatever course she would take to have them."[58] She was holding them, as a modern biographer points out, as a form of blackmail over the queen.[59] Anne well understood this strategy. When asked whether the Duchess of Marlborough was cheating in her capacity as mistress of the privy purse, the queen apparently replied in a comment that the duchess later cited to defend herself against mismanagement of the queen's finances: "Everybody knows cheating is not the Duchess of Marlborough's crime."[60]

The queen never responded to Sarah's long narrative except to say that she had "not yet had leisure to read all your paypers" but would write some "answer" when she found the time.[61] Although she perfectly understood the duchess's threat of blackmail, the queen may have decided that the duchess had more to lose by publishing those letters than she had. In any case, the queen decided to respond by refusing to reply, imitating Sarah's own long-standing strategy of freezing out someone she was angry with. Sarah then followed up with another letter, this time using Delarivier Manley's *New Atalantis* as an excuse once again to raise the issue of lesbian friendships in order to make the queen feel shamed enough about possible damage to her reputation that she would dismiss Abigail.

■

WHEN MANLEY'S *New Atalantis* became the talk of London by late October 1709, the duchess did not purchase or read a copy of the work but asked Arthur Maynwaring to read it for her. He promptly wrote back with a synopsis of the whole, in which, as he explains, "the favourite characters are Abigail[,] Mr. Harley and Lord Peterborough." Maynwaring hopes that the author's depiction of Abigail will make her laugh as it did him: "Hilaria (that's her name) is wedded to all the virtues; has a soul fitted for grandeur; a capacious repository for the confidence of royal favour." He further disparages "this stupid book" by recounting what the author (whom Maynwaring still believed to be male) writes of Robert Harley: "Speaking of Don Geronimo de Haro (as the fool calls him), he begins his character thus: he was honest! He was brave!" Manwaring interjects, "Could any one but an idiot call him honest in a good sense?"[62]

Despite his mockery of Manley's work, Maynwaring, himself a writer of satirical verse and pamphlets, seemed reluctant to prosecute the author even before he learned that it was the playwright Delarivier Manley, whom he might well have met through his own connections and those of his mistress, Anne Oldfield. At the start of his letter to the duchess, Maywnaring observes in a general way (overlooking his own satirical pamphleteering), "The license of the press is too great, and I hope some proper way may be found to restrain it this winter." He then adds caution about prosecuting the author of this work: "but I would not have the rise taken from this trifling books, which, as you observe truly, would only make it spread more." Maynwaring further mocks "the fine style" of the prose which "can only be fit to be laughed at."[63]

This response to a letter from Sarah, which (like almost all of hers) was destroyed at her own request, suggests that she, like Maynwaring, felt that harassing the author of this "trifling book" would only increase its popularity. Yet if Sarah recognized the imprudence of bringing legal charges against the author of *The New Atalantis,* she did not recognize the imprudence of writing a satirical letter of her own to Queen Anne citing the work.

In a letter to the queen written about the same time that the Earl of Sunderland arrested Manley, the duchess informs Anne of a new book that "is not well written" but that spread rumors about the queen and Abigail. Although Maynwaring had told the duchess that the book was complimentary to Abigail, the duchess suggests that the book was a satire about Abigail and that it "shews that the notion is extensively spread among all sorts of people" about the queen's preference for her bedchamber woman. The duchess misleadingly refers to the book as a "dialogue between Madam Maintenon and Madame Masham," which she describes as a conversation in which the French courtesan, Madame Maintenon, thanks Masham for her "good endeavours to serve the King of France here" and "her friendship for Mr. Harley." She adds that "there is stuff, not fit to be mentioned, of passions between women."[64]

In claiming to refer to Manley's *New Atalantis,* for which she and her printers were now "under prosecution," the duchess misleadingly gives it the title of an earlier court satire, one not written by Manley: *The Rival Dutchess: or, Court Incendiary. In a Dialogue between Madam Maintenon and Madam M*———. In insinuating that this was the title of Manley's publication Sarah is able to press the idea that the queen's (ostensibly lesbian) relationship with Abigail was the talk of the town. In fact, *The Rival Dutchess,* which may have been written by Arthur Maynwaring, is a satirical dialogue in which Madame M. (Abigail) explains to the French courtier Madame de Maintenon how she and Harley are promoting French policies at the English court. The dialogue is more about Machievellian politics than sex, and it depicts Abigail as working with Harley behind the scenes to help the French. It is nothing like Manley's complimentary treatment of Abigail in *The New Atalantis.* Nor are lesbian relationships the main focus of either work. There is one anecdote about lesbianism in *The Rival Dutchess,* but not in reference to anyone at court, and Manley includes a lesbian cabal in her *New Atalantis,* but it is a cabal of Whig women writers, including Manley's former friend Catherine Trotter and Trotter's literary patron, Lady Sarah Piers. Neither work depicts a relationship between Abigail and Queen Anne. As Sarah well knew, from Maynwaring's summary of Manley's work, Abigail is rendered in heroic terms in *The New Atalantis,* saving Sarah herself from a mob of angry rabble.

In mentioning the new book that "all sorts of people" would be reading, Sarah was assuming that the queen would not have read Manley's *New Atalantis* herself. Otherwise she might have been more careful in her reference to the work. She would have had to get the title right; she would also have had to acknowledge that she, not Abigail, bore the brunt of Manley's satire. Sarah knew that the queen did not love works of satire; Anne found Jonathan Swift's *A Tale of a Tub* disrespectful toward established religion, despite its serious critique of religious hypocrisy. But Sarah should have realized that Abigail Masham would very likely have read Manley's best-selling secret history, especially once she heard that the work satirized her haughty cousin and complimented her. As Sarah well knew from noting the change in tone and vocabulary in some of Anne's letters, Abigail also appeared to be advising the queen on her correspondence. So Abigail likely would have seen Sarah's letter, which might have motivated her to secure a copy of Manley's book and inform the queen that there were no lesbian scenes between the queen and the figure for Abigail—and that the only lesbian scenes were about Whig women writers and their Whig patrons.

Sarah had not only been writing to the queen herself but also asking her husband to write on her behalf. Since Marlborough was about to lead the troops into battle at Malplaquet the day he received one of Sarah's requests, the duke deferred writing to the queen at that time. When he did write to Anne in October, about giving away some of Sarah's rooms at Kensington Palace, the queen wrote back to place the blame squarely on Sarah, insisting, "I believe nobody was ever so used by a friend as I have been by her ever since my coming to the Crown. I desire nothing but that she will leave off teasing and tormenting me."[65] The queen also wrote to Sarah directly, two days before Manley was arrested for libel, telling her, as Sarah summarized later, after destroying the letter, that "she would always behave herself to me as the D: of M:s wife, & as her groom of the Stole & she desires me once more not to torment her about Masham."[66] It was just a few days later that Sarah took up her pen again to torment the queen about Abigail, using Manley's book as an excuse, insisting that "I hope you no longer think . . . I was the only person that discerned the private way of conversing with Mrs. Masham, since all that matter is now in print, and notwithstanding the prosecution, I suppose sold at every shop."[67]

Sarah's logic in asserting the publicity around Anne's ostensible passion for Abigail is difficult for modern historians to understand. Ophelia Field, writing in *The Favourite,* acknowledges the intensity of Anne and Sarah's friendship, even in an era when romantic language between female friends was typical.[68] In an early draft of her memoirs, Sarah describes how Anne "used to say *she desired to possess her wholy*" and how her emotions rose "even to the jealousy of a Lover." Sarah distinguishes between Anne's "passionate *Love*" for her and her "sincerest *Friendship*" for Anne.[69] Anne Somerset, Queen Anne's most recent biographer, dismisses the idea that there was ever a sexual intimacy, despite the passionate language in Anne's early letters to Sarah. As Somerset explains in *Queen Anne: The Politics of Passion,* Sarah felt that "lesbianism was a disgusting vice, with which she had never been tainted." She felt that Anne's friendship for her was "inspired purely by an admiration for her intellect and forthright character. Since Abigail lacked such attributes, it followed that Anne had been attracted to her for different reasons," that is, for "indulging her baser appetites."[70] Moreover, Somerset adds, Anne never invented private nicknames for Abigail (as she had done, in having Sarah write as Mrs. Freeman to her Mrs. Morely); she always addressed Masham simply by her last name as she would a servant.

Further evidence to bolster skepticism about Anne's putative lesbianism is a letter that Sarah would write to Anne's doctor, the Whig Sir David Hamilton, in December 1710, when she had given up on the strategy of trying to manipulate the queen into removing Abigail. In this later letter, Sarah refers to some satires "lately come out which they said were not fit for me to see, by which I guess they are upon a subject that you may remember I complain'd of to you." Rather than acknowledging that she had previously agreed with the gist of these satires (about Anne's relationship with Abigail), Sarah insisted, in what was probably an attempt to reconcile herself with the queen, that "really it troubl'd me very much, upon my own account as well as others, because it was very disagreeable, & what I know to be a lye."[71]

In addition to what she knows is a "lye" about Anne's lesbianism, the logic of Sarah holding Anne's prior letters over her was to shame the monarch by showing that she had broken the bonds of friendship and loyalty. In her 1742 memoir, *An Account of the Conduct of the Dowager Duchess of Marlborough,* the duchess emphasizes the significance of Anne's befriending her. For most monarchs, she explains, "Friendship is an offensive word; it imports a kind of equality between the parties; it suggests nothing to the mind of crowns or thrones, high titles, or immense revenues."[72] Sarah felt honored at the place of equality the queen had long granted her, and she gave it resonance as a type of Whig virtue, making Queen Anne into a monarch gladly sharing power with equals. But for all of Sarah's Whiggish principles, she—like most court Whigs of her era—did not mean for equality to extend beyond her own social rank. Part of her complaint in trying to shame the queen about her relationship with Abigail was that Abigail had been working as a domestic servant for the Earl of Rivers before Sarah took her in as a charity case and found her a position as bedchamber woman to the queen. She considered Abigail, her own first cousin, to be of a lower social rank. The public humiliation Sarah asserted was not just about the ostensible lesbianism but about Anne's associating with someone inferior. But the queen, for all her Tory traditionalism, was not at all a snob and greatly valued her loyal household servants, including Abigail.

Had Sarah been able to consult her husband, still in The Hague waiting for the wind to change, about sending such insinuating letters to the Queen, the ever diplomatic duke would not have thought it a good idea. He had already advised her, in an August letter, against reproaching the queen about the rooms at Kensington Palace. He had observed that "in disputes, especially in that of kindness and friendship, that all reproches, though never so reasonable, do serve to no other end by the making the breach wider."[73] In fact, when Sarah met in person with Anne about the rooms in October, after Abigail had left court to give birth, she only offended Anne further—shouting at her in a manner that startled footmen in adjacent corridors.[74]

Sarah felt that she was no longer writing merely to torment the queen about Abigail for personal reasons but for the good of the nation. Just as the queen's decision not to wear jewels at the thanksgiving ceremony for the Battle of Oudenarde in August 1708 had become the talk of Europe—and encouraged Louis XIV in thinking the Allies would lose support for the war if Anne lost confidence in Marlborough—so rumors of the queen's treatment of the Duchess of Marlborough were still being tracked by diplomats from foreign courts. The queen had heard this argument before and had spent a few months in 1707 putting on an act of behaving with warmth and friendship toward Sarah in public while treating her coldly in private. Anne saw Sarah less frequently in 1709, since Sarah often avoided court, but Sarah felt that she would be sensitive to the gossip in *The New Atalantis* that was being "sold at every shop" and recognize how this gossip would have played in courts across Europe. Sarah wrote to Maynwaring that the "truths" she was telling Anne, although they might make "her hate me," would make it "easier for the ministers [cabinet members] to govern her."[75]

■

By 10 November, the day the Duke of Marlborough finally returned to London, the fourth printing of Manley's *New Atalantis* had just been "wrought off" the presses and "seiz'd on" by government authorities. With the book now scarce, public interest in it would only increase in the months to come.[76] Two days later, an observer of the Sacheverell affair reported: "Notwithstanding the Majority of ye Court of Aldermen at London were, when propos'd, against printing Dr. Sacheverell's Sermon, yet 'tis now actually in the Press at London."[77]

Normally, sermons preached before the city leaders would be printed with their approval. However, many of the City of London aldermen listening to Sacheverell were aware that it would be controversial, and voted against printing it. Whether or not the lord mayor wanted him to publish it is less clear, but Sacheverell himself clearly intended to publish the text of his sermon, having spent a week correcting it and reviewing his text with three different lawyers, who "perused and examined" it in respect to ecclesiastical and civil law.[78] His care in preparing the publication ensured that it would be difficult to prosecute him for seditious libel.

The first edition of the sermon, which was available for sale by 25 November, was an expensive one, at 1 shilling for a pamphlet running to fifty-five pages. About eight hundred copies of this edition were printed and sold in London, Oxford, Litchfield, and Derby. By 1 December the printer, Henry Clements, was bringing out a cheaper, thirty-one-page version in smaller type. He printed between 35,000 to 40,000 copies of this version. Two days later he produced a further printing of this second edition. Clements realized a tidy profit "from one of the most successful minor publishing *coups* of the century" before the pirated editions (with even smaller type) began appearing through which unauthorized printers made their own profit.[79]

Had the sermon not been printed, there likely would have been no legal or political consequences. But by the middle of December, about 50,000 copies of it were being read and shared. As one historian explains, "A sermon which had originally been heard by a few hundred people was now going to be read, at the most narrowly conservative estimate by at least a quarter of a million men and women, in other words by a number equal to the whole electorate of England and Wales."[80] The Whigs in Parliament recognized that the sermon itself would encourage other high church clergy to preach against the Whigs and against the Act of Toleration. And Sacheverell himself was now even more popular as a preacher, attracting mobs of auditors. When he was invited to preach on the last Sunday in November at St. Margaret's Lothbury, a small church adjacent to the Bank of England and half a mile from St. Paul's Cathedral, a great mob filled the streets. An observer describes the scene outside St. Margaret's, where there "was so great a Concourse of People that they had like to have pull'd down the Church Doors and Windows to hear him."[81]

The Whig MP Arthur Maynwaring, a firm supporter of a free press, had found amusing the fictional scene of rabble rising up against the Marchioness of Caria (Duchess of Marlborough) in Manley's *New Atalantis.* However, when actual mobs swelled in the streets outside the Bank of England to welcome Sacheverell to St. Margaret's Lothbury, Maynwaring, along with the other Whigs in Parliament, must have shuddered.

4

The General Who Would Be King

When the queen moved the court in early November 1709 from its summer residence at Windsor to St. James's Palace in London, the Duchess of Marlborough kept her distance, often staying at Windsor Lodge (the elegant country house that was a perk of her position as ranger of Windsor Park) to avoid the queen and Abigail at court. But she returned to St. James's so that she would be in town to meet her husband on his return from the Continent. The Duke of Marlborough had endured a "tedious passage" by boat, first stuck in Dunkirk sands and then forced to land at Aldborough in Suffolk on 8 November, although when he arrived at St. James's Palace on 10 November he looked "as well as ever," according to one contemporary.[1] Shortly after his return to court, he sought an audience with Queen Anne to speak with her again about being appointed captain-general for life.

When Marlborough had first made this request of the queen in person the previous spring, Queen Anne declined to give him a direct answer. He had sought advice from both Sidney Godolphin and Sir William Cowper, lord chancellor of Britain, who told him there was no precedent for such an appointment. Despite their dissuasion, Marlborough felt he needed the security of the position to maintain his power in negotiations in Europe. When he wrote to the queen about the matter in an October letter, he complained that he knew he had lost influence with her since Abigail had replaced the Duchess of Marlborough as her favorite. Refusing to grant him that "mark of favour" in her written reply, Queen Anne left open the possibility that if he asked her again when he returned home, she "would comply" with his desires. At the same time, she also denied that Abigail or anyone else had influenced her in her decision. She insisted, "What I said was my own thoughts." She also requested his help in ensuring that the Duchess of Marlborough "behave with the decency she ought, both to her friend and Queen."[2]

Given her suggestion that he renew his request when he returned home, Marlborough tried one more time in person after his return to London in November. He understood that the Tories wanted a swift peace. As his descendant Winston Churchill explains, granting Marlborough the position for life "might have given him the authority which he needed to bring the war to a satisfactory end."[3] Although their meeting was no doubt polite on both sides, given the natural courtesy of each, the queen once again refused Marlborough's request.

Having spent over half of each year on the battlefields of Europe, Marlborough was thinking in terms of a European balance of power and a sense of European fairness to each of the Protestant Allies. In early November he had spent a few days in The Hague lobbying against a proposed buffer arrangement, the Barrier Treaty between Britain and the Dutch Republic, which he felt was unfair to the Prussian interests in the Grand Alliance. Marlborough was not only thinking like a European, he was doing everything he could to "preserve that confidence in himself on the Continent without which neither the armies nor the signatory states could be held together," even if that meant working against his fellow plenipotentiary, Charles Townshend, who was lobbying for the treaty.[4]

Queen Anne, by contrast, had been struggling throughout her entire reign less concerned with the European balance of power than with a simple balance between Tories and Whigs in her own cabinet. The queen certainly recognized the European situation, and she understood the need to keep in check an expansionist Catholic monarch who was encouraging, and financially underwriting, her own Catholic half-brother's attempts to gain the British throne. But Anne was more of a pragmatist than an idealist. The Whigs themselves, including the Duchess of Marlborough, had cried wolf too often, insisting at every turn that if the Whigs were not placated, the Pretender would soon be seated on her throne. It was already clear by 1709 that whatever shape the final peace treaty would take, it would include a clause requiring the French to expel the Pretender from France and recognize the Hanoverian succession to the English throne following Anne's death. Meanwhile Anne was growing impatient with the war and feeling harassed by the Whig Junto as well as by the Duchess of Marlborough. She was in no mood to agree to the Duke of Marlborough's request for a life command.

Not achieving success in his meeting with the queen, the duke repaired with the duchess and their friend Sidney Godolphin to Oxfordshire for a few days to inspect the progress made on Blenheim Palace.[5] This "*Superbous* Palace," as Delarivier Manley had mocked it in *The New Atalantis,* had initially been suggested as a country estate for the Marlboroughs, in honor of the Battle of Blenheim (1704), in lieu of an imposing column or monument in London. When Marlborough was granted the dukedom that same year, he and his wife were concerned at not owning the sort of country estate that other English dukes would have inherited. This palatial home, on a royal estate granted to the Marlboroughs for a nominal yearly rent, would become both the seat of the Duke of Marlborough and a monument to the victory at Blenheim.

It was understood that some public money would go toward the construction costs, but in 1704 no one imagined that costs would soar much beyond the initial outlay of £60,000. The difficulty was that Marlborough had chosen the Whig dramatist John Vanbrugh to design the building. Vanbrugh was not a trained architect but a designer who had worked with architects to create Castle Howard. His plans for a baroque-style palace were ostentatious and extravagant. The Duchess of Marlborough was continually squabbling with him over the costs of construction; meanwhile, many workers were not being paid, as the Marlboroughs delayed payments, thinking Parliament might grant further funding. By 1709 Blenheim was less than half completed; there was not even a portion finished where the duke and duchess might reside temporarily. Queen Anne, who had not allocated public money to rebuild Whitehall Palace (partially destroyed by fire in 1698) or to finish the renovations she envisioned for Hampton Court Palace, was balking at the continued requests for contributions. Making everything more difficult was the fact that although the victory against the French at Blenheim in 1704 had been stunning, it did not bring the anticipated swift end to the war. Five years later, following the terrible loss of Allied troops at the Battle of Malplaquet, the end of the war was still not in sight. Such an expensive tribute to that long-ago victory now seemed inappropriate, especially as the Marlboroughs continued to lose favor with Queen Anne.

In their initial attempt at avoiding the ostentation of a sculpted monument to Blenheim in London, the Marlboroughs had created a much greater embarrassment. The extravagance of the plans for the palace continued to fuel rumors that the Duke of Marlborough considered himself "King John the Second"—rumors only enhanced by his having been granted the title of Prince of Mindelheim, a city-sized princedom in Bavaria, by the Holy Roman emperor in 1705.[6] He was allocated the £2,000 annual income princedom and granted an exemption from the annual £6,000 in wartime imperial taxes. Marlborough may not have been King John of England, but he was already a prince with a palace under construction; he was a general and a plenipotentiary who sometimes felt he had a right to ignore diplomatic instructions, as he did in distancing himself from the Barrier Treaty—a move that even biographer Winston Churchill described as "open to stricture."[7] Although little was probably known to the wider public about Marlborough's unsupervised diplomatic maneuvering in Europe, Delarivier Manley accurately noted the resentment rising against the Marlboroughs by 1709. Rather than public opinion turning against Queen Anne because of Abigail Masham, as Sarah had hoped, public opinion was turning against her and her husband for their own imperialist attitudes, which seemed contradictory to her Whig principles.

On 15 November 1709, Anne officially opened Parliament, reading the Queen's Speech, in which she described the Battle of Malplaquet as "a most remarkable victory" and suggested that France was more "in need of a peace than before."[8] These words, however, had been written and approved by a parliamentary committee. And the queen, who usually read such speeches with emotion in her voice—a voice so beautiful that Charles II had arranged for the famed actress Elizabeth Barry to give Anne elocution lessons when she was a young girl—did not put her usual effort into her delivery that day. As Arthur Maynwaring reported afterward, writing to the duchess, "It was observed that she spoke it in a much fainter voice than she used to have, and her manner was more careless and less moving than it has been on other occasions."[9]

On 17 November, Marlborough was given a more enthusiastic hero's welcome in the House of Lords. On 22 November the queen attended a thanksgiving service at St. Paul's Cathedral to celebrate Marlborough's victory at Malplaquet, a service well attended by Whigs at court and in Parliament. The dean of Peterborough Cathedral preached on Luke 17:17, in effect comparing "the opponents of the ministry [Anne's Whig cabinet] to the nine healed lepers who had neglected to give thanks to Christ."[10] One Tory commentator snidely described the occasion as a celebration of the "late Glorious Victory (as the Duke of Marlborough and his Friends are pleas'd to style our prodigious Loss)." He added cynically that its only purpose was to "get large Summs of Money from them that the War may still be prosecuted to ye Benefit of ye Duke of Marlborough & c."[11]

Marlborough's enemies continued to whisper that he was extending the war for his own personal advantage and for the advantage of Whig merchants and money lenders supplying the war, which was funded by land taxes that fell hardest on Tory landowners. There were also rumors falsely insinuating that Marlborough was embezzling the percentage of supply funding allocated for espionage, but Parliament nevertheless voted £6 million to continue the war. By 25 November, Marlborough was reporting to a European ally that "our Parliamentary business is going wonderfully [*à merveille*]."[12]

■

ON THE SAME DAY that Marlborough expressed his optimism in a letter to Europe, the first printing of Sacheverell's sermon appeared in booksellers' windows. By the first week of December, tens of thousands more copies would be sold in more affordable editions, reaching many thousands more readers. While readers were now easily able to acquire Sacheverell's sermon, it was harder to find a copy of Delarivier Manley's *New Atalantis.* Manley had been released on bail and was awaiting trial, scheduled for early in the new year. Her *New Atalantis,* so talked about in London, was now even more difficult to purchase, following the government seizure of the most recent print run. By 12 November, Lady Mary Pierrepont was relieved to hear that a friend had obtained a copy of the second volume, and she asked to borrow it; in exchange, Lady Mary promised to get her one of the printed keys identifying the real persons represented by the pseudonyms.[13]

Even before she managed to borrow the second volume, Lady Mary was well aware of the concerns the government had about "the liberty" Manley "uses in her memoirs." Pierrepont sympathized with Manley's situation. "Miserable is the fate of writers," she observed to her friend, "if they are agreeable, they are offensive; and if dull, they starve." A Whig herself, Lady Mary was nevertheless worried that the arrest of a Tory satirist like Manley would dissuade writers of either political party from writing satire or telling the truth about those in power. She feared that Manley would "serve as a scarecrow to frighten people from attempting any thing but heavy panegyric."[14] Pierrepont was right to be concerned about this sort of government crackdown on the press for political partisanship. The Earl of Sunderland, previously true to his Whig principles in disinclining to censor, now continued in apprehending Tory writers suspected of supporting the Jacobite cause. He arrested six more authors and printers for seditious libel within the week after Manley was released on bail.[15]

The Whig journalist Richard Steele, a satirist in his own right and a former friend of Manley, underscored the Whig change of attitude toward prosecuting satirists. In an early September issue of his essay-style periodical *The Tatler,* Steele sneeringly referred to an unnamed writer's use of "some artificial Poisons convey'd by Smells" in order to bring "many Persons of both Sexes to an untimely Fate."[16] His allusion to "Persons of both Sexes" makes clear that he is referring to Manley's work, whose full title was *Secret Memoirs and Manners of Several Persons of Quality, of Both Sexes. From the New Atalantis.*

Lady Mary Pierrepont may not yet have read the second volume of Manley's *New Atalantis,* but she had read Steele's complaints about it in "that vile paper the Tatler."[17] Steele's objection to Manley's book was partly personal. He clearly resented his own depiction as Monsieur Le Ingrate and was annoyed that she had aired his past scandals in her secret history. At first he kept his resentment private, complaining to Manley in a letter of her satirical treatment of him while insisting that he would not retaliate publicly because of her gender and social rank: "Your Sex, as well as your Quality of a Gentlewoman (a Justice you would not do my Birth and Education) shall always preserve you against the Pen of your provok'd, *Most humble Servant.*"[18] By the time of Manley's arrest, however, Steele may have been wondering why he was continuing to treat her with such chivalry.

As the editor of the government newspaper *The Gazette,* Steele was the beneficiary of the Whig's patronage. He had also launched his own periodical, *The Tatler,* in which he reflected on art, literature, social morals, and the standards of good taste. Regardless of whatever sympathy he might have retained for Manley as a former friend, he followed Sunderland's lead in his public references to Manley's *New Atalantis.* In *The Tatler* of 10 November 1709, Steele offered the Whigs a literary justification for their punitive treatment of Manley by making a distinction between genuine satire and mere libel. He explained, "The Satyrist and Libeller differ as much as the Magistrate and the Murderer. In the Consideration of human Life, the Satyrist never falls upon Persons who are not glaringly faulty, and the Libeller on none but who are conspicuously commendable."[19] Steele insinuated that Manley should be pursued for libel because she was tarnishing the reputation of persons otherwise "commendable." Whether such "commendable" persons included himself, the Duke of Marlborough, Sidney Godolphin, or the many other prominent figures Manley satirized, his point was that while genuine satire has an appropriate role in civil society, mere libel does not. In making this distinction, however, Steele may not have persuaded his fellow Kit-Cat Club member Arthur Maynwaring—who recognized the satirical humor in *The New Atalantis*—that Manley had in fact written a dangerous libel.

■

IN NOVEMBER 1709 *The Tatler* was not the only literary venue being influenced by partisan discord. The very choice of plays performed on stage reflected recent court politics as well. One month earlier, when Manley's *New Atalantis* was making the queen's new favorite, Abigail Masham, the talk of London, the Queen's Theatre revived a tragedy called *The Unhappy Favourite,* about Queen Elizabeth I and her former favorite, the Earl of Essex, "at the Desire of several Persons of Quality."[20] On 12 November, this play was staged again with the same cast, in which Anne Oldfield, Arthur Maynwaring's mistress, played Essex's wife.

The play is based not on the actual events of Essex's treasonous rebellion but on a 1690s romantic fiction in which Queen Elizabeth tragically discovers Essex's innocence just after his execution. It is impossible to trace who requested the productions of the play that autumn, but it is conceivable that Maynwaring or some other ally of the

Marlboroughs requested the performance on behalf of the Duchess of Marlborough, who had long believed she had been maligned and misrepresented by Abigail Masham to the queen. Staged again just two weeks after the Duke of Marlborough's return to England, the play contains scenes that broadcast the sorrow of a wronged favorite. For example, the Earl of Essex, the unhappy former favorite of Queen Elizabeth I but maligned to the queen by the Countess of Nottingham, intones at the end of Act III:

> But if ill Fate, and thy own Merits bring
> Thee once to be a Favourite to a King,
> It is a Curse that follows Loyalty,
> Curst in they Merits, more in thy Degree,
> In all the sport of Chance its chiefest Aim,
> Mankind's the *Hunt,* a Favourite is the *Game.*[21]

The haunting verse in the 23 November production would have echoed the feelings of the Duchess of Marlborough, now herself feeling a wronged former favorite. Even if the production had been requested on her behalf, however, it is unlikely that either Sarah herself or her husband was in the audience. The painful evocation of a favorite's fall from favor would have stung too much.

Ten days later, on Saturday, 3 December, the Duke of Marlborough might have attended the Drury Lane Theatre's production of William Congreve's comedy *Love for Love,* in which the dancer Hester Santlow, with whom he was rumored to have been having a liaison, performed as an actress, not merely a dancer, for the first time. The Marlboroughs' eldest daughter, Henrietta Godolphin, likely would also have been in the audience since she was a close friend and patron of Congreve and was widely believed to be his lover. The Duchess of Marlborough—who was infuriated at Henrietta for her closeness to Congreve and the risk she was posing to the family reputation, and still angry at her husband about the rumors concerning his liaison with Santlow—almost certainly would not have attended the play that afternoon.

Congreve's *Love for Love,* like so many of his works, depicts the problem of parents forbidding their children to marry merely for the sake of love. Although this play was written in the 1690s, long before Congreve was acquainted with the Marlboroughs, he portrays the difficulty faced by many in the gentry, including the situation in the 1670s for John and Sarah Churchill when John's parents would not give him permission to marry Sarah because they wanted him to marry the heiress Catherine Sedley. The future Duke and Duchess of Marlborough were unusually lucky that a change in financial circumstances (the death of Sarah's brother giving her a share in a small estate) had made it feasible for John's parents to give their permission for the love match. The Duchess of Marlborough, however, did not allow her own children the same opportunity to choose their spouses that she and John had finessed.

Each of the Marlboroughs' daughters was married while still in her teens into an influential Whig family. These matches secured the social bonds between the most powerful Whigs at court: Henrietta at age sixteen was married to Sidney Godolphin's only son, Francis; Anne, at age seventeen, became the second wife to the third Earl of Sunderland, the most outspoken member of the Whig Junto; Mary Churchill was married at sixteen into the Whig Montagu family (with the promise that the queen would make her father-in-law a duke so that her husband would inherit the title); and Elizabeth was married at fifteen to the fourth Earl of Bridgewater, heir to another important Whig family.

There is no reason to assume that Henrietta disliked Francis Godolphin, the son of her parents' best friend, whom she had certainly known since she was a child. But Henrietta had her mother's wit and interest in the world of ideas. Francis Godolphin, although the son of two highly educated parents, once claimed he only ever read two books in his life, Gilbert Burnet's very Whiggish *History of His Own Time* and the actor Colley Cibber's *Apology for the Life of Colley Cibber.* This self-deprecating comment makes Godolphin sound less intelligent or energetic than he clearly was. He was not only MP for Helston, Cornwall, and (simultaneously) an MP for Oxford but also steward of the Duchy of Cornwall and cofferer of the royal household, joint registrar of the Court of Chancery, and lord warden of the stannaries. Since the only two books owned by many families at the time would have been the Bible and the traditional conduct manual *The Whole Duty of Man,* the only two books that Godolphin would later claim he had read (neither of which was published before 1720) signal not his indolence but his progressive Whig stance both on history (in Burnet's book) and on moral conduct (in the actor Cibber's colorful memoir); however, they do not indicate any passion for poetry or the theater. Like his father, Francis was clearly a tireless administrator; he also took after his father in his main passion outside government: trading and breeding a line of Arabian racehorses.[22]

There are no known accounts of Henrietta Godolphin ever making any disparaging comments about her husband. William Congreve, however, was an entirely different sort of person from Francis Godolphin: not a government administrator or an aficionado of racehorses but a writer. He wrote poems and several successful comedies for the stage in the 1690s and, since 1703, had been busy managing the new Queen's Theatre, along with the Whig dramatist and architect John Vanbrugh, who also served as the architect for Blenheim Palace.

Married to Francis Godolphin in 1698, just shy of her seventeenth birthday, Henrietta had given birth to five children by the time she was twenty-three. In 1703, Congreve wrote *The Tears of Amaryllis* for the Duchess of Marlborough on the occasion of the death of her son and heir John, Henrietta's younger brother. The poem focuses on the plight of Amaryllis, a mother, grieving over the loss of Amyntas. The poem depicts Amaryllis in agony, experiencing the grief of a "Mother's moan." Her grief is so overpowering that she chides the wind, the sun, and the "cruel Earth" for taking him. "Did ever Youth so immaturely end?" she cries, as she lies down on top of his grave, tears flowing.[23]

The only consolation in this poem are the tears themselves, which, as winter turns to spring, produce a "lively springing Green." The poem ends with Amaryllis amazed at the garden of flowers produced by her own tears:

> And *Amaryllis* saw with wond'ring Eyes
> A flow'ry Bed where she had wept, arise;
> Thick as the pearly Drops the Fair had shed,
> The blowing Buds advanc'd their purple Head
> From ev'ry Tear that fell, a Violet grew,
> And thence their Sweetness came, and thence their Mournful Hew.

The poet urges young nymphs to pay tribute to the "peaceful Grave" where these flowers first grew.[24]

Congreve dedicates his poem not to the Duchess or Duke of Marlborough but to Sidney Godolphin, signaling that Henrietta was the poem's likely intended audience. Henrietta lived with her husband and children at Godolphin House in London and found her father-in-law more patient and sympathetic than her own mother. If Henrietta had not yet come to know Congreve well, this poem would certainly have caught her attention for the beauty of the language and the hopeful image of new life springing from grief.

It is possible that Congreve already knew Henrietta better than her mother would have liked by this time. In the preface to the published poem, Congreve makes a point of repudiating a rumor that he had had a hand in the recent verse *A Satyr against Love,* whose title page indicates that it was "Revis'd and Corrected by Mr. Congreve." This poem, for which no printer's name is listed on the title page, describes a young nymph as "a reckon'd Virgin but a real Whore" who falls into the snares of a swain who persuades her that there is "no real Happiness in Love" without "Liberty." The poet bemoans: "The Virgin-treasure watch'd so long in vain / by careful Parents is surrender'd then." When she is married to the man her parents choose, the nymph "pukes and whines and does nothing but Complain" about the "Drudgery of Life."[25]

Congreve, a handsome man and athletic in his youth, although losing his vision to cataracts by 1709, was rumored to have been the lover of the actress Anne Bracegirdle in the 1690s, but the rumors about seducing a woman into adultery in 1709 would not have referred to Bracegirdle, who never married and bore Congreve no children. By 1704 the Duchess of Marlborough was complaining that Henrietta had "a great mind to be thought a Wit" and was associating with "Mr Congreve & several Poets, and in short the worst company that a Young Lady can keep."[26] By 1711 rumors were flying that Henrietta had "latly been in Pickell for her sins."[27] At the time of her brother's death in 1703, gossip about her friendship with Congreve may already have been circulating.

It might seem hypocritical on Sarah's part to complain that Henrietta might enjoy the company of someone capable of matching her own taste for satire and poetry since Sarah herself regularly enjoyed the companionship and wit of Arthur Maynwaring. Sarah could have responded that she was not rumored to be romantically involved with Maynwaring, while there were certainly rumors about Henrietta and

Congreve. Sarah was concerned about the family reputation, and even concerned that Henrietta might have an illegitimate child who could be heir to the Marlborough title, which would pass to Henrietta after her father's death. Henrietta's husband, however, was more tolerant of his wife's behavior than her mother was.

Francis Godolphin, like his father Sidney, was a patient and empathetic man. Francis's mother, the beautiful Margaret Blagge, had kept up an intense philosophical epistolary correspondence with the writer John Evelyn during the ten years of her engagement to Godolphin. After Margaret's death, Evelyn had even taken charge of Francis Godolphin's upbringing and education during the years when Sidney was preoccupied with operations in the Treasury, where he held positions of increasing responsibility at court. So Francis was raised in part by the highly literary admirer of his dead mother, and he seemed accepting of his wife's own literary connections. When she gave birth to a daughter in 1723, twenty-two years after the birth of their last child, Francis would lovingly raise the daughter as his own, even though everyone presumed the child had been fathered by Congreve—a presumption seemingly confirmed by Congreve's bequeathing the bulk of his estate to Henrietta, who in turn bequeathed the value of it to her daughter, Mary.[28] Demonstrating his sympathetic tolerance for his wife's relationship with Congreve, Francis Godolphin was executor of both Congreve's and Henrietta's wills.

Since gossip about Congreve and Henrietta Godolphin was already familiar by 1709, it is somewhat surprising that Delarivier Manley makes no mention of it in her *New Atalantis,* in which she recycles so much old gossip in tarnishing the reputations of Sidney Godolphin and the Duchess of Marlborough. Manley's discretion on this subject suggests that she may have known Congreve from when they were both writing plays for the stage in the 1690s. She likewise avoided any mention of Maynwaring's liaison with Anne Oldfield, suggesting that she may also have known them or at least have had mutual friends through the theater. When Maynwaring read Manley's book for the Duchess of Marlborough, he did yet know who the author was. But by suggesting that the duchess herself would have found some scenes amusing, Maynwaring signaled both his support for a fellow satirist and his Whiggish support for free speech in the matter of satire. His support for free speech, however, did not extend to the queen's right to continue to converse freely with Abigail Masham as an inside court favorite, given his interest in removing her from court. Maynwaring, like the Duchess of Marlborough and the Earl of Sunderland, did not always act out of Whig principles.

A further paradox for the Duchess of Marlborough was that as a Whig, she opposed the principle of monarchy by divine right and the principle of passive obedience to authority. As a parent, however, she appeared to prefer the Tory model of passive obedience. To justify Parliament's voting in 1689 to replace James II with William and Mary, it was essential that the right to remove a tyrannical monarch be enshrined in English political thought. When John Locke wrote his *Two Treatises of Government* (1689), a publication that helped retroactively justify the Glorious Revolution, he reminded readers that God had not granted dominion of the earth solely to Adam but to Adam and Eve jointly, in the first granting of shared power. Locke thus asserted that paternalistic monarchy by divine right was a thing of the past—and power sharing with Parliament was central to the principles of the Revolution the Whigs so valued. It was Sacheverell's preaching in favor of passive obedience that infuriated the Whigs because such "obedience" repudiated the very Revolution principles that had put William and Mary, then Anne, on the throne.

The Duchess of Marlborough, who had received little education in her youth, took up more serious reading in the 1690s and was certainly familiar with Locke's theories of government. She was also proud to have been considered by the queen to have been a "friend" rather than a mere "subject" because friendship "imports a kind of equality between the parties."[29] Regardless of her appreciation for power sharing and equality in government, Sarah nevertheless expected obedience and respect from her family members. Her children, when quite young, would write letters to her begging forgiveness when they sensed her displeasure, even when they were not certain exactly what they had done wrong. Henrietta Godophin, who had obeyed her parents at age sixteen by marrying their best friend's son, could not prevent herself from falling in love outside the bounds of obedience or virtue when she met

William Congreve. The poem *A Satyr against Love*, falsely attributed to Congreve, explains that "even Virtue" may be "by Love betray'd." When this happens, "blind Obedience" thus becomes "its Captive made."[30]

■

BETWEEN THE PRODUCTION of *The Unhappy Favourite* in late November 1709 and *Love for Love* ten days later, the publication of Sacheverell's sermon on 25 November would have drowned out most news about the theater and any gossip about Marlborough seen admiring Hester Santlow or about Henrietta Godolphin spotted at the theater, enjoying the production of Congreve's *Love for Love*.

The duchess was keeping a low profile at court in early December 1709, but the Duke of Marlborough was back in the thick of political squabbles, trying to help the Whigs decide how best to proceed against Sacheverell's sermon. The Earl of Sunderland was certain that Sacheverell ought to be punished soundly and was pleased to observe the Duke of Marlborough's anger about the sermon on his return from war.

The other ministers in the queen's cabinet had been impatient for Marborough's return while they sought to decide how to proceed in the Sacheverell affair. Their discussion after his return was about political strategy for the Whigs, which they would not have thought "a proper matter to debate before the Queen in full Cabinet."[31] The Whigs had other venues for political discussion, in particular the Kit-Cat Club, a celebrated Whig literary and political club that took its name from its initial meeting site, the Cat and Fiddle Tavern, where members enjoyed the pastry chef Christopher Cat's mutton pies, washed down with ample libations, as they discussed political theory, poetry, and satire. Horace Walpole, in commenting on Godfrey Kneller's portraits of the Kit-Cats, describes them as "generally mentioned as a set of wits," although their members were in reality "the patriots that saved Britain" from a return to Catholicism.[32] The club's political activity also cemented Whig party cohesion.[33]

The Kit-Cats included the writers William Congreve and Richard Steele, powerful Whigs in the House of Commons and the House of Lords, including the Earl of Sunderland and Lord Chancellor Cowper, and the writers and MPs Arthur Maynwaring and Joseph Addison. Neither Sidney Godolphin nor the Duke of Marlborough, still nominally

Tories, were members. But around 8 December 1709 they were both admitted as members "extraordinary" to a meeting at the house of the financier Sir Henry Furnese, MP for Sandwich.[34] There were no minutes for this gathering, as there would have been for a cabinet meeting, but a contemporary, Alexander Cunningham, made notes about what happened, and later recorded it in his *History of Great Britain*.

There was general consensus that Sacheverell's sermon deserved censure. The Duke of Marlborough proposed that Sacheverell be prosecuted "lest such preachers as these should preach us all out of the kingdom."[35] Here Marlborough was pointing out the dangers of clergymen undermining the Revolution principles of 1688 and the Protestant line of succession. The Whig cabinet members present at the Kit-Cat Club that evening generally agreed on the need to prosecute, but they debated whether they should prosecute Sacheverell for seditious libel at the Court of the Queen's Bench or impeach him in the House of Commons. There were concerns that prosecution for seditious libel—the same charge brought against Manley for her *New Atalantis*—might not be successful, in light of the slippery wording of the published text. That difficulty made impeachment a seemingly more feasible option since the Whigs presumed that precise textual evidence was not necessary for that proceeding—an assumption that would come back to haunt them later in the process.

Impeachment was essentially a parallel judicial process to the crown's control of justice at the Court of the Queen's Bench. Through this process, "Parliament could prosecute and try individuals, usually holders of public office, for high treason or other crimes and misdemeanours."[36] Although not intended to remove a monarch, and never used against a prime minister, the procedure could be deployed against anyone except a monarch (and "perhaps" another member of "the royal family"), even a private citizen. In 1660, for example, William Drake was impeached for writing a pamphlet against Parliament.[37] Yet typically impeachment was used against royal officeholders carrying out unpopular policies; it became an indirect check on the monarch by allowing Parliament to assert that a certain royal adviser was misleading the monarch. In more general terms, as Frank Bowman has observed, it served as "a mechanism for bending the kingdom's basic constitutional order away from absolutism and toward representative government." Although "sometimes employed for petty or ignoble purposes," Bowman acknowledges, "it was invented as a mighty weapon against executive tyranny and as a powerful tool for preservation of the constitution."[38]

Impeachment actions were taken against royal councillors during the reigns of Edward III, Richard II, and Richard III but were less frequent during the reigns of the powerful monarchs Henry VIII and Elizabeth I. The practice was revived in the 1640s, when Parliament deployed "its ancient right" in its struggle against Charles I's administration, at a time when impeachment was "the only means by which Parliament could dismiss an individual holding office under the Crown."[39] However, across four centuries of the practice in British history, it was unusual to impeach a clergyman. One of the very few precedents for Parliament in 1709 was the example of the clergyman Dr. Mainwaring, who was impeached for preaching seditious libel in 1628.[40]

Baron John Somers, a gifted lawyer and former Lord Chancellor of England as well as former president of the scientific body the Royal Society, warned against acting in anger. Somers—who, like Godolphin and the Marlboroughs, was a target in Manley's *New Atalantis*—addressed Sidney Godolphin directly, advising the usually mild-mannered lord treasurer to "take care not to consult your passions or affections more than your own dignity and usage" and in punishing Sacheverell to "let no hatred, revenge, anger or passion interpose."[41] Somers knew whereof he spoke: in 1701, he had been one of five Whig party leaders against whom impeachment proceedings were taken by Tories (after the Whigs had fallen from favor in the last year of William III's reign) for "having misused their powers and given bad advice to the crown."[42]

Although Somers was ultimately acquitted by the House of Commons, he understood the disadvantage of impeaching for political reasons. He recommended impeaching only if the sentence matched the crime. Otherwise, he argued, "I think it best to make use of that method of process which our laws have provided," meaning a charge of libel. Alexander Cunningham noted that Somers's "opinion, which tended to clemency, was not agreeable to the Duke of Marlborough's friends, and especially to the earl of Sunderland," so the Kit-Cats at that meeting chose impeachment instead.[43] Here we see how much emphasis the Whigs still placed on Marlborough's opinion. Sunderland was certainly going to press for impeachment, but his pressing for it would have additional weight if it was seen as what Marlborough preferred. Cunningham's phrasing also indicates Marlborough's preferred method of proceeding in political squabbles, which was to let others suggest his preference rather than make a bold public declaration himself. Marlborough was direct, if cunning, as a military leader. In matters of politics, he preferred indirection, allowing others to proceed with vehemence (as his wife often did in her letters to the queen) while he exuded politeness, reserve, and diplomacy.

The Kit-Cat Club gathering was not a formal cabinet meeting, but the ministers in the queen's cabinet were accustomed to meeting once or twice per week in the secretary of state's offices in the Cockpit at Whitehall Palace (the same part of the palace that had once been Princess Anne's apartments and whence she had fled, with Sarah Churchill, in November 1688), in addition to their usual Sunday afternoon Privy Council meeting with the queen. Thus the decision was "laid before the Council" in such a meeting, but not in the queen's presence at an official meeting where minutes were taken.[44] Nor were most MPs aware that a decision to impeach had been made.

Impeachment in the English tradition was a two-step process in which the House of Commons voted on an impeachment, which would be tried in the House of Lords.[45] On Tuesday, 13 December, the Tories in the House of Commons were stunned to see the MP John Dolben rise with marked-up copies of two of Sacheverell's sermons and move that a vote be taken that the sermons were "malicious, scandalous, and seditious libels, highly reflecting upon her Majesty and government the Protestant Succession as by law established and both Houses of Parliament."[46] The chancellor of the exchequer, John Smith, then moved to add "the phrase, 'the late happy Revolution' to Dolben's catalogue of what Sacheverell had 'highly reflected on.'"[47]

The following day the House of Commons called Sacheverell to the bar and interrogated him about who had given him permission to have the sermon printed. Then they allowed him to express his regret at having "fallen under the displeasure of this House." But the main debate was between the Tories and the Whigs. The Tories felt that if a libel suit was unlikely to succeed, "they thought it very unreasonable, by an impeachment in Parliament, to make a man criminal that by the law of the land was innocent." But the Whigs felt that these "Highflying clergymen had been sheltered too long behind their cloth and behind the unwillingness of courts to convict for libel."[48] Meanwhile, Sacheverell remained in the custody of the House of Commons.

On 24 December, Sacheverell petitioned the House of Commons to be released on bail. Bail was not granted, and he appears to have spent Christmas in the custody of the sergeant-at-arms for the House of Commons. Yet sympathy for him was already swelling. During his incarceration Sacheverell was chosen to be "lecturer" at the nearby church of Newington-Butts, a position valued at £80 per annum, a sign of support and a salary that would have helped defray his costs while confined (chargeable to the prisoner in this era) and his legal fees.[49] This second post, at a church not far from St. Saviour's in Southwark, would also give Sacheverell one more church in which to preach to eager crowds, as soon as he was released on bail.

■

On Monday, 9 January, as MPs continued to return to London after the Christmas holidays, John Dolben laid the four articles of impeachment against Sacheverell on the table in the House of Commons. Each article focused on something Sacheverell "doth suggest and maintain" in contradiction of established Whig ways of viewing the Revolution of 1688 and the religious Toleration Act of 1689. The first article objected to Sacheverell's suggesting that "the necessary means used to bring about the said happy Revolution were odious and unjustifiable." The second article asserted that Sacheverell maintained that "the aforesaid Toleration, granted by law is unreasonable." The third article objected to Sacheverell's suggestion that "the Church of England is in a condition of great peril and adversity under her Majesty's administration." The fourth article objected to Sacheverell "falsely and maliciously" suggesting "that her Majesty's administration, both in ecclesiastical and civil affairs, tends to the destruction of the constitution."[50] The very wording of these articles, in using the verbs *suggest* and *maintain,* showed how delicate a case the Whigs were pursuing. Sacheverell was not being accused of treason; he was merely being charged with suggesting that he opposed the standard Whig version of history since 1688.

In light of the thin textual evidence against Sacheverell, it is not surprising that Tories found objections to the articles of impeachment and demanded to know "on what specific passages" the articles "were grounded."[51] An observer reports that "Mr. Harley spoke long and well upon this occasion in Behalf of the Dr. [i.e., Sacheverell]." Harley, who was born a Dissenting Presbyterian and had begun his career as a Whig, was certainly no fan of Sacheverell's high church bluster. But at this point he was playing opposition politics, and he was playing it with language that would make it as hard to pin him down as it was to pin down Sacheverell's crime in his printed sermon. Alexander Cunningham reports that those who heard Harley criticize Sacheverell's sermon as "a circumgyration of incoherent words without any regular order" felt he did so by making use "of a *circumgyration* of incoherent words, as he himself had before condemned in Sacheverell" such that "the house could not certainly discover from his expressions whether he spake for him or against him."[52]

Despite the concerns, however incoherent, of the Tories, the Whigs prevailed. The articles were read a second time in the Commons late on Wednesday, 11 January 1710, and approved by a vote of 232 to 131.[53] Sacheverell was ordered to be removed from the custody of the sergeant-at-arms of the Commons—which happened so swiftly that he did not pay his fees for the month's confinement—and placed into the custody of the gentleman usher of the black rod for the House of Lords.[54] Once in the custody of the Lords, Sacheverell requested to see a copy of the articles against him and to petition for bail. When he was finally released on bail, set at £6,000, on the morning of Saturday, 14 January, the Whigs had another glimpse of the populist excitement aroused by Sacheverell's case. On the following morning, such crowds gathered around St. Saviour's Church in Southwark, expecting to hear him preach, that "the parishioners could not get near their seats." Only the strategy of telling the crowds that he would be preaching at Newington-Butts "carried the mob thither."[55] In fact, Sacheverell was not preaching at either church but was busy working on his answers to the articles of impeachment.

His written answers—in which he contradicted a central principle of the Glorious Revolution by insisting on the "illegality of Resistance"—would not assist his legal case, but the case he seemed most interested in building was one of popular support. As a high church Tory opposed to acts of political resistance, he should have been ideologically opposed to grassroots political uprisings. However, now that such uprisings were enacted on his behalf, he appeared to appreciate the value of resistance. He and his legal team also realized that time was on their side: "The longer the trial could be postponed, and the longer thereafter it could be spun out, the more likely did it seem that the powerful currents of opinion" would become a torrent.[56]

During the initial debate in December about Sacheverell in the House of Commons, a Whig MP was heard to exult that they were going "to roast a parson," but as the Tory Lord Ailesbury reported afterward, it "proved a fatal dish for them and their adherents."[57] The central paradox of Sacheverell's sermons was that his anger and bombast in delivering his message of passive obedience to authority seemed designed to incite populist mobs in protest against the Whigs, mobs that were in no way passive or obedient to authority. As Alexander Cunningham explains, "The clergy flocked together, and traversed town and country to inflame the spirits of the multitude." Not just high church clergymen were involved in these riots but "the butchers also, and the dregs of the city . . . ran together in crowds."[58]

The Whigs have been faulted by many historians, who felt they rashly overreached in their prosecution of Sacheverell. In hindsight, they have been accused of "the grossest political folly and myopia." Yet "there were early and disturbing signs that Sacheverell might develop very rapidly into a dangerous demagogue."[59] The Whigs who prosecuted him were thoughtful men genuinely concerned about an uprising that might topple a government. The civil wars, followed by the Restoration of 1660, had shown them that any revolution could be overturned. Having experienced (and in Marlborough's case, having helped facilitate) the Glorious Revolution, they were concerned that this most recent victory of Protestantism over Catholicism might also be reversed. The Whigs who had clipped the wings of the monarchy in 1688 did not necessarily want to extend Parliament's power to include the voice of the masses. Nevertheless, the optics of prosecuting a popular clergyman in the national church were not good for the Whigs.

Marlborough himself expressed concerns in early January; he was now "not so sure" how far they should proceed in this prosecution.[60]

Marlborough was right to be concerned about where the Whig prosecution would take things and right to be concerned about how this trial would play out for a Tory and high church queen, even one who owed her throne to the Glorious Revolution. His own relationship with Anne was growing increasingly strained. Not only had she not seen the need to grant him life tenure as captain-general, she also was undermining his command in subtler ways. Although Marlborough was in favor of punishing Sacheverell, he began to see the dangers in the prosecution and hoped to keep his public distance from it, even though his perceived initial support had been important in rallying the Whigs to proceed with impeachment.

■

ON 10 JANUARY, the same day that the House of Commons was engrossed in debate over Sacheverell, Algernon Capell, Earl of Essex, died unexpectedly at age forty, leaving vacant his position as lieutenant of the Tower of London. It was a position normally filled on the advice of the captain-general of the army; another vacancy normally filled by the captain-general was also open, commander of the Oxford regiment. To the Duke of Marlborough's great surprise, Queen Anne gave the lieutenant position to Earl Rivers rather than to a commander of Marlborough's own choosing. Anne was also rumored to be planning to give Abigail Masham's brother, Jack Hill, command of the Oxford regiment. As Winston Churchill explains, "It was obvious that an insult of the most carefully studied character was intended by the Queen's secret advisers. But the issue ran much deeper than this."[61] He continues, "The appointment of Mrs Masham's brother to a regiment over the heads of many more competent and experienced colonels was nothing less than a signal to the Army that Marlborough no longer possessed the confidence of the Queen." It was not merely that the queen was putting in someone unfit and untrustworthy for the command; her choice would have signaled that the captain-general was no longer in charge. Churchill opines, "The evil of such a demonstration would swiftly extend to the Allies, spreading doubt and discouragement as it travelled."[62]

In shock over Anne's decision to fill the position of lieutenant of the Tower without waiting for his recommendation, Marlborough met with the queen to make his case for appointing a commander he could trust to the position she intended to give to Abigail's brother. He made every argument for his case, with his usual courtesy and politeness. But, as the Duchess of Marlborough wrote afterward, "he could not draw one kind expression from her, nor obtain any answer, but that he would do well to advise with his friends." Nor did Godolphin have any success in persuading the queen to see Marlborough's position. As Sarah later observed, "The scheme of the Queen's new counsellors to make her ministers quit her service or engage her to discard them, began now to appear without disguise."[63]

On Sunday, 15 January, the day of the weekly meeting of the Privy Council, Marlborough left St. James's Palace with Sarah for Windsor Lodge, absenting himself from court without taking the usual ceremonial leave of the monarch or offering any reason for skipping the Privy Council meeting. The queen made no comment on his absence, and no others attending spoke up to ask her to reconsider her military appointments. From Windsor, Marlborough drafted a letter to the queen, which he ended by expressing his "hope that your Majesty will either dismiss Mrs Masham or myself."[64] We do not know how Anne would have chosen between them had he sent this letter directly, but Marlborough did not send the letter to the queen.

Following his cautious political style of allowing others to speak for him, Marlborough sent the letter to Godolphin to ask his opinion and have him show it to the Whig ministers, to let them know of his plans, and then deliver it to the queen himself. But Godolphin was likewise cautious and did not rally the Whig ministers to present a united front. He instead asked Lord Somers to speak to the queen. Somers eloquently expressed what Marlborough himself had already pointed out: that "all the eyes of Europe are fixed upon him, and business is transacted with him under the notion of one who is honoured with your Majesty's entire trust and favour."[65] Somers's eloquence had no effect on the queen. Meanwhile, express messengers, along with Marlborough's confidential military secretaries, were now carrying messages on horseback back and forth between London and Windsor, but the matter remained unresolved.

The Marlboroughs wanted other Whigs to press privately to have Abigail dismissed, but more outspoken Whigs, including Sunderland, wanted to introduce a measure in Parliament demanding her removal. The Duke and Duchess of Marlboroughs both thought this a terrible idea, and other Whig peers felt the plan was probably unconstitutional. The queen, having heard rumor of this plan, began calling in ministers and MPs one by one to express her displeasure at it. She met with numerous members of the House of Lords, begging them "with tears in her eyes" to oppose any such motion.[66] She "declared with great spirit and courage" that she would take such a motion "as an indignity to herself."[67] As Robert Harley had observed early in her reign, "There is no one party, nay not both of them, can stand agst. the Queen's frowns."[68] Such a parliamentary maneuver against the queen's bedchamber woman was therefore not introduced, and Marlborough decided to send his original letter, without the ultimatum, for the queen to choose between him and Abigail.

Meanwhile, the queen walked back her plan to appoint Jack Hill commander of the Oxford regiment. She asked Godolphin to let Marlborough know that she would allow him to appoint his own choice of commander if he would return to town. He returned on the understanding that the Whigs would put further pressure on the queen (but not by an act of Parliament) to dismiss Abigail, but the Whigs never rallied around a method for doing this. Arthur Maynwaring was keen for them to take a stand, but the Whig ministers seemed to have lost their nerve in venturing to ask the queen to dismiss her bedchamber woman. Nor would it necessarily have worked. The queen had already demonstrated in 1692 how loyalty to a female favorite, Sarah, prompted her to enter voluntary exile from court. As monarch herself, Anne certainly appreciated the Whig principle that she owed her throne to Parliament. She never advocated for the Tory idea of a divine right monarchy, but she was a traditional Tory in the sense of her value for the personal loyalty a monarch owed her friends and favorites. The lords and MPs she asked not to defy her in this regard understood her right to choose her own household. The Marlboroughs, particularly John, who still considered himself a Tory, ought to have remembered Anne's sense of personal loyalty. They should have remembered how hard Anne had fought, at her marriage in 1683, to persuade her father and her uncle to have Sarah appointed as a lady-in-waiting to her household. The Marlboroughs had long taken for granted Anne's loyalty to them, as the close friends who helped bring about the Glorious Revolution and ensure her right to the throne. What they never acknowledged was her right to transfer her political and personal loyalty from one favorite to another.

Since Abigail was not dismissed, it clearly would have been better for Marlborough had he not left town at all. Sarah later wished, as she wrote to Maynwaring, that Marlborough had stayed in town, attended the Privy Council meeting, treated the queen with public coldness, and "declared to all the world how he was used, and that he served till the war was ended only because he did not think it reasonable to let a chambermaid disappoint all he had done."[69] John would have preferred that the Whig ministers work privately and quietly behind the scenes on his behalf. But neither a public route nor a private route was taken to embarrass the queen. Moreover, Sarah's own attempt to hector the queen in private letters about her ostensible lesbianism had clearly not achieved its intended effect.

The queen greeted Marlborough with public smiles and words of gratitude—easy for her since she knew she had triumphed over the Whigs, having Marlborough return to town for very little concession on her side.[70] Meanwhile, Abigail Masham may have been feeling buoyed up by Manley's flattering descriptions of her in *The New Atalantis,* which continued to encourage public mockery of the Marlboroughs and Godolphin.

■

Anne's cabinet ministers—including her lord treasurer, her secretaries of state, lord privy seal, and lord keeper, among others—served at her pleasure. Her initial scheme, early in her reign, was to maintain a balance between Whigs and Tories—a plan that made sense for a Tory who owed her throne to the Whig-engineered Glorious Revolution but that suited neither party, particularly not the Whig Junto, which often held military funding hostage to demands for more representation in Anne's cabinet. By 1709 the Whigs, with the support of the Duchess of Marlborough, had forced themselves to a majority in her cabinet, having ousted Robert Harley as a secretary of state in a partisan coup in 1708 (though he remained a member of Parliament), which obliged Anne to seek advice in secret from Harley through his visits to his cousin Abigail Masham at court. Rumors of these secret meetings then infuriated the Whigs, who had failed in engineering Abigail's removal from court.

After Anne's death in 1714, her successor, the German-speaking George I, would not be nearly as involved in the daily business of governing as Anne was, writing letters and running cabinet meetings, in part because of his limited command of the English language and in part because Robert Walpole effectively consolidated power as "first" minister in the 1720s (acting as de facto prime minister, in modern terminology). Anne, however, always insisted on running her country herself despite her physical limitations, her relative lack of education, and the political challenges following the Glorious Revolution. As Beatrice Curtis Brown, the editor of Anne's letters, points out, Anne found herself in a political situation that would have challenged "even Queen Elizabeth." As Brown explains, "On the one hand, Parliament had, in 1688, set up effective checks on free government by the Crown; on the other hand it was not yet prepared to accept the responsibility for government itself, and expected the sovereign to be his own Prime Minister."[71] Moreover, Anne's impulse to lead through a cabinet balanced between Whigs and Tories was a perfectly reasonable approach to leadership.

Anne was well aware that she was not quick to put her thoughts into words. In her correspondence with her sister, Mary, Princess of Orange, in the months leading up to the Glorious Revolution, she continually reassured both Mary and William of her loyal Protestantism, but she also admitted her verbal deficiency: "Though I am not good at saying much for myself, yet believe my heart as sincere as it is possible."[72] Once she took the throne, she was serious about governing, even if at first she relied on Sidney Godolphin to instruct her in her role in cabinet meetings and in the daily tasks of running a country. She was regularly in pain from gout, but she wrote many letters by hand every day, both letters of business to ministers and letters to friends. Her handwriting is unfailingly even and legible, in sharp contrast to the hasty, often illegible scrawl of the Duchess of Marlborough.

Despite her gout and obesity, Anne remained physically active, indulging her taste for hunting in a chaise when she was no longer able to ride horseback. At Hampton Court and in royal hunting parks, she added new roads designed to accommodate the two-wheeled one-horse chaise she used to follow the hunt in inclement weather. Jonathan Swift describes her as hunting, on a rainy summer day, "in a chaise with one horse, which she drives herself, and drives furiously, like Jehu, and is a mighty hunter like Nimrod."[73] As plagued as she was by the gout by 1710, it is not clear how often she was well enough to hunt in this one-horse chaise, but Swift's metaphorical point about the subtlety and strength of Anne's power is significant.

Although Anne did not indulge in extensive building or renovation projects at her palaces (possibly because of the frugal tendencies of the Duchess of Marlborough as mistress of the privy purse), we may glean some insight into her character from some of the modest changes she effected at Hampton Court, where William and Mary had left their own mark on both gardens and palace. Although she spent more time at Kensington and St. James's Palace, Queen Anne refurbished and updated the Chapel Royal at Hampton Court in her own style, choosing architectural designs by Christopher Wren and Nicholas Hawksmoor. Her daily attendance there was an opportunity to see and be seen, since she did not participate in the public dressing ceremony (the *levée*) that male monarchs made a morning ritual. The central ceiling of the chapel was redone with "a playful scene of cherubs in the heavens holding aloft a crown and a sword."[74] She also commissioned Antonio Verrio to paint a regal portrait of her on the ceiling of the Queen's Drawing Room. Given her strong dislike of William and Mary, it is significant that when Anne redesigned the Great Parterre and the Great Fountain Garden at Hampton Court, she reduced the number of fountains from thirteen to one, adding instead larger stretches of ornamental water. The layout, which she chose on the advice of her royal gardener, Henry Wise, produced a simplified design "more English in taste than the French inspiration" of her sister and brother-in-law.[75] This decision emphasized her preference for understatement, a preference that she was also adapting as a strategy in dealing with the Marlboroughs.

As soon as the Duke of Marlborough returned to court on 23 January, he was anxious to distance himself from the Sacheverell proceedings and keen to get back to Europe to smooth over any misunderstandings in Europe about Britain's commitment to the war. He thus requested the queen's permission to leave for Europe, which she duly granted. In the first few weeks of February, before his departure, his allies in the House of Commons had wanted to send him to Europe with a statement from the queen acknowledging "the great and unparalleled services of the Duke of Marlborough." When Sidney Godolphin approached her with suggested wording for her agreement with this declaration by Parliament, Anne would agree only to say that she had "already given the necessary directions for his immediate departure," and that she was pleased that the House of Commons concurred with her "just sense of the Duke of Marlborough's eminent services."[76] Just as she had reduced the number of fountains in gardens at Hampton Court designed by William and Mary, so Queen Anne now edited down the verbal praise she would shower on her most celebrated general.

5

A Female Satirist in Court

While the Marlboroughs were in retreat at Windsor Lodge in mid-January, hoping to dissuade Queen Anne from appointing Abigail Masham's brother to a regimental command, the Court of the Queen's Bench—where the libel trial against Delarivier Manley would take place—opened the docket for Hilary term, the law session starting after the feast of St. Hilary on 14 January. The attorney general in charge of the court was Sir James Montagu, a Whig MP, younger brother to the Earl of Halifax and a member of the Kit-Cat Club. James was also cousin to John, Duke of Montagu, husband of the Marlboroughs' daughter Mary.

The Court of the Queen's Bench (or King's, depending on the monarch's gender) was housed in Westminster Hall, the cavernous medieval great hall, first completed in 1097 for William II, son of William the Conqueror. The hall boasted the largest wooden hammer-beam room, commissioned by Richard II at the end of the thirteenth century. Built of massive timbers and weighing 660 tons, it was protected by a decorative mantle of lead weighing 176 tons. The roof would endure over four centuries. By the time of Queen Anne's reign, the roof was intact, but just barely. By the 1740s it would be extensively propped up with wooden posts while restoration work was undertaken.

In early medieval times, justice was meted out by the monarch while seated at the King's Table, a hefty rectangle of Purbeck marble. When the king presided, he sat in a marble chair, although in the centuries following passage of the Magna Carta in 1215, justice was increasingly delegated to judges rather than the monarch. In Queen Anne's era, Westminster Hall was divided into three court areas during legal terms: Common Pleas was situated by the door on the north wall, while Chancery and the King's Bench were convened at opposite corners of the south wall. Justices were seated at raised wooden benches twenty-seven feet long; there were lower benches for lawyers and litigants.

Bars of oak plank defined each court's space, explaining the etymology of the phrase "called to the bar." These wooden benches and bars could be removed for trials requiring the attendance of both houses, or grand banquets or other occasions. Most notably, it was in Westminster Hall that King Charles I was tried by Parliament and found guilty of treason in 1649. At about this time, the Purbeck marble table of justice disappeared, probably intentionally broken up, as a symbol of the monarch's ruptured authority; during Cromwell's protectorate, the Court of the King's Bench was known as the upper bench. The Courts of Chancery and the King's Bench (returning to its former name after the restoration of the monarchy in 1660) retained their locations in the corners of Westminster Hall until they were moved to nearby buildings in 1820.

Manley's was not the first trial of Hilary term in 1710. She and the printers arrested for *The New Atalantis* would not approach the oak bar of the Queen's Bench until mid-February. Meanwhile, the Duke of Marlborough, during his standoff with the queen, continued his regular correspondence, in English and French, with European courtiers and military leaders. He wrote to the Austrian Count Philipp Ludwig Wenzel von Sinzendorf (chief negotiator for the Holy Roman emperor) from Windsor Lodge on 20 January during his brief remove from court to assure him of his "zeal for the good of the common cause" (*zèle pour le bien de la cause commune*). Four days later, back at St. James's Palace, Marlborough wrote again to Sinzendorf, mentioning that he was already beginning to think of his return to Europe. In this phrase, Marlborough chose the French verb *songer*, meaning not just to think but to dream or to long for: "I begin already to dream of my return" (*je commence déjà à songer à mon retour*).[1] These letters, written just two months after his return to London, indicate the extent to which Marlborough was thinking like a European. Queen Anne—not active on the battlefield, as a male monarch would have been in this era, or involved in the regular negotiations with European military—was increasingly susceptible to the more narrowly Anglocentric view of the world promoted by the Tories at her court.

The Whigs in Parliament meanwhile were delayed in pursuing the impeachment proceedings as they waited for Dr. Sacheverell to finish writing his answers to their charges and to secure a new legal team, after two of his lawyers resigned after reading his written responses. On 17 January 1710, he petitioned the House of Lords for an extension of the time allowed for his response.[2] They granted him one additional day, but he would again delay before submitting his response. As they waited, public interest in the affair continued to rise. On 23 January, Sacheverell's sermon was published in Scotland. One Tory court watcher observed that the sermon was likely "to produce a great Number of Converts unless a most vile, anti-monarchical Book" by Mr. Hoadly be likewise "carried over" to Scotland, "as an antidote against it."[3]

Benjamin Hoadly, rector of St. Peter-le-Poer, a parish church about a half mile northeast of St. Paul's Cathedral, was a staunch defender of Whig principles. In 1704 he had preached a sermon on the anniversary of Queen Anne's accession in which he emphasized that Anne's taking the throne was directly connected to the Glorious Revolution; he also exhorted his parishioners to "true Christian Moderation."[4] This sermon caught the attention of the Duchess of Marlborough, who lobbied Queen Anne for a position for Hoadly at Canterbury Cathedral. Anne was less thrilled with the sermon than Sarah was and did not appoint Hoadly to the position, but Sarah became Hoadly's financial patron, and Hoadly continued to preach anti-Tory sermons, repudiating the doctrine of passive obedience. In mid-December 1709, Hoadly published his most thorough defense of Revolution principles, *The Original and Institution of Civil Government Discussed,* in which he followed John Locke in refuting the idea that monarchy required passive obedience to paternalistic authority. It was this publication, "the most extensive political treatise published in this period," that would have served as an "antidote" to Sacheverell's bombastic defense of passive obedience.[5]

On Wednesday, 25 January, Sacheverell finally submitted his written response to the articles of impeachment to the House of Commons.[6] It was clear, however, that he had finished his response much earlier in January since a privately published edition of *The Answer of Dr. Henry Sacheverell D.D. to the Articles of Impeachment* was already circulating among prominent Tories. As a contemporary account of the Sacheverell affair made clear, the document "was first handed about in Manuscript, then printed privately, and at last sold publickly to incense the People and prepossess them in his favour." The writer complains that "Parliament took no notice" of Sacheverell's public relations strategy, "tho they certainly they might have done it to the Doctor's disadvantage."[7]

Sacheverell's written response was lengthy; some of the published editions of his *Answer* ran to over twenty pages. It was clearly designed as much for public consumption as for his own defense. The handwritten version he delivered to Parliament was made of eighteen bulky parchment sheets stitched together. He delivered it to the House of Lords on 25 January with great ceremony, arriving in a coach and dressed in his most expensive clerical gown. An anonymous broadsheet printed shortly after the event describes how Sacheverell arrived at the Court of Requests, waiting to be summoned into the Lords Chamber. He was soon surrounded by "clergyman, gentlemen and several officers in new scarlet clothes, adorned with gold loops and buttons."[8] Entering the Lords Chamber, with its elegant red upholstery and golden monarch's throne, he submitted his bulky parchment manuscript to the clerk. It took the clerk forty-five minutes to read it aloud. When this was done, the Lord Chancellor, William Cowper, asked if Sacheverell had anything to add, but Sacheverell merely replied, "I will abide by my Answer," which he signed and then left the chamber. As he left, his supporters outside the Lords Chamber and also outside Westminster Hall "gave three great huzzas, as many in Westminster Hall, as many in the New Palace Yard outside." As he mounted his coach, "50 or 60 coaches followed after" him in his support.[9] The Whig spin on these huzzas for the clergyman was that they were "*impudent,*" as Tory diarist Thomas Hearne sarcastically observed in his own ironic spin on that spin.[10]

Sacheverell's very public *Answer* demonstrated that he was "totally unrepentant" about the main points he had made in his sermon.[11] He denied any "seditious Intent" in his sermon at St. Paul's, but he defended the premise of passive obedience by insisting that "the Illegality of Resistance" was "the Doctrine of the Church of England," as well as the doctrine "taught in that University whereof he hath been for more than Twenty Years a Member." Although there was nothing apologetic about his written reply, Sacheverell nevertheless put up a veneer of modesty, averring that "if this Doctrine should be declared Erroneous" and if "it should please God that he should suffer for Asserting it, He trusts that God will enable him to shew his steady belief of this

Doctrine by a meek and patient Resignation to whatever shall befall him on that account."[12]

Sacheverell also remained unrepentant about the matter of toleration, insisting that "upon the most diligent enquiry he has not been able to inform himself that a Toleration hath been granted by law." Here he was splitting hairs by pointing out that the Toleration Act of 1689 allowed Dissenters certain exemptions from taking communion in the Church of England but, in his opinion, did not actually make religious "Toleration and Liberty of Conscience" the law of the land "upon all Occasions." He further took issue with the charges against him insofar as they were based "not on his Maintaining or Asserting but on his barely *Suggesting* what is therein maintained," thus emphasizing the central weakness of the case against him.[13]

Sacheverell was correct that he was being impeached for *suggesting* views that contradicted Whiggish Revolution principles. But his written statement—in its assertion that the Act of Toleration did not actually guarantee religious toleration and that passive obedience was still the guiding principle of nation after the Revolution of 1688—was nevertheless provocative, even reckless. Two of his four lawyers returned their fees and "refused to assist him" because of his written response, phrased "without either submission or common respect."[14] The lawyers who resigned would have preferred "a short answer, as non-committal as possible, leaving the counsel the maximum field for manoeuvre during the trial."[15] Most legal minds of the day believed that Sacheverell "never had a due regard either for the authority of parliament, or the liberty of the people of England."[16]

Sacheverell's abrasive style was not working to his legal advantage, but the Whigs were simultaneously undermining their own case in the court of public opinion. During the last week in January, Lord Sunderland arrested Sir Seymour Pile, a Mr. Westby of the Six Clerks' Office, a public legal office, and "Mr. Nichols, a wholesale grocer," for drinking to Dr. Sacheverell's health. Sunderland's logic here, given that merely raising a glass to Sacheverell was not a crime, was that in this public display of support for the clergyman, they were apparently "by force imposing it on others."[17] On Friday, 27 January, a request for habeas corpus was presented to the Court of the Queen's Bench and the men were released on bail. In an era when freedom of the press and religion were new ideas, even the Whigs who generally supported these principles were struggling to understand the extent to which freedom of speech should be allowed in public. The English Bill of Rights, signed into law in 1689, included freedom of speech in Parliament but did not extend to freedom of speech everywhere. Nevertheless, most Britons would have assumed that a clergyman in the pulpit was free to avow obedience to the queen and that his supporters could freely raise a toast to him.

Until the lapse of the last Licensing Act in 1695, there had been no freely published newspapers, other than one controlled by the government, or pamphlets other than those securing approval by the government licenser. However, there had been relative freedom of the press since 1695, and the "prerogative powers of the crown were gone forever," but Parliament had the power to exert control, notably through a charge of seditious libel, or occasionally by a move such as impeachment.[18] It seemed reasonable enough in 1709 for Parliament to sanction a clergyman preaching against many of the laws and precedents of the land. However, the way events were turning out, whatever sanction was taken, it would not be a simple private affair confined only to Parliament. "By the beginning of February," the historian Geoffrey Holmes observes, "things had not gone entirely to plan."[19]

Once Sacheverell's reply was received by the House of Lords, that chamber sent it to the House of Commons; a committee then promptly wrote a report acknowledging that the *Answer* did not absolve the clergyman of the charges, particularly since he only reaffirmed his commitment to passive obedience and religious intolerance. The committee asserted in its replication (reply) that "there were many Things in" Sacheverell's Answer "not warranted by the Proceedings" and "unbecoming a Person impeached." To prevent further delay, the committee did not detail those further points of offense but merely concluded that "the said *Henry Sachverell* is guilty in such a manner as he stands impeached." The Tories objected to this reply, saying that "it merely asserted the Answer's inadequacy without demonstrating it," but the votes were with the Whigs, and the replication passed by 182 votes to 88 and so was sent to the House of Lords. The Whigs still felt that things were "under reasonable control" when the report on Sacheverell's response was sent back to the Lords. The House of Lords moved to proceed with the impeachment trial "at the Bar of this House."[20]

Meanwhile, on 4 February 1710, attendance in the House of Commons swelled with an influx of MPs, including many country Tories who did not regularly attend Parliament, for a vote on an unrelated matter.[21] This swelled Commons unexpectedly voted 192 to 180 for a Tory proposal that Sacheverell should be given a public trial with both chambers of Parliament in attendance. The House of Lords felt obliged to agree to this plan, although some members of the Whig Junto recognized the peril of a public trial that would greatly increase the public impact of the proceedings and might increase support for the clergyman.

Since neither the Lords Chamber nor the Commons Chamber was large enough to accommodate all the politicians, the impeachment proceedings would have to take place in Westminster Hall. The House of Lords officially sent the queen a request to approve the construction of scaffolded seating to accommodate the four hundred or five hundred members of both Houses of Parliament. The lord steward returned the queen's reply to approve the construction, supervised by her surveyor general, the eminent architect Sir Christopher Wren.

Westminster Hall would have to be repurposed from its usual setup of wooden benches and bars for three courts in different corners to a single central court; the vendors' stalls against the walls would also be temporarily removed. The Whig peers, realizing that every day of delay was increasing enthusiasm for Sacheverell among his supporters, summoned Wren to ask how swiftly he could transform the great hall. Working with fifty workmen, day and night, the seventy-seven-year-old Wren anticipated a full fortnight. By 14 February he had made such good progress that he thought they could schedule the trial for the following week. But, as excitement gathered in town, peers in the House of Lords wanted to guarantee that each of them could bring up to eight guests as spectators. No trial had attracted this much attention since Charles I's trial in 1649. Meanwhile the queen, who planned to attend, "was positive she wou'd have no body over her head," a comment with the result that "the house laught coming so pat to what had lately been the discourse of the town," the Queen's outmaneuvering Marlborough in his scheme to have Abigail removed.[22] Instead of wrapping up his work, Wren was ordered to "cause as many Places to be prepared, on the Scaffold now erected in *Westminster Hall,* as can possibly be."[23]

On 20 February there was a further delay when a House of Commons committee inspected the structures and found they had seating for only for 327 persons, seventy too few for the number of MPs currently in town. Sacheverell, meanwhile, had brought a request to the House of Lords asking for assistance in replacing the two lawyers who had quit his defense team. He added an elderly commercial lawyer, a civil lawyer, and a little-known third lawyer. His legal team, thus composed, was not intimidating. The House of Commons in the meantime had added the MP Robert Walpole, then treasurer of the navy, and Lieutenant-General James Stanhope, returning from the battlefields in Spain—both adept legal minds.

Despite the expertise of the Whig legal team, Sidney Godolphin and the Duke of Marlborough were starting to see the dangers of the Whiggish zeal in prosecuting the clergyman. From the outset they had preferred a narrower set of charges against the clergyman, excluding a charge for preaching against "passive obedience," although Sunderland had insisted on it.[24]

■

Marlborough's own behind-the-scenes attempts to persuade the Whigs to force Abigail Masham out of her court position had only emboldened the Tories in their defense of Sacheverell. The queen's private meetings with MPs and peers to prevent parliamentary actions against Abigail had sent some of the Tories "running to Court with faces full of business and satisfaction, as if they were going to get the government into their hands."[25] The queen's "demonstration of independence" about Abigail mistakenly persuaded them that this was "a token of her favour towards the Doctor's cause."[26]

The "Doctor" may have not secured a very formidable legal team, but he was generating increasingly positive publicity, particularly on the part of the women of London, who were feeling sympathetic toward his cause. He had found time that winter to sit for an oil portrait by the painter Thomas Gibson, in which he is depicted with scowling mien and rigid jaw.[27] Gibson's portrait of Sacheverell was adapted and engraved for an appealing mezzotint, which was printed and sold in the weeks leading up to the trial. The mezzotint print offered a substantially softened portrait of the clergyman: he was no longer scowling, merely looking thoughtful. The print caught the standard of masculine aristocratic beauty, which allowed a fleshier face, framed by a large powdered wig. The clergyman who heard Sacheverell preach on Guy Fawkes Day and was so taken aback by Sacheverell's red face and wild eyes acknowledged that on other occasions he has seen Sacheverell's face "Fair and *Effeminate* enough."[28]

As a quick aside, it is worth noting that the one-shilling prints were designed for the ladies of rank who could afford them, but they would have been widely shared with their female attendants and others in the household. Their distribution, as one newspaper reported, certainly increased "concern both for the Church and the afflicted assertor of its rights" among "the fair and tender-hearted sex."[29] Even the female night strollers were rumored to have taken Sacheverell's case to heart. One anonymous pamphleteer in *The Officers Address to the Ladies* describes "the *Strowler in the Strand,* who never pray'd for her Self in her life," as avowing, "God bless the Doctor."[30] This pamphlet, printed by the Whig printer Abigail Baldwin (who had been running the family printing business on her own since her husband's death in 1698), was an anti-Sacheverell tract designed to warn women that in supporting this clergyman, they were unwittingly putting their nation and their way of life at risk. Subtitled *To their Brightness the Ladies of Great Britain; the Humble Address of her Majesties Officers,* this pamphlet advised the women of rank who were drawn to Sacheverell's sympathetic visage to beware the political forces they were unleashing by supporting him.

According to this pamphleteer, women who supported a Tory clergyman who favored passive obedience were abetting the return of the Catholic pretender to the British throne and the return of an autocratic French Catholic style of government.[31] The doctrine of passive obedience would also "destroy the Liberty and Priviledges of *Wives* and *Daughters,*" including the "Antient Priviledge," occasionally granted to a long-suffering wife, of a "separate Maintenance" agreement. By contrast, their "own *Dear* Doctor's" (Sacheverell's) response to a dangerous or intolerable husband would certainly be: "when you are married, *you are married,* Obey your Husbands and be D——to you." On a lighter note, the pamphlet reminds women that they ought to be attracted to the dashing military man, not the effeminate clergyman with a resonant speaking voice: "all his *Manhood* is in his face. . . . Surely a good Voice is not the only thing you admire?" The pamphleteer prevails upon women to forget the clergyman and return to "your former favourable opinion" of soldiers" and that they, the officers writing this address, will "remember the *Church*, the *Queen*, Duke of *Marlborough* &c." and will "*Toast* all your *Ladyships' Healths and Inclinations*, provided that the Doctor has no Share in the latter."[32]

Whig pamphlets like this one were attempts to turn public sentiment against Sacheverell, but his cause was increasingly popular, not only with women attracted to his plight—and to the mezzotint print of his face—but also with populist mobs angry because of the strain war refugees were placing on charities for the poor. In particular, more than 12,000 German-speaking refugees had arrived from the Palatine region since the previous spring, claiming to be Protestant refugees fleeing the destruction of land and crops by Louis XIV's Catholic troops. As Bishop Burnet, a Whig historian and friend of the Duchess of Marlborough, observed, "It was a time of dearth and scarcity, so that the poor were much pinched." The previous summer, "ten or twelve thousand poor people of the Palatinate, who were reduced to great misery, came into England." When these refugees first arrived, "they were well received and supplied, both by the queen and by voluntary charities of good people." But, as Burnet noted, this generosity toward the new arrivals "filled our own poor with great indignation; who thought those charities, to which they had a better right, were thus intercepted by strangers."[33]

Certain Whigs, including Sunderland and Marlborough, had long felt that Britain's economy and its colonies would prosper with a larger population, and they welcomed immigrants in general. Queen Anne fully supported this policy. The previous winter Parliament had passed the Naturalization Act, which was approved by the queen in March 1709. The act allowed foreigners who had taken communion in any Protestant church within the past three months to be naturalized as English citizens merely by taking an oath of allegiance and paying a fee of one shilling. In February 1708 a few hundred immigrants from the Palatinate and neighboring regions arrived in London, even before the passage of the Naturalization Act. They were welcomed by charities, and the queen paid to transport many of them to American colonies.

This generous treatment of them resulted in rumors in the Palatine region that the queen of England would pay the passage to the American colonies of immigrants from Europe. These rumors were reiterated in a new edition of a German book, printed in Frankfurt, about advantages of immigrating to the American colony of Carolina. Three editions of this book appeared in 1709, featuring a picture of Queen Anne on the cover and a title page embossed in gold; it included the new (if false) claim about Queen Anne's promise to pay their passage to America. Most who emigrated would not have owned or even seen a copy of the book, but they all had heard of the "'golden book' with Queen Anne's picture on the cover" and her promise to pay their passage to America.[34] Given the otherwise prohibitive cost of travel across the Atlantic, many thousands of impoverished German peasants decided they might mange to transport themselves to a port in Holland and beg passage on a ship to England.

The Tory landowners and high churchmen "tended to distrust foreigners and foreign connections"; they were also concerned, following the immigration of many skilled Protestant artisans from France (Huguenots) in 1685, that these new immigrants might displace British artisans. In fact, these new immigrants were the rural poor, not skilled artisans. The Earl of Sunderland, writing to the Board of Trade, envisioned the newcomers as "Religious Temperate and hard Industrious" and "perhaps the fittest Nation in Europe to be encouraged to come among the Britains."[35] Moreover, he and Marlborough made it possible for these migrants to board the ships arriving from Britain transporting soldiers to the Continent for the war; on their return journey to the English coast, such ships would carry these German-speaking migrants. The Whigs thus championed this new immigration policy—and when it backfired, the consequences would be laid at their doorstep.

On 12 May a fleet with 1,283 people set sail from Rotterdam to London. Although Sunderland knew these immigrants had dreams of emigrating to America, he had hopes they might help expand the economy of Britain. The Board of Trade commandeered barges to help them disembark and found barns on farmland just south of London in which to house them. Within the next few months, 10,000 to 12,000 impoverished rural German speakers flooded into England. Not all of them were Protestant; about one-third were Catholic, belying the claims that they were fleeing "Popish Persecution."[36] Most of them erroneously believed the queen would be funding their passage to America. They were not all from the Palatine but hailed from a variety of small German principalities. Feeding and housing them swiftly overwhelmed the charitable resources of London. They were housed temporarily in tent camps at Blackheath and Camberwell, outside London. The queen, still sympathetic to their plight, allotted money to feed them and employed some in digging canals. Others joined the military. However, their presence was fiercely debated in public.

In a city of about 600,000, an influx of more than 10,000 impoverished foreigners caused a sensation. British visitors flocked to Blackheath to gawk at them, their poverty, their ragged clothing. Daniel Defoe, writing for Sunderland and Godolphin, took up the cause of "the poor Palatine refugees" in *A Brief History of the Poor Palatine Refugees,* which first appeared in August 1709. Defoe "disregarded the immigrants' varied origins and different religious backgrounds . . . he ignored their wishes to continue on to America." But the refugees themselves accepted the label of "poor Palatines" rather than acknowledge "what they really were: peasant opportunists bent on acquiring free land," as a modern historian describes them.[37] Daniel Defoe offered his empathetic description of the "poor Palatines," but others were soon labeling them "Gypsies."[38] Public sentiment swiftly turned against them, and mobs of English peasants sometimes attacked them. When Henry Sacheverell provocatively offered rabble-rousing pleas for passive obedience to the monarch, he also tapped into mob resentment of the Whig policies toward immigration and naturalization. By the autumn of 1709, even Lord Sunderland had begun to view them as "Vagrant destitute people," and immediately sent any new arrivals back to the Continent.[39]

While the Whigs were being outmaneuvered by populist protest in the debate over immigrants, the Duke of Marlborough continued in his regular correspondence with courtiers and military leaders among the Allies in Europe, passing reassurance from Queen Anne about Britain's continued efforts on their behalf. On 7 February 1710 he wrote to his confidential military envoy, Lieutenant-General William Cadogan, assuring him that all necessary "horses, clothing, recruits for the foot, and whatever else is necessary from hence, is appointed for the end of the month, at farthest."[40]

■

While the best of the Whig legal minds were taken up with Sacheverell's written answer and the parliamentary maneuvers about the impeachment proceedings, Delarivier Manley and her printers were brought to the bar of the Court of the Queen's Bench sometime in the first two weeks of February 1710. We know from contemporary accounts that they appeared before the judges on Monday, 13 February, the last day of Hilary term. We do not know how many times, if any, they were called before the judges before that date. There are no extant records of the interrogation either in the parchment Controlment Rolls for the Queen's Bench trials that year or in the Bag Rolls, containing miscellaneous related handwritten papers looped onto a string and wrapped in parchment. These rolls should contain information about all trials, regardless of outcome, in a given regnal year—the year that begins on the date of a monarch's accession, which for Anne, was 8 March. Perhaps in the flurry of excitement around the Sacheverell trial and the need to relocate the benches in the courts in Westminster Hall (as well the fatal illness of Chief Justice Holt, who died on 5 March), omissions were made in the usual bookkeeping for the final weeks of Anne's eighth regnal year, which ended on 7 March 1710. Aside from the warrant for her arrest and some contemporary references to it, our only details about the trial itself stem from Manley's own account in her fictionalized autobiography, *The Adventures of Rivella.* Manley is a biased source, certainly, but the extant arrest warrant and newspaper references confirm most of the facts of the events as she describes them.[41]

The arrest warrant, signed by Sunderland in late October, charged Manley and her printers with spreading "many false, malitious and scandalous Reflections upon Several of the Queen's Liege Subjects and highly tending to the Disturbance of the publick Peace and Quiete of her Majesty's Government."[42] We have no record of exactly which passages Sunderland objected to most, but he must have been concerned about her reference to the death on the battlefield of Britain's most valiant general and the scene in which she describes a mob of resentful rabble rising up against his wife.

John Churchill, first Duke of Marlborough, with his chief engineer, John Armstrong, after Enoch Seeman, oil on canvas, ca. 1720. (© National Portrait Gallery, London)

[*Top left*] Sarah Churchill (née Jenyns), Duchess of Marlborough, after Sir Godfrey Kneller, oil on canvas, ca. 1702. (© National Portrait Gallery, London)

[*Top right*] Sidney Godolphin, first Earl of Godolphin, by Sir Godfrey Kneller, oil on canvas, ca. 1705–7. (© National Portrait Gallery, London)

[*Bottom right*] Charles Spencer, third Earl of Sunderland, by John Simon, after Sir Godfrey Kneller, mezzotint, 1724 (1720). (© National Portrait Gallery, London)

Queen Anne, by Michael Dahl, oil on canvas, ca. 1702. (© National Portrait Gallery, London)

Unknown woman, formerly known as Abigail (née Hill), Lady Masham, by unknown artist, oil on canvas, ca. 1700. (© National Portrait Gallery, London)

Robert Harley, first Earl of Oxford, by Sir Godfrey Kneller, oil on canvas, 1714. (© National Portrait Gallery, London)

Frontispiece engraving, *The New Atalantis,* by Delarivier Manley, second volume, 1709. (Reproduced with permission from the private collection of Carole Sargent, PhD, Georgetown University, Washington, DC)

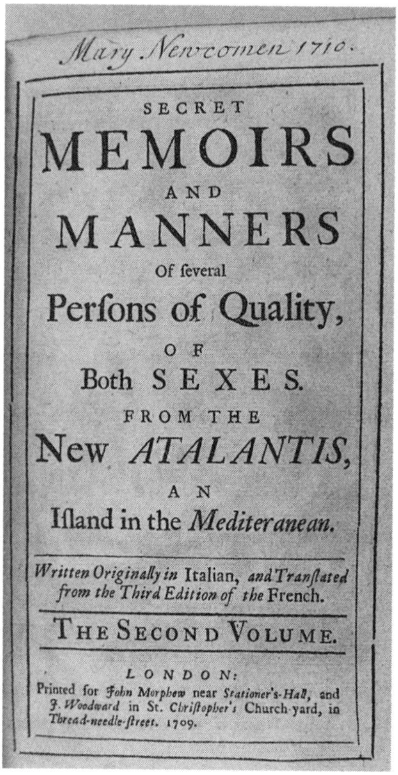

Mary Newcomen 1710.

SECRET
MEMOIRS
AND
MANNERS
Of ſeveral
Perſons of Quality,
OF
Both SEXES.
FROM THE
New *ATALANTIS*,
AN
Iſland in the *Mediteranean*.

Written Originally in Italian, *and Tranſlated from the Third Edition of the* French.

THE SECOND VOLUME.

LONDON:
Printed for *John Morphew* near *Stationer's-Hall*, and *J. Woodward* in St. *Chriſtopher's* Church-yard, in *Thread-needle-ſtreet*. 1709.

[*Left*] Title page, *The New Atalantis*, by Delarivier Manley, second volume, 1709. (Reproduced with permission from the private collection of Carole Sargent, PhD, Georgetown University, Washington, DC)

[*Top right*] Henry Sacheverell, fellow at Magdalen College, Oxford, by Thomas Gibson, oil on canvas, 1710. (Reproduced by permission of the Fellows of Magdalen College)

[*Bottom right*] Henry Sacheverell, by John Smith, after Anthony Russel mezzotint, 1710. (© National Portrait Gallery, London)

Trial of Dr. Sacheverell, engraving, nineteenth century. (Private collection; © Look and Learn/Bridgeman Images)

Sacheverell's Triumph, design for playing card, 1710. (Lebrecht History/Bridgeman Images)

Destruction of Daniel Burgess's Presbyterian Meeting House, engraving from *The Whigs Unmask'd* (London, 1714). (Archival Services, University Libraries, The University of Akron)

Sir Richard Steele, by Sir Godfrey Kneller, oil on canvas, 1711. (© National Portrait Gallery, London)

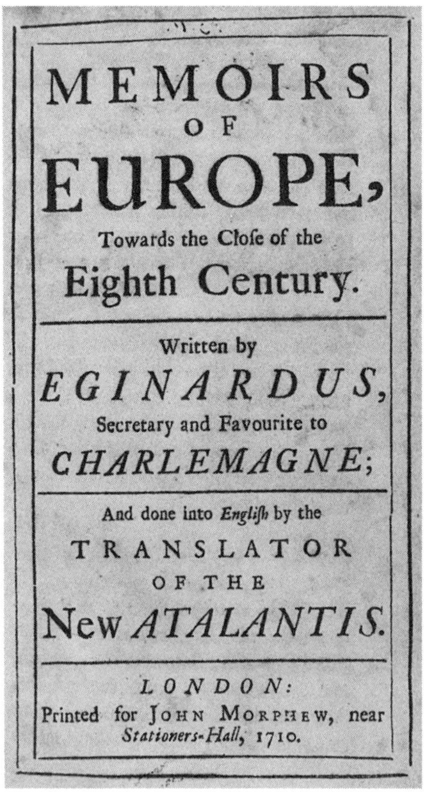

MEMOIRS
OF
EUROPE,
Towards the Close of the
Eighth Century.

Written by
EGINARDUS,
Secretary and Favourite to
CHARLEMAGNE;

And done into *English* by the
TRANSLATOR
OF THE
New *ATALANTIS*.

LONDON:
Printed for JOHN MORPHEW, near
Stationers-Hall, 1710.

Title page, *Memoirs of Europe*, by Delarivier Manley, 1710. (Reproduced with permission from the private collection of Carole Sargent, PhD, Georgetown University, Washington, DC)

Jonathan Swift, by Charles Jervas, oil on canvas, ca. 1718. (© National Portrait Gallery, London)

Arthur Maynwaring, by Sir Godfrey Kneller, oil on canvas, ca. 1710. (© National Portrait Gallery, London)

William Congreve, by Sir Godfrey Kneller, oil on canvas, 1709. (© National Portrait Gallery, London)

Henrietta ("Harriet") Godolphin (née Churchill), Duchess of Marlborough, by Francis Kyte, after Sir Godfrey Kneller, mezzotint, early eighteenth century. (© National Portrait Gallery, London)

In his initial interrogation in his office in Whitehall in early November, Sunderland tried to pressure Manley to divulge which "Persons" had assisted her "in writing her Books; or at least from whom she had receiv'd Information of some special Facts, which they thought were above her own Intelligence." Here she refused to give any names, insisting that she wrote from "*Inspiration*" and merely "for her own Amusement and Diversion." Manley in fact may not have had a specific "source" for leaks of court secrets, but John Barber, the printer with whom she lived, was well connected in Tory circles. He probably invited to dine the writers whose works he was printing, including John Freind, physician to the Earl of Peterborough, a Whig military commander who had been recalled from his position on account of misconduct and misappropriation of funds. Freind's published account about Peterborough, printed by John Barber, suggested that he had been unfairly treated by the Whigs and helped render him a sympathetic figure for the Tories.[43] Manley reiterated this sympathetic depiction of Peterborough in her *New Atalantis,* giving Sunderland the impression that the disgruntled military commander might have been her patron. There is no evidence, however, that Manley was in contact with Peterborough before writing *The New Atalantis.* Only in 1711 did she call on him to introduce herself and beg for patronage for her efforts for the Tories.[44]

Manley also had her own friends among the gentry, including George Granville, Baron Lansdowne, whom she had known when they were writing plays together in the 1690s. In her earliest publication, *Letters Writen by Mrs. Manley* (1696), a travelogue about a stagecoach journey she took from London to Exeter in 1694, Manley cites from Granville's then unpublished translation of Thyestes. Echoing him echoing Thyestes, she pleas for retreat from the corrupt politics of court: "Place me, ye Gods, in some obscure Retreat / Oh! keep me innocent: Make others Great."[45] Here she suggests that her two-year stint in the West Country of England was for reasons of political purity rather than the more practical reasons (such as a lower cost of living) that probably motivated her exile from London.

Such a loyal Tory that he would not accept a position at court under William and Mary (because he had previously sworn allegiance to James II, who was still alive in 1689), Lansdowne came to court when Anne took the throne (one year after James II died in exile in France) and was elected MP, becoming a strong ally of Harley and the Tories. We do not know if Manley and Granville were corresponding at this time. But Manley may have met him at a soirée or gaming table at the home of a society mistress—the sort of venue where she may have seen the Duke of Marlborough and others in that social strata. Granville was a strong critic of Whig military policy and could have informed Manley's Tory critique of the War of Spanish Succession and might have passed along information about Godolphin's increasing lack of influence with the queen.

Manley, of course, as the daughter of a royalist military officer and historian who spent her childhood and adolescence in the governor's residences at military outposts from Portsmouth to Landguard Fort in Suffolk, may not have needed others to guide her critique of Whig military policy. Her father had spent several decades employed by European armies while in exile, after fleeing imprisonment as a royalist during the English civil wars. He well knew the Dutch-French border on which the War of Spanish Succession was playing out. He had also written several books (in Latin) on military history. Dinner table conversations with her father or between her father and other military officers would have given Manley an intimate knowledge of military strategy and European history. While Marlborough and the Whigs may have been optimistic that they could eventually bring Louis XIV to his knees, Manley could well have decided on her own that this was unrealistic.

Sunderland, for all of his erudition, seems not to have seen Manley as a full person, only as a Grub Street hack, doing someone else's bidding. Nor did he expect her, if she had sources, to have enough of a sense of honor to protect them. When she concealed her sources with the reply that her only source was inspiration, Sunderland showed his temper, insisting that "*Inspiration* us'd to be upon a good Account, and her Writings were stark naught." Acknowledging that there were "evil Angels as well as good," Manley insisted "that nevertheless what she had wrote might still be by *Inspiration*."[46] Here she is not only protecting any inside sources who might have conveyed information to her or to John Barber, she is also speaking the truth. Her style of gossipy satire was in fact a literary inspiration—an inspired literary mash-up combining at least three prior literary forms. By her very title, *Secret Memoirs and Manners of Several Persons of Quality, of Both Sexes. From the New Atalantis,* Manley signals two types of books she is echoing: secret court memoirs about earlier English monarchs and Francis Bacon's *New Atlantis* (1627), a scientific and philosophical travelogue about the utopian island of Atlantis. In her preface, Manley claims her connection to a third mode of writing: satire in the style of Varro.

Any book title starting with *Secret Memoirs* would conjure up the *Anekdota,* Procopius's unpublished gossipy history of the sixth-century Byzantine emperor Justinian and empress Theodora, available in English translations, including *The Secret History of the Court of the Emperor Justinian* (1674). This work inspired similar secret histories about Charles II and his mistresses, emphasizing how easily Charles was manipulated by the Duchess of Cleveland, reminding readers of how he had been manipulated and bribed by Louis XIV in a corrupt agreement to return England to Catholicism.

As a Tory, Manley was tweaking and reworking this style of Whig secret history into something much more playful. She did not have a single story line—as was typical in secret histories about Charles II—or even a single cast of characters. By organizing her gossip about prominent courtiers in a travelogue in the style of Bacon's *New Atlantis,* Manley wove a patchwork quilt of gossip about adultery and corruption among prominent Whigs from 1688 to the present day. She included gossip from the early days at the court of Charles II, focusing on anecdotes about young courtiers, such as the Marlboroughs and Godolphin, who had grown to power and influence four decades later.

Anecdotes in which the particular details were invented but the overall tale was true were hard to prosecute for libel. Thus Manley's bathing scene in which the young John Churchill is seduced by Barbara, Duchess of Cleveland, was a fiction but was based in the truth of Churchill's youthful affair with the king's mistress. In thus mocking the Whigs, Manley created an amusing if dystopian vision of the current court. She was mocking not only the heroism but the whole Whig notion of progress, both scientific and political. While Francis Bacon had imagined his New Atlantis as an island on which scientific knowledge developed through open-mindedness, tolerance, justice, and reason, Manley describes her New Atalantis (England) in the Kingdom of Utopia (Great Britain) as anything but virtuous. Nor do its inhabitants act from knowledge or reason but from lust, greed, and self-interest. This amusing if cynical portrait would pose the same difficulty for legal prosecution for libel as Parliament faced in impeaching Sacheverell. Like Sacheverell's sermon, Manley's secret history suggested rather than asserted an antigovernment viewpoint.

Manley made the case for prosecution even harder by including a dedicatory essay to the second volume in which she describes her satire in the classical terms used by male satirists of her day. The "very Soul of Satire," she pronounces, citing John Dryden's essay on satire, "is [the] scourging of Vice, [and the] Exhortation to Virtue." It is "the Poet's Office," she insists, echoing Dryden, to prevent "others" from "falling into" the "Crimes and Follies" of "vicious Men."[47] For the Queen's Bench to succeed in its prosecution of Manley, the government lawyers would have to demonstrate that she was doing something other than satirizing vice to promote virtue. Yet Manley organized her whole book as a moralizing whirlwind tour of the "New Atalantis" and "Angela" (London) given by the goddess of virtue, so disappointed in the world in its present state, to her daughter Astrea (goddess of justice) visiting Earth from the heavenly spheres of the gods.

Manley's dedicatory essay to the second volume, whose publication provoked her arrest, burnished her credentials as a classically influenced satirist. Her dedicatee, the Duke of Beaufort, was a Tory with Jacobite sympathies (for the exiled Catholic line of Stuarts), but she framed her work within the classical tradition of satire. She locates the precedents for her particular style of "Varonian" satire, as she labels it, in the works of "Ennius, Varro, Lucian, Horace, Juvenal, Persius, & etc." Her scholarly authority is Dryden's "Discourse concerning Satire," the dedication to his translation of Juvenal's satires in which he defines the style of various classical satirists. Manley could not draw directly on Varro as a source since few of his complete works survived to the eighteenth century, but in the dedication she paraphrases Dryden's description of Varro's style of writing in a way that also describes her own style in *The New Atalantis:* "written like Varonian Satyrs, on different Subjects, Tales, Stories and Characters of Invention, after the Manner of Lucian, who copy'd from Varro." By situating her work within the tradition of serious classical satire, she could deflect concerns that she was predicting (or wishing for) Godolphin (as Count Biron) being reduced to a mere "*Ghost* of his own *departed* Genius" or the famous general (Marlborough) having died during a recent battle in the war for which he would not agree to an "*Honourable* Peace."[48]

In the case of "predicting" Marlborough's death, Manley was borrowing a trope from her former friend, Richard Steele. Earlier in the year he had announced in his thrice-weekly journal *The Tatler* that he would feel comfortable announcing the premature deaths of those whose conduct he felt was lacking humanity. In such cases, "tho' the Legs and Arms, and whole Body, of that Man may still appear and perform their animal Functions; yet, since, as I have elsewhere, observ'd, his Art is gone, the Man is gone." He ended the first issue of his *Tatler,* published in April 1709, with the following warning: "I shall, as I see Occasion, proceed to confute other dead Men, who pretend to be in Being, that they are actually deceased. I therefore give all Men fair Warning to mend their Manners, for I shall from Time to time print Bills of Mortality; and I beg the Pardon of all such who shall be nam'd therein, if they who are good for Nothing shall find themselves in the Number of the Deceased."[49]

In her dedicatory preface, Manley cites Steele's published praise of satire for its ability to sanction "Ingratitude, Avarice, *and those other* Vices, *which the* Law *does not reach.*"[50] Here Manley is citing a recent publication by a Whig member of the Kit-Cat Club, the very same group that had met at the home of Sir Henry Furnese in early December to determine to impeach Dr. Sacheverell. Most of them presumably had not been consulted about arresting Manley, or those who knew her might have alerted Sunderland that she was an educated gentlewoman. Had the Kit-Cats Richard Steele or Arthur Maynwaring or William Congreve been individually consulted, they might have advised Sunderland not to attempt prosecution of a satirist citing a fellow Kit-Cat member in her own defense. Although Manley also insulted Steele in her *New Atalantis,* he was perfectly capable of responding to her satire with his own satirical retort in *The Tatler* in September.

■

Having already been interrogated by Lord Sunderland in his office in early November, before she sued for habeas corpus and was released on bail, Manley returned for her trial at the Court of the Queen's Bench in mid-February. As she describes it in her fictional memoir, she was "several Times exposing her in Person to walk cross the Court before the Bench of Judges, with her three Attendants, the *Printer* and both the *Publishers.*" In this brief account of her experience at the Court of the Queen's Bench, Manley emphasizes her self-consciousness about her physical presence in walking in front of the judges' oak benches in Westminster Hall. She also underscores her sense of justice in taking full responsibility for the anonymous work, admitting to the judge that her printers "*had receiv'd the Copy from her Hand.*" In this retelling, she suggests that she had initially made a decision "to surrender her self into the *Messenger's* Hands" so that she could "discharge those honest People from their Imprisonment."[51] Here she is not quite accurate, according to the dates of the arrest warrants. In Sunderland's warrant book in the National Archives, the warrant for the trade printers (whose names were on the title page of *The New Atalantis*), dated 28 October 1709, precedes the warrant for "____ Manley & John Barber Printer," which was probably issued at the same time since it is worded merely as "accused & c. (in the same words of that above)."[52] In other words, Manley may have taken responsibility for her work in court, but she did so only after being arrested for it.

Manley's self-promotion here is consistent with her depiction of herself elsewhere in her *Adventures of Rivella.* In that memoir, she presents herself not only as honest in taking responsibility for the printers who published her work but also as "immoveable" in her desire to "serve her Country, and the ancient Constitution." She is, according to her own account, descended "from a long untainted Descent of Loyal Ancestors," meaning that her father was a royalist during the civil wars and stayed loyal in exile for over a decade until returning to England after the Restoration.[53]

Manley organizes her fictional memoir as a conversation between two courtiers discoursing in Somerset House garden: the Chevalier d'Aumont, a relation of the duc d'Aumont, the French ambassador to Great Britain, and a fictional personage, Sir Charles Lovemore, who ostensibly knew Manley from childhood and had been in love with her since he was a youth.[54] When the news breaks out about *The New Atalantis,* she confesses to this lifelong admirer that her printers were arrested for libel that she "her self was Author of the *Atalantis.*" She also adds that "she was proud of having more Courage than had any of our Sex, of throwing the first Stone, which might give a Hint for other Persons of more Capacity to examine the Defects, and Vices of some Men who took a Delight to impose upon the World, by the Pretence of publick Good, whilst their true Design was only to gratify and advance themselves." When her admirer asked "how she would like going to *Newgate* [Prison]?" she claims to have replied, "Very well; since it was to discharge her Conscience."[55]

Despite her willingness to cast the first stone against the Whigs in power and face trial alongside her the printers, when she appeared at the Queen's Bench on Monday, 13 February, she "was discharged," as the Whig diarist Narcissus Luttrell observes, offering no more detail.[56] Thomas Hearne, the Tory diarist, makes no mention of her trial (though he does collect a list of the identifications of the persons satirized in *The New Atalantis*). Manley herself simply observes that the attorney general "dropt the Prosecution," although "not without a very great Expence to the Defendants."[57] Her point about the costs incurred for legal fees is significant. Seditious libel, when used as a deterrent against antigovernment publications, was punishable by a large fine, time in pillory, and imprisonment. In 1702 the pamphleteer Daniel Defoe suffered all three punishments for his mockery of a high church clergyman's intolerance of Dissenters—the pamphlet probably inspired by Sachverell's early sermons. Even if a prosecution was eventually dropped, as in Manley's case, those who had been charged would have incurred substantial costs in legal fees, sending a clear message to other writers and printers that considering a potentially libelous publication would be expensive.

Describing how she had to "walk cross the Court before the Bench of Judges" is all the detail Manley provides of the trial itself, except to speculate as to "Whether the Persons in Power were ashamed to bring a Woman to her Trial for writing a few amorous Trifles purely for her own Amusement, or that our Laws were defective, as most Persons conceived, because she had serv'd her self with Romantick Names, and a feign'd Scene of Action?"[58] What she does not mention in her memoir is that every judge and lawyer at the Court of the Queen's Bench that week would have been preoccupied with preparations for one side or the other in Sacheverell's impeachment. Moreover, everyone at the courts in Westminster Hall would have been displaced by Christopher

Wren and his team of fifty workmen toiling around the clock to prepare the space for the impeachment trial. Although she makes no mention of it in her memoir, Manley was perfectly attuned to the impeachment proceedings in the spring of 1710. In *Memoirs of Europe,* her sequel to *The New Atalantis,* which she may have begun writing even before the libel charges against her were dismissed, Henry Sacheverell becomes a heroic figure, vaunted alongside Abigail Masham, to whom she would dedicate the second volume.

■

In mid-February 1709, as Manley returned home after the charges were dropped to celebrate with the printers and their associates in Lambeth Hill, the Duke of Marlborough was finalizing his preparations to sail for France. The Whigs who had looked to him for support and gravitas during the proceedings against Sacheverell were disappointed. As one eighteenth-century historian observed, "The Duke of Marlborough made many pretences to excuse himself from coming to the parliament, as he was busy in preparing the war, and that his duty called him to Holland." He persisted in this plan, even though it "gave offense to his friends who could not so well answer for the success of their proceedings, and the event of the trial in his absence." This observer sums up, "However, such was his pleasure, and such was their respect to his dignity, that they acquiesced." Yet up until the very moment of his departure, "when he was in his chariot," petitions were being presented to him "entreating him to put off his journey," but these he "politely" waved off." Not only were the Whigs putting their reputations on the line by bringing an unpopular public impeachment case against an increasingly sympathetic clergyman, Marlborough himself was putting his own dignity and reputation at risk. In this account, published many decades after these events first occurred, the author already acknowledges the change in attitude toward Marlborough: there were many who felt "that he never had a due regard either for the authority of parliament, or the liberty of the people of England, or the majesty of the sovereign; that he above all things consulted his own interest."[59]

The Marlboroughs, who had risen to power through their allegiance to Anne before she came to the throne, did not yet seem to have understood how public opinion was turning against them as they lost the queen's favor. The Duke of Marlborough was heard complaining that others had spoken disparagingly of him behind his back. Meanwhile, court gossips took note that, on 6 February, the Duchess of Marlborough "did not make her appearance at Chappel with the Queen her Birth day, wch most of the Ladys of the Bed Chamber did."[60]

That same week the House of Lords passed measures instructing Sir Christopher Wren to add yet more scaffolded seating to Westminster Hall. By Thursday, 16 February, both houses of Parliament had agreed to the wording of the address to the queen as she formally offered her order to Marlborough to depart for Holland, conveying their hope that "negotiations for peace will suddenly be renewed" even as they expressed their concern that "crafty and insinuating designs of our enemies . . . might create divisions" among the Allies. The joint statement also praised Marlborough's "unparallel'd service" and applauded "your majesties great wisdome in having honoured the same person with the great characters of general and plenipotentiary."[61]

Marlborough did not wait long enough to hear the queen's understated rejoinder to Parliament in ordering his departure. By Saturday, 18 February, the Duke of Marlborough and his wife were already on their way to Harwich, where he would depart, with seven men of war, for The Hague. He would not be present on Monday when the queen's message, in which she noted that she was glad to find that Parliament concurred with her "in a just sense of the Duke of Marlborough's eminent services," would be read in Parliament. Her cutting understatement, while not ideal public relations for the captain-general as he sailed to The Hague, was only a minor setback for the Whigs compared to the crisis of public opinion that would be unleashed against them as the impeachment trial opened against Sacheverell.

6

Impeachment and Public Opinion

AFTER SEEING her husband off at Harwich, the Duchess of Marlborough returned to London just in time to watch the Sacheverell trial. The queen and the Marlboroughs had agreed in January (following the standoff over military appointments) that Sarah would nominally retain her positions as mistress of the privy purse and groom of the stole, but that she would rarely be in attendance at court. The hostility between the queen and the duchess was running too high for Sarah's presence ever to be helpful either to Marlborough or to the Whigs. Queen Anne, however, still feared that if she dismissed Sarah, or allowed Sarah to resign her court offices, the duke would also resign as captain-general. The queen was starting to acknowledge that the peace treaty they could achieve in 1710 might be as advantageous as they could ever achieve and that further years of fighting would be useless and cripplingly expensive. Moreover, Anne's increasing aversion to Sarah was only making her more sympathetic to the Tory view of the war, but she was not yet ready for Marlborough to resign. Queen Anne still hoped that the Allies might pull off a stunning victory during the coming campaign season—a victory without the murderous casualties of Malplaquet—that might achieve an "honorable Peace" with France and Spain that would be equally pleasing to the Whigs and Tories. She also still hoped for harmony and balance between both parties in her government.

By retaining Sarah in her court offices, Anne's message to European diplomats at her court was that she was still pursuing the war with full force. Her simultaneous message to Marlborough, through the subdued version of her well-wishes to him on his departure, was that his favor was slipping, as was her patience with the war. Marlborough was worried that the queen's treatment of him might make the Allies doubt his confidence and send them to attempt separate peace treaties with France that would undermine the Alliance. But he was nevertheless confident in his own powers, pleased to "become again Prince, General, Plenipotentiary, with the magnates of Europe waiting upon his action, and brave armies impatient for his presence," as Winston Churchill describes him, and delighted to "quit the darkening scene in London."[1]

When Sarah returned from the coastal port of Harwich after saying good-bye to her husband, she could have chosen to return to Windsor Lodge or to her own house at St. Albans, rather than to her apartments in St. James's Palace. However, she was fully caught up in the partisan fervor of Sacheverell's trial. As one of Anne's attendants (with a reserved seat in Anne's royal box) and the wife of a member of the House of Lords (and so eligible for eight additional spectator tickets), the duchess would have had no difficulty securing a seat, but she was about to cause difficulties for herself by the manner in which she took that seat.

Public opinion was already turning against her even before the start of the impeachment proceedings, as shown in Manley's depiction of her in *The New Atalantis,* particularly the scene in which "the *Rabble* . . . rush'd altogether like an impetious Torrent upon her *Superbous* Palace."[2] When Manley referred to this "*Superbous* Palace," everyone would have thought of Blenheim. But by 1709 ground has also been broken just around the corner from St. James's Palace in central London for Marlborough House, on a plot of royal land leased to the Marlboroughs by the queen. Less fanciful than the baroque extravaganza still under construction at Blenheim, Marlborough House is more reminiscent of the smaller but still substantial brick mansion on the Sunderland estate at Althorp. Having engaged the Tory Sir Christopher Wren, Anne's surveyor general, the duchess informed him that "I mortally hate all Grandeur and Architecture."[3] The result is an impressive but understated two-story mansion of Dutch red brick with simple channeled stone quoins and straight-headed windows; there is decorative carving only on the central first-floor window. The painter Louis Laguerre was retained to decorate the public entrance hall, ceiling, and stairwells with painted scenes of the Duke of Marlborough at the Battle of Blenheim and other momentous battles. The duchess interacted largely with Wren's son, Christopher, and Wren's deputy, the architect Nicholas Hawksmoor, on the project, pressing them to keep the process moving forward. By August 1709, Lady Wentworth, well connected at court, wrote to her brother, living abroad, that Marlborough House "advances prodigiously."[4] By transferring money from the privy purse to her own account, the duchess was able to pay in cash and receive a better price for the construction, and ensure its swift completion.

It seems remarkable, in light of the insulting and offensive letters the duchess had been writing to the Queen since 1708, that Anne had granted her the land and allowed her to borrow the money to speed the construction (if she was aware at the time of Sarah's manipulation of the funds). Although she still had lodgings at St. James's Palace and Kensington and the lifetime use of Windsor Lodge, Sarah knew that she would need a London residence whenever the queen finally determined that she should be dismissed from her court positions. For the same reason, Queen Anne likewise recognized the need for the duchess to have her own house in London, which probably explains why she agreed to the advantageous lease of land.

Realizing that she could lose her court positions in the near future, Sarah had already pressed Anne that winter about a prior promise to retain as ladies-in-waiting her daughters Anne Sunderland and Henrietta Godolphin even if she herself were dismissed. While Sarah thought Anne had renewed that promise on behalf of her daughters in January, Anne felt she had been vague enough as to have assured no promise at all—a misunderstanding that would come to a head later that spring.

The Marlboroughs' lavish public building projects, particularly the construction site of Marlborough House, so visible in London, would have raised public ire against the duchess, never known for her charity or generosity. Such resentment would have been exacerbated in a year when the cost of grain had risen astronomically because of the harsh previous winter, which had compromised the crops in the summer of 1709. Since the war began, public expenditure had risen from £3 million to £13 million in Britain. Land taxes, which hit large landowners (many of them Tory) harder than merchants (many of them Whig), fueled resentment against the war. The national debt would rise from £10 million at the start of Anne's reign in 1702 to £50 million by the time of her death in 1714.[5] Delarivier Manley's fictional scene in *The New Atalantis* about rabble chasing the Marchioness of Caria was eerily prescient about the possibility of mob violence in London, even if the violence would not be specifically directed against the Marlboroughs but more generally against the Whigs, who had initiated impeachment proceedings against Sacheverell. Living above John Barber's printing shop in the crowded district south of St. Paul's Cathedral, where the streets were lined with printers and booksellers, Delarivier Manley would have picked up rumors of public discontent not only with the Marlboroughs but also with the Whigs' decision to prosecute Sacheverell.

Sir Christopher Wren, as surveyor general, had been at the beck and call of Parliament since late January, with demands for configuring Westminster Hall for the impeachment trial—one reason why his son and his deputy surveyor, Hawksmoor, were taking the lead with Marlborough House. Wren had charged the Treasury £3,000 to convert the interior of the cavernous Westminster Hall, which Daniel Defoe had described as "a great barn of three hundred feet long," into a magnificent public arena.[6] Wren would have charged only for the workers and the materials. His own salary, as surveyor of public works, had been held hostage for more than a decade in an attempt to speed up the pace of work on St. Paul's Cathedral. The cathedral, under reconstruction since the Great Fire of 1666, would finally be declared complete only in 1711, after which Wren would begin receiving his back pay.

The hold on his salary seems not to have deterred Wren's creative spirit in transforming Westminster Hall into a stage befitting the seriousness of the impeachment proceedings. The center of the room was framed with eighty-foot-long oak benches, terraced in height so that the four hundred or so members of the House of Commons could squeeze onto nine scaffolded benches on one side of the room; members of the House of Lords and their guests had nine benches on the other side. Framed by these scaffolded benches was a central carpeted area with benches for lawyers and judges, echoing the layout of the Lords Chamber in Parliament, with a throne for the queen (which she did not occupy since she was attending only as a visitor, ostensibly incognito, not as the arbiter of justice on a throne), flanked by two curtained boxes, one for her and her closest attendants, another for her ladies-in-waiting. This ceremonial courtroom was edged along the length of two walls with high shallow galleries, designed for spectators who would pay three to five guineas for tickets—although, given the pressing demand, these seats would in fact be taken up by the ticketed guests of the members of government.

Christopher Wren was a Tory, which was one of the reasons why the Duke of Marlborough chose the Whig dramatist John Vanbrugh rather than Wren to design Blenheim Palace, but he was not known for expressing partisan sentiment in his designs. The Duchess of Marlborough chose Wren rather than Vanbrugh for Marlborough House in part because she found Vanbrugh too extravagant. Although she would later complain that Wren likewise was unable to control the expenses of the builders, she expressed admiration for his work ethic, pointing out that Wren "was content to be dragged up in a basket three or four times a week to the top of St. Paul's, and at great hazard, for 200*l.* a year."[7] Despite his Tory politics, Wren, a scientist and architect—he was not only surveyor general but also a former president of the Royal Society—could not have been impressed with Sacheverell's incoherent and provocative sermon. It is unlikely that Wren was expressing any particular partisan sentiment in the floor plan for Sacheverell's trial. He was merely crafting a venue suitable for the gravity of occasion, the royal presence, and Parliament's demands for the maximum number of seats. In doing so, regardless of his own political views, Wren created an elaborate formal staging ground for the most attended trial in over a century, an arena that would make the public spectacle of it, including the reactions of its spectators, the talk of the town for years to come. The trial, already a philosophical revisiting of the Glorious Revolution, was set to become high political theater.

Sacheverell and his high church Tory supporters appeared to grasp the optics of the moment more readily than their Whig prosecutors. While Whig MPs and barristers were working furiously behind the scenes to craft their speeches for the prosecution, Sacheverell's friends and allies were scheming to create the greatest possible public impact. Friends of the clergyman arranged lodgings in the Inner Temple (one of the Inns of Court where students and members resided) so that he would be surrounded by sympathetic lawyers and law students. One friend lent a special carriage with an unusually extensive set of glass windows that would provide the public, already lured by the mezzotint print of his portrait, a continuous view of him as the carriage made it stately way from the Inner Temple, just above the Thames and slightly west of St. Paul's Cathedral, along the full length of the Strand toward Westminster. Sacheverell, vain of his appearance and dress, confident in himself and his Tory view of his country and its national church, would enjoy every minute of the attention he anticipated.

■

IN THE WEEKS before the trial, as Westminster Hall was being readied and the London public was scrambling to procure spectator tickets, clergymen were drawing larger crowds than usual while preaching on themes of passive obedience and resistance. Printers and booksellers were selling pamphlets for and against Sacheverell and on topics of obedience, resistance, and the Glorious Revolution. The Whig printer Abigail Baldwin printed *A Letter to the Good People of Great Britain*, in which she reminded her readers how lucky they were to be the beneficiaries of that "late Happy Revolution." She begins this pamphlet, signed A.B. (suggesting that she may have written it herself), with a nod to the nation's recent freedom from press censorship: "It is a pleasure that I am free to write, and you to read without danger, everything that concerns the Common Good of our Country." She reminds readers of a certain age that "it is in our memory, when all wrong was done with Impunity." Yet, she warns, there are "secret and base" forces at work, including "some of your Preachers" who are instilling "Doctrines, under pretence of Religion, destructive of your Laws and Constitution," and threatening the "present happy Settlement under her Gracious Majesty." Mrs. Baldwin, the printer-author, is warning her readers to be careful how they read and how they respond to the "Cry of Danger to the Church." Her advice, ultimately is to "be watchful for your Country, and for your Posterity" and "beware of those who have been diligent to divide and enflame you."[8]

Many Tories believed that Queen Anne must have supported Sacheverell, given the independence she had demonstrated in standing up to Marlborough over military appointments in January, yet the queen had told Bishop Burnet in January that Sacheverell's "was a bad sermon and that he deserved well to be punished for it."[9] When Abigail Masham, a Tory supporter of Sacheverell, asked her whether she would give her opinion publicly about the trial, Anne told her that "she did not meddle one way or other, and that it was her friends' advice not to meddle." Abigail tried to press the queen to find out "who she called her friends?"[10] In this era, a "friend" might also refer to a political ally—and for most of her adult life, Anne's friends and political advisers were Sidney Godolphin and the Marlboroughs. Anne certainly knew that she owed her throne to the Glorious Revolution and to those friends (the Whigs) who had brought it about. She specifically rejected the high Tory defense of monarchy by divine right, asserting on at least one occasion that it "was unfit to be given to anybody."[11] Yet, as a high church Tory, she also loved and wanted to protect the Church of England. The friends she was now taking advice from no longer included the Marlboroughs, but she also had friends other than Abigail Masham and Robert Harley, including many bishops in the Church of England, such as the Whig Henry Compton, bishop of London, who had guided Anne on horseback, armed with pistols, during her midnight flight from Whitehall Palace in 1688. When she gained the throne, Anne made Compton a member of her Privy Council.

By contrast, those churchmen in favor of Sacheverell were seduced by the cry of "the Church in Danger," and many felt, as did Reverend Maurice Wheeler, that "in him the Church will be sentenced either to stand or fall."[12] On 26 February 1710, the day before the trial, prayers were said for Sacheverell at St. Bride's Church and "several other" churches in London.[13] An anonymous handbill was nailed to the great front door of St. Paul's Cathedral, giving voice to the general fear: "THIS CHURCH IS TO LET; ENQUIRE AT THE COMMONS' HOUSE AND YOU MAY KNOW FURTHER."[14]

On the morning of 27 February, much of London was astir at five or six in the morning—long before dawn at that time of year. Coaches were rolling in by seven o'clock to New Palace Yard in front of Westminster Hall, disgorging the well-connected gentry and nobility with tickets to the proceedings, who queued until the doors opened at nine o'clock. Ladies eager to see "the Doctor" had dressed in finery, knowing they were there "to see and be seen."[15] The members of the House of Commons had begun with the usual morning prayers in their own chamber and passed one small unrelated piece of legislation, to fund improvements to a royal park at Farnham. While the sergeant-at-arms checked the low passages connecting St. Stephen's Chapel in Westminster Palace to Westminster Hall, the names of the MPs were read out by the clerk, in alphabetical order of counties (first those in England, then Wales, then Scotland), ensuring that the MPs filed in an orderly fashion through the passage and thence to the nine long scaffolded benches on their side of Westminster Hall. By ten o'clock the four hundred–some members of the House of Commons had filled the oak benches on their side of the hall and were awaiting the formal procession of the members of the House of Lords, in their ceremonial scarlet robes, with the number of ermine bars publicizing their rank.

At the center of this public courtroom were three woolsacks—large red woolen cushions, usually stuffed with horsehair—one for the lord chancellor, the Whig William Cowper, and two others for the twelve judges. Behind these was the royal throne, which the queen would not occupy (since she was not presiding), and on either side were the royal boxes for the queen and her ladies-in-waiting to observe the proceedings. The only person occupying one of the queen's boxes on the first morning of the trial was the Duchess of Marlborough. The queen was not planning on arriving at the trial until about four in the afternoon, around the time her presence would be needed give the required assent to the acts of impeachment.

The members of the House of Lords—119 Lords, including fifteen bishops—filed in, in reverse order of rank and seniority, followed by the Lord Chancellor William Cowper, whose family Manley had so scathingly mocked that his mother, Lady Sarah Cowper, had been relieved to find that she as "Lady Volpone" came off "well" by comparison with the rest of the family.[16] The sergeant-at-arms called, in the name of "Our Sovereign Lady the Queen," for all assembled to "keep Silence, upon pain of Imprisonment." He then commanded the defendant to come forward: "Oyez! *Henry Sacheverell,* Doctor in Divinity, come forth save thee and thy Bail, or thou forfeitest thy Recognizance."[17] Sacheverell appeared "immaculately gowned, bands crisp and white, exuding self-confidence," and knelt before the bar, with his defense team of counsellors, including three of the queen's chaplains.[18]

Lord Chancellor Cowper opened the proceedings by addressing Sacheverell directly, reminding him that, while released on bail, he had been allowed all the time he had requested to prepare his defense and that "their Lordships" showed him "all the Indulgence" that he might "reasonably expect."[19] Cowper then instructed the clerk to read the charges of impeachment and Sacheverell's written response. During the hour or so that it took for the clerk to read out these lengthy documents, all eyes turned toward the Duchess of Marlborough when she left her seat in the royal box and found a seat at the end of one of the House of Commons' benches. She perched next to the stand for the managers of the trial—those members of the House of Commons chosen to manage the trial in the House of Lords. This dramatic movement certainly reminded everyone present of her unqualified support for the Whigs prosecuting Sacheverell, but it was also embarrassing for them and inconvenient; her move prompted others scrambling for a place on any bench to seek seating on the House of Commons' benches, causing headaches for the deputy clerk and the sergeant-at-arms to keep "strangers" off the benches for the MPs.[20]

Sarah's move to the House of Common's bench, moreover, would only have encouraged the gossip about her well-known avarice. Claiming a place on a crowded bench when she already had an entire box to herself was at one with building a mansion in town on royal land while waiting for the completion of her private palace on another plot of royal land and retaining apartments in three royal palaces, as well as the entirety of Windsor Lodge.

Once the charges were read, the first days of the proceedings were taken up by the prosecution proving the charges against Sacheverell. The first to speak was Britain's attorney general, the Whig lawyer and MP James Montagu, who had recently dismissed the libel charges against Manley and her printers at the Court of the Queen's Bench. Any Whigs thinking about newspaper coverage would have been relieved that there were few mentions in newspapers of Manley's trial in February. At least there were no further journalistic attacks on the Whigs for harassing a witty lady satirist in the same week when so many pamphlets were defending the "Fair" preacher.

Montagu laid out the central thread of the reason for impeaching Dr. Sacheverell, namely, that he had, "with a Wicked, Malicious, Seditious Intention," attempted to "Undermine and Subvert Her Majesty's Government, and the Protestant Succession"; "Traduce and Condemn the late happy Revolution"; and "create Jealousies and Divisions amongst Her Majesty's Subjects," inciting them "to Sedition and Rebellion." In particular, Montagu asserted, Sacheverell had laid down as "a general Position, *that it is not lawful, upon any Pretence whatsoever, to make Resistance to the Supreme Power,*" which "by other passages, he explains to be the Regal Power." Refuting Sacheverell's fantastical assertion that the events of 1688 did not constitute any sort of resistance to the government, Montagu reminded those present that "Every Body knows, that knows any thing of the Revolution, That the Prince of *Orange* came over hither with an Armed Force." Montagu queried, "Was there any Occasion at that time to be so earnest to cry down Resistance, and Preach up Passive Obedience?"[21]

Montagu was followed by the eminent barrister Nicholas Lechmere, queen's counsel, who continued making the case that Sacheverell had opposed the very foundation of Britain's current system of government, which came into existence because of the resistance and overthrow of the previous government. "That glorious Enterprize," as Lechmere termed the Revolution of 1688, "which his late Majesty [William III] undertook with an armed Force to deliver this Kingdom from Popery and Arbitrary Power," was in fact an act of resistance, and one in which many "Subjects of the Realm" had participated "in Aid of that Enterprise." He further pointed out that these events clearly founded "that Power, and Right of Resistance which was exercised by the People at the time of the happy Revolution," and which led to "a limited Monarchy, wherein the Supreme Power is communicated and divided between Queen, Lords and Commons." Lechmere then invoked the "History of *Magna Charta*" to remind his auditors that "our Ancestors" established themselves as "Masters of Franchises that were truly their own, and which no Earthly Power had Right to extort from them." He then alluded to the unwritten but "Excellent Constitution of our Government" and "the true Spirit of the *English* Nation," both of which had been preserved by "the late happy Revolution" in the face of "Danger being Imminent, not only to the Laws and Liberties of the Kingdom, but the Protestant Religion." He further insisted that the House of Commons agreed that "the Toleration of Protestant Dissenters" was "one of the earliest and happiest Effects of the late Revolution, wisely calculated for the Support and strengthening the Protestant Interest."[22] Here Lechmere deftly refuted the Tory rallying cry that religious toleration was placing the "Church in Danger."

As Montagu and Lechmere established the government's rationale for prosecution, their speeches offered a public defense of the Revolution of 1688 and the Toleration Act of 1689. While it may seem odd that either of these would have needed defending two decades after that relatively peaceful revolution changed the monarchy from Catholic to Protestant and ushered in an era of relative toleration for Dissenting Protestants, sentiment remained divided about this moment in history, even though it was responsible for placing on the throne the much-loved Queen Anne. Many in the audience and among the larger public had not yet come to accept the swift ideological shift that enabled the Glorious Revolution, even if they were happy to be rid of the threat of a Catholic monarch.

The Tory diarist Thomas Hearne complained that during the impeachment proceedings the "Doctrine of Passive Obedience was decry'd as a pernicious, Slavish Doctrine." By the third day of the trial, Hearne was asserting that the proceedings "were manag'd by the Party with all the aggravating Circumstances that could be invented by Diabolical Malice."[23] But the trial was nowhere near complete. It would continue for several more weeks, and the spectators would continue to line up before dawn every morning. One Londoner noted the good effect of the trial on making ladies of fashion rise unusually early: "Secheverell will make all the Ladys turn good huswivs, they goe att seven every mornin."[24] There would be plenty of time for the Doctor to further impress the ladies and gentlemen in attendance when he raised his own mellifluous voice in his own defense.

After Lechmere finished his opening remarks, Attorney General Montague then asked that the dedication to the printed version of Sacheverell's sermon, given at Derby in August 1709, and the entire sermon Sacheverell delivered at St. Paul's Cathedral on Guy Fawkes Day in 1709 be read aloud to the two thousand persons in Westminster Hall. By then it was almost three o'clock in the afternoon. The Lords and the Commons adjourned to their separate chambers. The House of Lords was awaiting the Queen, who would give her assent to the acts of impeachment. Her arrival was somewhat delayed, however, by the crush of a crowd that surrounded her sedan chair while she was being carried from St. James's Palace to Westminster Hall—a journey of slightly less than one mile. She had embarked on this short journey at about half past three, but soon found herself surrounded by a crowd of people, some shouting "*God bless your Majesty and the Church,*" others shouting "*We hope your Majesty is for Dr.* Sacheverell."[25] A smaller number were also heard shouting "No Presbyterians!" or "No meetings!"[26]

For all of her high church sympathies, the queen had never expressed intolerance of Dissenting Protestants. Her late husband, whom she adored, was a Danish-born Lutheran who retained his own separate Lutheran chapel at court. She would not have wanted a populist crowd agitating under any circumstances, and certainly not in favor of a clergyman who had preached against the Revolution principle of resistance that had taken her to the throne. And yet the crowds of this first day felt certain that they understood the queen's political leanings. Not surprisingly, she looked "subdued when she reached the entrance" to the House of Lords.[27]

If Anne had not anticipated the uprisings of intolerant, anti-Dissenting populists on the first day of the trial, she could certainly not have anticipated how the dilatory pace of the trial itself would abet and increase such uprisings. Already the delay in waiting for the seating to be built in Westminster Hall had given time for the pamphlet wars to raise partisan fury on both sides. Had the trial taken place within the confines of Parliament, and not on display for a public audience, things might have played out more swiftly. But, in the context of a public trial, the defense took four full days to present its case (27 February to 2 March), while the defense took five days (3–7 March). The Prosecution then asked for an adjournment for two days (9–10 March) which then expanded into eleven days, counting weekends, as the House of Commons and the lords came to their separate judgments. The lords then deliberated on the final judgment and the punishment, spinning the trial out until 23 March—almost an entire month. During this time "all other business was at a stand; for this took up all men's thoughts."[28]

■

THE MOST IMPORTANT day of the trial for the prosecution was the second day, Tuesday, 28 February, during which time the six most impressive Whig speakers articulated the case for the prosecution. The

Queen arrived at 11 a.m., in a procession of halberdiers carrying her in a purple-covered sedan chair. She was dressed in purple and, attending incognito as an observer, wore "a thin hood over her face."[29] Just before she arrived, spectators had been amused by the spectacle of the sergeant-at-arms. brandishing an order from the House of Commons, requesting that "the duchess of Marlborough and a group of other ladies" be removed from the Commons' benches.[30]

Back in the royal box, the duchess experienced a further difficulty. She and the other ladies-in-waiting usually would not sit down in the queen's presence unless she gave them leave to do so. Anne was not so inhumane as to want to have wished her ladies to stand for seven to ten hours per day for more than two weeks. However, she apparently forgot to give the order to sit—so no one sat, until the Duchess of Marlborough asked if she might sit down. The queen gave permission, but only the duchess and two other ladies-in-waiting took a seat. Sarah subsequently believed that the other ladies-in-waiting, particularly the Duchess of Hyde and the Duchess of Somerset (who refused to sit but stood behind the queen), had somehow conspired to make it appear that she had "done something that was impertinent." When Sarah approached the queen at St. James's Palace early the next morning to confirm that the ladies could sit, the queen retorted sharply, "If I had not liked you should it, why do you think I would have ordered it?"[31] For the duration of the lengthy trial, all the ladies-in-waiting would sit, with the queen's permission, in her presence, but Sarah still felt there had been a conspiracy against her.

The prosecution was represented by Sir Joseph Jekyll, who spoke for almost an hour about the "clear sense and meaning" of the most disturbing passages in Sacheverell's sermon. He also pointed out the dangers posed to the very foundation of government implicit in Sacheverell's challenge to the legality of the Revolution of 1688. As he explained, "if the Justice of the Revolution be establish'd," then there could be differences of opinion about religious toleration: some would rejoice in it, others might object, but it would be accepted or "acquiesc'd in by all." While there might still be disagreement between different political parties, he argued, there would not be the level of "Disputes and Factions" as would follow, in Jekyll's estimation, if the validity of the

Revolution were denied. When that validity was denied, as in Sacheverell's sermon, the level of disagreement and dispute between parties was bound to rise to such a degree that "a total Subversion of our Constitution" would follow. Jekyll also made clear that the requirement of passive obedience of "Submission" was not only to the monarch, as Sacheverell would have it, but also to the rule of law. Jekyll praised the "Temper and Prudence" of those who in 1688–89 articulated the foundation of the nation's government as resting "not only on Royal but on Legislative Authority." He also praised both Parliament and William III for implicitly condoning the resistance to James II that brought about the Revolution. Thus, in "condemning" that "Resistance," Sacheverell "cast Black and Odious Colours on the late King and the Revolution."[32]

Jekyll was followed by Robert Eye, solicitor-general, who detailed the weakness of Sacheverell's written answer to the impeachment, insisting that in that *Answer,* Sacheverell once again was reiterating the doctrine of nonresistance. He pointed out that "if the Resistance at the Revolution was illegal," then "the Revolution settled in Usurpation." If William and Mary and now Queen Anne were now usurpers to thc crown, then "the Friends of the Pretender" would be emboldened to "advance his Title to the Crown, and call him King."[33] Although it may seem counterintuitive that disallowing the right of resistance could result in the overthrow of the current monarch, that was, in essence, the prosecution's rallying cry.

Then the comptroller of the household gave a "short but effective speech," and the MP Robert Walpole followed with remarks that were "robust, combative, well-honed" and "spiced here and there with mordant humour."[34] He began by acknowledging the strangeness of his (and the Whig position), which was to assert that as "a Loyal Subject and Faithful Servant of the best of Queens," he was in an awkward situation "in speaking in Defence of the Necessary and Commendable Resistance used at the Revolution," since "his Arguments may be misconstrued, and misrepresented, as maintaining Antimonarchical Schemes." As he continued in his address to the judges, Walpole ironically echoed Sacheverell's own insulting prose style in the string of adjectives he deployed when he expressed his hope that their "Judgment in this Case will convince the world that every *Seditious, Discontented, Hot-headed, Ungifted, Unedifying Preacher* (the Doctor will pardon me for borrowing one String of Epithets from him, and for once using a little of his own Language), who had no Hopes of distinguishing himself in the world but by a matchless Indiscretion, may not advance, with Impunity, Doctrines destructive of the Peace and Quiet of her Majesty's government."[35] Walpole reminded his auditors that the "Doctrine of unlimited, unconditional Passive Obedience, was first invented to support Arbitrary and Despotick Power, and was never promoted or countenanc'd by any Government that had not Designs some time or other of making use of it."[36]

The next speakers for the prosecution focused on the second article of impeachment, concerning the legality of toleration for Dissenting protestants. Sir Peter King reminded Parliament and the visiting spectators that "the Act relating to the Toleration" was one that "every one" remembers "the Necessity for" and has "experienced the Benefit of it." However, "the Doctor," he said, suggested and maintained "that the Toleration granted by Law is unreasonable, and the Allowance of it unwarrantable." King observed that "it is almost difficult to be serious in giving a Reply to that part of his Answer" wherein Sacheverell asserted "that he cannot inform himself that a Toleration hath been granted by Law."[37]

Spencer Cowper—brother of Lord Chancellor William Cowper and the same MP satirized by Manley with respect to the rumors surrounding the drowning of his lover, Sarah Stout—seconded this argument about toleration, by observing that "it is unnecessary at this time . . . to justifie the Reasonableness of the Toleration granted to Protestant Dissenters." He insisted "that this Indulgence is required from us as Christians, and as we are Men professing Humanity and good Will towards one another." Concluding the last speech of that second day of the trial, he stressed the seriousness of the challenge Sacheverell offered to the political status quo: "Many are the Seeds of Sedition which he has Sown, and the Fruit to be expected is Civil Discord and Confusion, unless some Remedy shall be applied to prevent it."[38]

The queen heard less of the prosecution's case than everyone else since she left to dine with Lord Halifax for about two hours in the middle of the day. All the other spectators, however, remained riveted. Even a ten-year-old boy sent a letter to his grandfather, the Duke of Marlborough, by way of the military chaplain Dr. Francis Hare, assuring his famous relation that he "should have thought it a very great scandal in me to have let Doctor Hare go without sending a letter by him." He wishes "there was to be Peace" but "if it please God to prolong the wars, may he prosper the arms of her Majesty and protect you." Young William Godolphin (whose other grandfather was Lord Treasurer Sidney Godolphin, also present at these proceedings) concludes his letter with a reference to the trial that was eclipsing every other event in London at that moment: "I have been at Doctor Sacheverell's trial every day and am against him."[39]

The third day of the trial, Wednesday, 1 March, began with Sacheverell appearing at the bar with his counsel, as on previous days. The prosecution continued with public statements, addressing in particular the third article of impeachment, Sacheverell's claim that the Church of England was in "great Peril and Adversity under Her Majesty's Administration."[40] The speakers, beginning with the MP William Thompson, were keen to dispute the familiar high church complaint that toleration of Dissenters placed "the Church in Danger." After refuting this accusation, Thompson begged the House of Lords to "exert your Power and Authority to Suppress that Audacious and Unparallel'd Insolence, that daily flies abroad from the Pulpit and the Press." In his mind, it was not the Dissenters placing the Church in danger but the intolerance of preachers such as Sacheverell who published "these Seditious Murmurs" from the pulpit and the press that "are become the Mints of Faction and Sedition."[41]

Henry Compton, bishop of London, reaffirmed "the extreme Danger from which our Laws and Liberties, and our Church and Constitution were Rescued" by William III when he forced James II's abdication. Compton further attested to the significance of the 1707 Act of Union, joining Scotland to England, in which "the same Parliament proceeded . . . with so much Vigour, as well as Prudence" that "in less than six Weeks," the union was recognized and had already shown its "good Effect all over *Europe*."[42]

The most rousing speech that afternoon was given by Sir Thomas Parker, a sergeant-at-law (one of an elite group of barristers qualified to argue in the Court of Common Pleas) and MP for Derby, who was very ill and feared he would not be able to stand long enough to complete his testimony. However, "well over an hour later he was still on his feet, holding even the hostile part of his audience captive with a display which for intellectual quality and power of analysis can rarely have been matched in any British political trial."[43] Parker laid out his case step by step to show that while Sacheverell pretended to be in favor of passive obedience to the queen, his sermon in fact undermined the authority of the current monarch by undermining the legality of the Revolution. The only fundamental "Principle" Sacheverell supported would be a principle that "*is fundamental* to the *Pretender,*" that is, Anne's Catholic half-brother, James Francis Edward Stuart. Parker then challenged the clergyman on his own choice of biblical passage, from Lamentations, which echoed in his reference "*Sion*" mourning "*in Bitterness*" and "*her Priests*" sighing. As Parker pointed out, offering a Bible lesson himself to the clergyman and two thousand spectators, that passage refers to the Jewish people when they were "inslav'd, their *King* in a *Foreign* Country, *strip'd of his Crown*"—the same circumstances the Pretender believed he had experienced while in exile in France. Yet only supporters of the Pretender would have described his situation that way. For loyal supporters of Queen Anne, the Pretender was merely her Catholic half-brother, or possibly an unrelated infant smuggled into the birthing chamber in a warming pan with no claim to the crown (following the fiction that Mary of Modena had faked the pregnancy). Parker concluded by observing ironically, "Thus has the Doctor, out of his *tender Concern for Her Majesty's Person and Government,* thought fit to express his Sentiments."[44]

In response to those who believed that Sacheverell was merely a clergyman doing his duty, Parker concluded his speech by pointing out that "*it is the Business of a Clergyman to preach Peace,*" not to be "*blowing a Trumpet* in *Sion,* to engage his *Country in* Seditions and Tumults, overthrow the *best Constitution,* and betray the *best Queen* that ever made a People happy, and this with *Scripture* in his Mouth." Sir John Smith, chancellor of the exchequer, closed the prosecution's testimony that day asserting that "we have made good our Charge" against Sacheverell and "'tis high time for the Justice of the Nation to put a Stop" to Sacheverell's dangerous behavior in raising "Jealousies," fomenting "Divisions," and stirring up "Sedition."[45] The Lords adjourned to their chambers, and the events inside Westminster Hall concluded for the day at about six o'clock, when Lord Treasurer Sidney Godolphin moved to adjourn for the day. Outside Westminster Hall, however, mobs in support of the Doctor were already assembling in the streets, as they had every day of the trial. And that night the mobs turned to acts of destruction that had been meticulously planned in advance.

■

ON THE FIRST morning of the trial, Sacheverell, in his borrowed glass-windowed coach, and his legal team (in eight attendant coaches) had been flanked on their route from the Inner Temple to Westminster by about four hundred supporters and well-wishers, in a crowd described as "vociferous rather than ugly." On that first morning, many of them cheered him along with shouts of "God bless you," "God send you a happy deliverance," and "They shall not hurt a hair of your head."[46] On Tuesday the mobs were larger, surging around Sachverell as he left Westminster Hall in the evening, after the trial ended for the day. As the mob followed Sacheverell, pausing as he "from time to time gave his hand out of the coach window to be kissed," the coaches of the prosecution, including that of the lord chancellor, were caught behind this ceremonial procession and slowed to a crawl.[47]

After accompanying him to the Inner Temple, some of the mob were overhead discussing in a "Council of War" a plan to demolish Daniel Burgess's impressive brick Presbyterian meetinghouse (as Dissenting places of worship were often called during this era), one of the best attended and most opulent in London. On Tuesday evening, after the trial, the mob smashed every glass window in the building that they could reach with sticks; they likewise smashed the windows in Burgess's private house. Burgess's son rushed to the secretary of state's offices at Whitehall, asking for protection against further destruction. Secretary Henry Boyle promised a guard would be placed outside the meetinghouse the following evening, but such a guard never appeared. The government either did not fully understand the extent of the threat or did not have adequate staffing to supply a guard.

On Wednesday morning the mobs were even larger and more provocative in their support for the Doctor, "falling upon those that did not pull off their Hatts to ye Doctor as he pass'd by."[48] By that morning the mob was larger than on previous days and infiltrated with "a hired company of butchers" serving as bodyguards to Sacheverell and other "reputedly paid thugs" from across the river in Southwark, Sachevell's parish.[49]

After the proceedings in Westminster Hall concluded, at about 6 p.m., the mob accompanied Sacheverell's coach to his lodgings; the mob leaders then led the crowd the four short blocks back to Burgess's meetinghouse. This mob was not merely a spontaneous gathering of Sacheverell supporters. It had been primed for violence by a printed broadsheet, hot off the press and distributed at the close of the trial, about "an imaginary prizefight" between the Whig clergyman Benjamin Hoadley and Sacheverell. Some members of the mob caught the MP John Dolben, one of the managers of the trial in Parliament, and threatened to hang him.[50] He only escaped by insisting he "was not Dolben nor a Parliament-man."[51] Although Dolben had carried the initial impeachment charges from the House of Commons to the House of Lords in early January, he was too ill, possibly from the stress of the proceedings, to participate in the trial itself. After the trial he retreated to the country for rest, where he died in May. The mob that evening was also enhanced by agents of destruction carrying crowbars, pickaxes, and other carpenters' tools. Several of these later admitted to having been enlisted in advance and promised payment for their work.[52]

These laborers, with their tools, set about dismantling Daniel Burgess's meetinghouse, a building tall enough that the mobs with sticks the previous evening had not reached all the windows. Those smashed the night before had been boarded over for protection, but a man in sailor's garb climbed up to an intact window above the main door. Some nearby who knew of the plans asked onlookers whether "they got in." Those watching the destruction confirmed that "they are pulling the pulpit down." One enthusiastic supporter of the plans was heard "snapping his fingers" and shouting "We have done it."[53]

The demolition of Burgess's meetinghouse was methodical. Several dozen men took down the pulpit, then hundreds of feet of wooden pews; they also unhinged the wooded doors. All of this combustible wood was carted out to a predesignated location. As one of the participants later admitted, "There were pullers down and there were carriers," as well as others specifically tasked with setting and lighting the massive quantities of combustible wood on fire, producing enormous bonfires.[54] Those carrying lighter materials—cushions, vestry chairs, and smaller boards—were seen dancing around the fire "two or three times" and "halooing for Sacheverell" before tossing in the combustible materials. The mob shouted incessantly "High Church and Sacheverell" as it cheered on the blaze.[55]

Far from repenting of this act of violent destruction, Sacheverell's supporters were clearly proud of it. An engraving of the scene (in which Dr. Burgess's meetinghouse is mockingly labeled "Dr. Burgises Theater") was included in a Tory publication, *The Whigs Unmask'd: Being the Secret History of the Calf's-Head-Club,* published three years later. The "Calf's-Head-Club" was ostensibly made up of those Whigs so loyal to the principle of resistance that they celebrated every year the execution of Charles I on 30 January by feasting on a calf's head. Edward Ward, the presumed author of the anonymous work, insists, as did Sacheverell, on linking the Whigs to the execution of 1649 rather than to the Glorious Revoution of 1688. Although to modern eyes, the scene shows the dangerous violence of the backlash against the Whigs, Ward describes the destruction as the Whigs' fault. In his extreme Tory version of events, it was the "Whiggish Managers Prosecution of Doctor *Sacheverell*" that was "provoking the Good People of *England* to shew their Resentments, in pulling down the Meeting-Houses." Ward further justifies this act of violence against Presbyterians with three lines of verse: "*For Bold Adventures, in so just a Cause, / Tho; done by Force, repugnant to the Laws, / Deserve eternal Mem'ry and Applause.*"[56]

The methodical approach to the destruction that Ward celebrates three years later indicates that it was carefully plotted in advance. This advance planning is also indicated by the move from one Dissenting meetinghouse to the next. After destroying Burgess's meetinghouse, portions of the mob then set off to the meetinghouse of the Congregationalist minister, Thomas Bradbury, and another huge bonfire was set aflame in Holborn. By eleven o'clock the mob was heading to Christopher Taylor's Presbyterian meetinghouse, tucked away in Leather Lane, and then to Jabez Earl's meetinghouse, off Drury Lane. The mobs then raged entirely out of control across an area from St. Paul's Cathedral west to Covent Garden and north to Clerkenwell Green. The usual constables and night watchmen had no means to stop this mass of rioters.

Lord Sunderland was busy with paperwork (and no doubt further preparations for the impeachment proceedings) in his office at the Cockpit in Whitehall Palace about 9 p.m. when Lord Chancellor Cowper and Lord Privy Seal, Newcastle, arrived to let him know of the riots and the bonfires. Sunderland took a sedan chair toward St. James's Palace, in the opposite direction from the conflagration, to warn the queen. It was too late in the day to convene a local militia. The only soldiers readily available to intervene immediately were the queen's own guards at St. James's Palace. Yet if her guards left to control the riots in central London, there would be no one guarding the queen should the mobs decide to head toward her palace. Sunderland expressed this concern to the queen. At first she was "seized with a paleness and trembling," but then commanded Sunderland to take her personal horse and foot guards, asserting that "*God would be Her Guard.*"[57]

Queen Anne is often depicted as a cipher, manipulated by others—first by the Marlboroughs, then by Abigail Masham and Robert Harley. This depiction is based, in part, on the Duchess of Marlborough's condescending recollections in her published memoirs. From a young age, Anne certainly lacked in confidence, and she herself admitted that she did not always readily find the words she needed to express her thoughts. But this does not mean she was stupid or the puppet of others. Sarah would later write in her memoirs that Anne's "memory was exceeding great," but that she chose to remember the trivia of "ceremonies and customs of court."[58] This does not necessarily indicate that she did not remember other more significant political details, merely that she did not always act in what Sarah considered was the Whigs' best interest. In explaining her own loss of influence, Sarah attributes Anne's change of heart to her "weakness credulity and inconsistency" in coming under the sway of Abigail and Harley. She does not give Anne credit for making a conscious choice as to whose advice she would choose in a given matter. Anne's power lay in deciding which adviser's advice to follow about any given decision or policy.

What is striking about the Queen's response in this moment of crisis on 1 March 1710 is that not only was she not scripted in advance and had no time to consult with either Whig or Tory advisers but that she made her decision before Sunderland—who was genuinely torn about what to advise her to do—could attempt to sway her one way or the other. Her decision at this point stemmed from a genuine religious faith—one possibly stronger than that felt by her closest friends or advisers. It is this religious certainty that may often have made her impenetrable to close friends, such as the Duchess of Marlborough and the Earl of Godolphin. Sarah describes Anne's trust in God in superficial terms, as "implicit faith and subjection, accompanied with the form and course of a sort of piety,"[59] but Sarah may simply not have fully appreciated the depth and power of Anne's faith.

As soon as he was back at Whitehall, Sunderland sent a note by a messenger to the commander of Her Majesty's Foot Guards. The commander, Brigadier Tatton, was not found, but an infantry captain was summoned to Lord Sunderland, who ordered him to go and disperse the mob. The aptly named Captain Horsey, according to his subsequent account, was extremely concerned about "any accident that might happen" and requested that he be given orders in writing, which Sunderland said he would deliver in the morning. Meanwhile, Horsey carefully interrogated Sunderland as "*Whether he was to Preach or Fight the Mobb?* If the first, *he desired some better Speaker might be sent along with him, for he was but an indifferent Orator; if the latter, Fighting was his Trade, and he would do his best.*" Secretary Sunderland replied that he would have to use his own best "Judgment and Discretion," using violence only "*in Case of Necessity.*"[60] Regiments of the Middlesex militia and the First Foot Guards and fourth troop of Horse Guards were held in readiness.

Captain Horsey clearly thought carefully about the orders he gave his own troops, and "thanks to the soldiers' superb discipline," the riots were contained without a shot being fired and with only about fifty casualties "from sword or saber cuts."[61] The horse guards rode in and pressed the rioters to the two sides of a street, gradually divided them into groups of fifty to one hundred, then dispersed them. Captain Orrell of the Horse Grenadiers kept up the pursuit until midnight, finally arriving at Samuel Wright's meetinghouse in Blackfriars just as a mob was about set alight an organized stacked of combustible pews and galleries cut "into pieces," with "straw, rushes and links under them."[62] The city was finally quiet by 3 a.m., with foot guards patrolling the streets, as they would for the next two days.

■

THE VIOLENCE that overtook London on Wednesday night did not bring the impeachment proceedings to a standstill. It appears instead to have confirmed the Whig managers in the appropriateness of their cause, although the proceedings would not resume until Thursday afternoon. On Thursday morning the House of Commons met separately to discuss the "insolence of the mob" and vote on an address to the queen, requesting that she issue a proclamation "to prevent such tumults" as were "fomented by papists, nonjurors, and other enemies to her majesties title and government." They urged the queen to offer "a reward to the discoverors of such incendiaries as have been the abettors thereof." The queen promptly replied that "she was sensible of the great concern they had for the publick on this occasion, and, as she had a just resentment of such tumultnary proceedings, so she would take care to suppresse and prevent the same, and would accordingly publish a proclamation to that end."[63]

The queen immediately convened the Privy Council, which issued a proclamation promising that "all such rioters, traitors, rebels, and *all their accomplices, adherents, abetters and advisors* shall be forthwith proceeded against according to the utmost severity of law."[64] What would be harder to prove in a court of law were the rumors that there were "many Gentlemen in Disguise" in the mob of rioters and that "the Rabble were further encouraged by Money thrown to them by Men of Figure out of their Coaches."[65] When the impeachment proceedings finally resumed about two o'clock the next afternoon, Nicholas Lechmere drew a connection between the impeachment charges against Sacheverell "stirring up Sedition, and exhorting to Rebellion" and the violence of the night before: "the Rebellion that has been rais'd, and that High-Treason that was committed, the last Night, by those Persons who abet the Prisoner." Yet he promised that they would continue to "discharge the great Trust reposed" in them by the House of Commons in continuing the "Progress of their Impeachment."[66]

Not much of substance, however, occurred during the trial that afternoon. Lechmere simply "summ'd up all the arguments, and told the lords that he hoped they had made good their charge against Sacheverell."[67] Or at least this is the version of events as told by the Whig chronicler Narcissus Luttrell. The Tory chronicler Thomas Hearne frames his version of Lechmere's summary arguments with a denigrating description of Lechmere as "a man of Parts but a most vile, stinking Whigg." He also snarls that Lechmere had concluded that "in some extraordinary Cases, such as that of the late wicked Revolution, Resistance is lawfull."[68]

Thomas Hearne's Tory view of the proceedings extended even to the violence of Wednesday night. He uses the mild verbal phrase "pulled down" to describe the mob destruction of the Presbyterian meetinghouses; he describes Daniel Burgess, pastor of the first such meetinghouse destroyed, as "that old Presbyterian Rogue." Even when describing how the organizers laid the bonfire, Hearne takes a swipe at the pastor, describing his pulpit, when placed atop the pile before it was lit, as "the Tub in wch he us'd to hold forth."[69] He also conveys skepticism about the Commons's assertion that "the Doctor himself is reckon'd the principal Cause of it." Of course, Whig chroniclers also expressed bias; the historian Abel Boyer described the death of a linnen-draper's apprentice as "Divine Justice" when the casement he was dismantling in Burgess's meetinghouse fell on him."[70]

Despite the difference between Whig and Tory views on the violence that transpired the previous day, the residents of London were shaken by the unrest. Even Sacheverell would have had to acknowledge that this mob violence was "an odd way of defending passive obedience and non-resistance."[71] Rather than incite the mob further with the visible reminder of his presence, he abandoned the glass-enclosed carriage for a sedan chair with the curtains drawn; eventually he settled on taking a more anonymous hackney coach.

■

ALTHOUGH WE MIGHT assume that public opinion would have shifted to favor the Whigs after the mob rioting against the Presbyterians and the destruction of their places of worship, opinion remained divided along partisan lines, with opponents of the impeachment continuing to insult the prosecutors personally. Then as now, religious intolerance was often spurred by provocateurs inciting hate for its own sake, rather than out of precise theological arguments. As the historian Geoffrey Holmes points out, "Most of the rioters lived not in the City proper," where churches were abundant, but "in the neglected suburbs," where they may not have attended "any Anglican service" and may have received "little or no religious instruction." Nor were the rioters necessarily directly affected by the immigrants from the Palatine, most of whom had by this point settled in the countryside or relocated to Ireland. Holmes, writing in 1973, suggests patronizingly that it is "difficult to penetrate the minds even of the highly literate classes of a past society, let alone those of the inarticulate masses."[72] The uprisings, however, were not spontaneous but incited by a preacher not speaking to peoples' "minds" but to their gut emotions and their fear of difference.

Social scientists find that "when people feel threatened, they want tighter social norms."[73] Michele Gelfand posits that people living closer to the edge of poverty and ruin desire strong moral rules and a strong leader, and are less tolerant of immigrants and cultural and religious differences.[74] Sacheverell first stoked populist fears with cries of "the Church in Danger" from toleration; he then addressed those fears by repudiating toleration and praising traditional passive obedience to authority rather than the newly asserted right to resist. Sacheverell tapped into a populist desire for more control, a desire that was expressed, paradoxically, by a mob raging out of the control of law and order. Wealthy educated Whig elites, particularly someone like the Earl of Sunderland, who would not have felt threatened by immigrants or by famine, may not have felt a need for a strong authoritarian leader. On the other hand, Whig fears of not defeating French and Catholic power on the Continent were stoking Whigs' own desire to prosecute clergyman such as Sacheverell and writers like Delarivier Manley for certain types of printed speech. Whigs like Sunderland were probably reacting so strongly to the Tory use of the new press freedoms because they had conceived of satirical secret history as a Whig propaganda tool, as it had been in the years leading up to and following the Glorious Revolution. Acknowledging that the Godolphin ministry was already unpopular before it put forth the unpopular plan of impeaching Sacheverell, historian Geoffrey Holmes points out that "politicians in the early eighteenth century rarely allowed such considerations" as the popularity of their policies "to influence important political calculations."[75] Only about 3 percent of the population could vote, but even nonvoters were finding ways to express opinions about those who governed them.

Tories, including the MP Robert Harley, had been harnessing the best satirists and journalists to make their case in public. Harley had been paying Daniel Defoe since 1703 as a hired pen to write in support of policies favored by Godolphin and Marlborough, including the 1707 Act of Union with Scotland. By September 1708, after he had been pushed out of his position in Anne's cabinet in February of that year, Harley had begun undermining the influence of Godolphin and Marlborough in pamphlets such as *A Dream at Harwich,* in which the nation is depicted as drugged into blindness, with its fingers plugging its ears, allowing a certain family (i.e., the Marlboroughs) to plunder its resources.[76] Soon Harley would enlist Jonathan Swift (originally a Whig, but who switched sides after Godolphin refused to support him for the preferment he sought in the Church of England) into the pamphlet wars against the War of Spanish Succession. Delarivier Manley would subsequently write for Harley when she joined forces with Jonathan Swift in writing pamphlets and periodicals in 1711.

Harley was sensitive to the need to manipulate public opinion in a way that the Marlboroughs and Lord Sunderland simply were not. Sacheverell, as a narcissist and provocateur who had always craved public attention, had a natural sense of how to play a crowd. On Saturday, 5 March, even before Sacheverell took the stand, Sidney Godolphin wrote to the Duke of Marlborough, regretting they had even started the proceedings. He observes that "the tryall" not only "takes up all my time, but very much impairs my health, and how it well yet end I am not at all certain. But I certainly wish it never had began, for it has occasioned a very great ferment, and given opportunity to a great many people to bee impertinent."[77]

■

SACHEVERELL'S DEFENSE was to have begun with Sir Simon Harcourt, a highly experienced barrister and MP (who had once represented Bossiney, Cornwall, alongside John Manley, Delarivier's cousin and bigamous husband) who had briefly served as attorney general, though he stepped down when Robert Harley was dismissed from Anne's cabinet in 1708. Harcourt was too ill on Thursday afternoon to attend. Certainly all the others in the room, including the queen, the lords, and the MPs, who had been up most of the night concerned about the riots, would have been exhausted and glad to postpone events to the next morning. Even on Friday, Sir Simon was accompanied to the proceedings by a medical doctor, but "every body desires to hear him," as Robert Harley's sister, Abigail Harley, wrote to their brother Edward.[78]

Harcourt himself recognized the difficulty of defending Sacheverell for condemning resistance and so challenging the legality of the Revolution of 1688. He described his speech as "like dancing upon the ropes: if he slipped, he was sure to break his neck; they watched his words so."[79] His speech, which lasted over two hours, was riveting—even more so as a performance than as a written document. He had a beautiful speaking voice, and he delivered his argument so as to leave the audience spellbound by "the cadences, and the strength, the justness and the beauty of the expression."[80]

Much more subtle than Sacheverell himself, Harcourt pointed out that Sacheverell had been speaking in "General Terms" about "the Illegality of Resistance to the Supreme Power or on any Pretence." An adept scholar, Harcourt cited numerous examples of Church of England practice and doctrine since Henry VIII established the church in 1533. He also pointed out that the written homilies of the church included clauses against disobedience. Moreover, he concluded that Sacheverell himself "is not the Person he has been represented, he hath no disloyal Thoughts about him."[81]

While this speech held everyone's attention, the subsequent speakers in Sacheverell's defense were less riveting. The queen left for a long dinner in the afternoon. On Saturday, the clerks read aloud the passages Harcourt had referred to from many well-known books, including Hooker's *Laws of Ecclesiastical Polity,* which certainly promoted obedience rather than resistance. The Whigs sometimes took the opportunity to have the clerks read passages from the same books, to cite passages where clergyman were warned against meddling in affairs of state. Monday's speeches were as little interesting to the public as those of Friday afternoon, as Tory lawyers struggled to defend some of Sacheverell's least defensible points in his written answer to the charges.

On Tuesday afternoon, however, Sacheverell himself was allowed to take the stand. The Whig managers assumed he would work himself up into his usual frenzy and give an offensive speech that would work against him. Instead, unexpectedly, he delivered a speech so different from any of his sermons that everyone in the room swiftly realized he had not written it himself. The Duchess of Marlborough later described him as a "tool" and alluded to the speech "full of impious piety" being "put into his mouth."[82] Many guessed that the speech had been penned and edited by the most erudite Tory divines, likely including Dr. Francis Atterbury. But before the duchess and others could pronounce him a mere "tool," Sacheverell had already made that point in his own defense.

Sacheverell began his carefully scripted speech by acknowledging that he himself understood that he was viewed as "*an insignificant Tool of a Party, not worth regarding.*" Yet he also explained that the "Design" behind his impeachment was "to procure an *Eternal and Indelible Brand of Infamy to be fix'd in a Parliamentary way on all those who maintain the Doctrine of Non-Resistance, and to have the Clergy directed what Doctrines they are to Preach, and what not.*" His impeachment, in other words, was a means of interference with clergymen doing their usual jobs in the pulpit of their own parishes—not something that most ordinary Britons would be happy about. Underplaying his usual narcissism, Sacheverell then observed, in a style of humility not usual for him, that "as *Insignificant* as I am in my *Self,* yet the *Consequences* of my Tryal (if rightly represented to your Lordships by some of *those Gentlemen*) are of the highest Moment and Importance."[83]

He portrayed himself ultimately as an obedient servant of the Queen. "So far was I from designing to *defame* Her Majesty's *Administration,* or to infuse any *undutiful Thoughts* of Her," he opined, "that I not only pay Her all Honour and Obedience, but am from the *bottom of my Soul* zealously, and affectionately *Loyal* to Her." He also insisted that it is his "Sincere and Hearty Prayer, that *God* would prolong the Life of *Her most Sacred Majesty.*" Rather than harboring "*Malicious,* or *Seditious Designs,*" his only aim was to "*instil* the *Principles of Loyalty,* and *Obedience*" into the souls of his "Fellow-Subjects." He begged the prosecution to consider the values of "*Moderation and Temper.*" And he asked the audience for pity on his "*Sufferings*" not only while imprisoned but afterward, while he "purposely avoided doing any Part of the *Duty* of my *Function,* or even *appearing in Publick,* lest it should Occasion any *Tumult* or *Disturbance.*" He added that unfortunately, such disturbances had already been occasioned by his "*necessary Attendance*" at the trial, thus portraying the mob violence as the fault of the prosecution rather than the fault of his provocative preaching.[84]

Ultimately, the words that Sacheverell read out, while moving, were not as memorable as his tone of voice and the visual impression he made on his auditors. The Duchess of Marlborough, with heavy irony noting Sacheverell's skill in brandishing a handkerchief, describes how his "good assurance, clean gloves, white handkerchiefs well managed, with other suitable accomplishments, moved the hearts of many at his appearance." Moreover, the formality of the occasion "and the solemnity of his trial added much to a pity and concern which had nothing in reason or justice to support them." She also sneered at the "weaker part of the ladies" who "were more like mad or bewitched than like persons in their senses."[85] Another contemporary describes how his "Studied, Artful, and Pathetick Speech, made no small Impression on many of the Spectators, and drew even Tears from some of the most tender-hearted among the Fair Sex." This same observer points out that the speech "had a contrary Effect" on other auditors, "who look'd upon it a kind of sly *Recantation* of what the Doctor had advanc'd in his Sermons."[86] The image of Sacheverell giving his speech remained such a fixture in the nation's cultural memory that an engraving of it was produced for a nineteenth-century history of England, showing Sacheverell in his clerical gown and wig holding the rapt attention of his auditors in a Westminster Hall filled almost to bursting with spectators.[87]

The formal speeches in Westminster Hall finally ended on Monday, 13 March, once the defense had finished its presentation and the prosecution had provided its response. Sir Thomas Parker summed up the prosecution and concluded ten days of legal and political argument, which encompassed over forty major speeches and more than 200,000 words. He concluded that Sacheverell was right that the impeachment was not just about Sacheverell's own behavior. Parker confessed that "*his* Punishment is not *all* we aim at." The prosecution's ultimate goal was to persuade Tory clergymen "not to preach the *Doctrine of Submission* in such a way as to *prepare* the way to *Rebellion*." Although the Whigs had gone to trial to defend the political right to resist, as the nation had resisted the Catholic monarch in 1688, they nevertheless ended with a plea to avoid the kind of rebellion against the principles established three decades earlier. In making Sacheverell "an Example for these impious Attempts against his Country," Parker suggested that they identify "the *Shame* of his Own Order."[88]

In responding to these concluding remarks, the Tory diarist Thomas Hearne was not concerned with the niceties of when resistance was more desirable than rebellion. His concern was instead that Parker "was very severe against Dr. Sacheverell, and us'd very ill Language upon the occasion, calling him an Imposter, a false Prophet, and said he had forfeited his Order, with abundance of other stuff."[89] Once again, his attacks treated a matter of political principle as a personal vendetta.

The Whigs remained more convinced than ever that Sacheverell was a fraud and a rabble-rouser, posing a threat to the nation and the Protestant line of succession. The Tories remained persuaded that the Whigs were unfairly prosecuting an innocent clergyman, putting the church and monarch in danger. Thomas Hearne copied out a verse ostensibly left on the queen's dressing table, titled "A Poem Found on the Queen's Toilet," begging the queen to "stop ye dire Proceedings er'e too late, / And see thy own in poor Sachev'rel's fate." Warning her that impeaching Sacheverell might be a prelude to her own downfall, the versifier alludes to Parliament's ordering the execution of her grandfather, Charles I: "Fatal Experience bids thee now be wise, / At him they strikc, but thou're ye Sacrifice, / Let one bless'd Martyr of thy Race suffice."[90]

Rather than tamping down the effect of his sermon and discouraging clergymen or writers who might have been attempting to foment discontent with the Whigs, the trial only served to harden the divide between the pro- and anti-Sacheverell forces, between the Tories and the Whigs. Yet the public suspense in March 1710 further increased as the Lords and Commons deliberated both about their verdict and about the appropriate punishment, particularly in light of the tinder box of public sympathy for the "Fair" Doctor.

7

Impeached but Triumphant

Once the managers in the House of Commons had made their closing arguments in favor of Sacheverell's impeachment, the members of the House of Lords prepared to file out of Westminster Hall back to the Lords Chamber to begin deliberations. On Friday, 9 March, just as they were about to leave Westminster Hall, however, the Tory Lord Nottingham stood up and surprised all the Whigs in the room by asking the right to pose a procedural question. Completely caught off guard by this request, the Duke of Devonshire, lord steward of the House of Lords and a Whig, requested that the lords adjourn to consider whether such a question should be put to both houses in Westminster Hall or considered in the Lords Chamber. The lords duly filed out and considered the request, leaving everyone in the room in suspense. The lords returned in short order, having agreed to hear the question in public, but the question itself would stun everyone in the hall.

The question was simple and should have been posed much earlier in the whole process rather than in front of an audience of two thousand spectators after several weeks of emotionally charged testimony. But this move on the part of the Tories again demonstrated that they were thinking about the trial not merely in terms of political principles but also in terms of public relations. Lord Nottingham turned to the eleven judges sitting on the judicial woolsack in the center of the room and asked "whether by the law of *England* . . . for Crimes and Misdemeanors by Writing or Speaking, the particular Words, supposed to be Criminal, must not be expressly specified in such *Indictment?*" In other words, could they impeach Sacheverell merely on the insinuated and implied intent of his published sermon, or could they prosecute only on his specific printed words? One by one, each of the eleven judges sitting in the center of that room gave his opinion, and each agreed that "by the Laws of *England*" the particular words "ought to be specified in such Indictment."[1]

Although no extant account describes the spectators' reaction to that moment, there was likely a collective gasp. Everyone there recognized that none of the charges was based on an exact citation from Sacheverell's printed text; rather, all the charges were based on what he suggested or insinuated. It was because of the lack of precise incriminating detail in the published text that impeachment was chosen rather than a libel suit. Yet no one had investigated the historical precedent for impeaching without precise written evidence. Without further ado, the lords adjourned and filed back out of the hall to their own chamber, where discussion on this topic continued that afternoon and into Saturday, 11 March. The queen joined them and listened to the entire debate. The canniest Whig legal minds in the House of Lords, including Lord Somers, Lord Halifax, and the Lord Chancellor William Cowper, introduced a distinction between whether they should be guided solely by the laws of England or also by parliamentary precedent. A compromise was proposed that their determination should follow "the Law of the Land, and the Law and Usage of Parliament."[2] This compromise was swiftly approved, and Lord Godolphin then requested that clerks be sent to find prior parliamentary precedents in this sort of indictment.[3] This legal hair-splitting would have quickly spread by gossip in society London, and by letter to friends and family around England and abroad.[4] Trying to specify the difference between "the laws of England" and "the usages of Parliament" would have struck many in the public as ludicrous. It may even have struck Queen Anne as stretching the bounds of credulity, although at this point, she, like the lords in the chamber, probably just wanted the process to end as swiftly as possible.[5]

■

BY TUESDAY, this research into parliamentary precedent had produced twenty-one prior cases of impeachment in the previous century, and only one, from 1628, seemed to be based on something other than the exact wording of a published text. The debate in the Lords Chamber grew increasingly raucous: "no bear garden was ever more noisy."[6] But the most powerful Whig lords were ruthlessly twisting arms, and by eight o'clock on Tuesday evening, 14 March, the Lords voted 65 to 47 that "the particular Words supposed to be criminal are not necessary to be expressly specified in such Impeachments."[7] The next day was a religious holiday; the lords attended a sermon in Westminster Abbey but considered no government business. On Thursday the debate began in earnest over whether or not to agree with the House of Commons on each of the individual articles, and subsequently whether to vote that that Sacheverell had committed high crimes and misdemeanors overall.

The Whigs had sensed Queen Anne's implicit support for impeachment when, on the death of Chief Justice Holt of the Queen's Bench on 5 March, she had replaced him with Sergeant-at-Law Thomas Parker, one of the most eloquent Whig speakers during the impeachment proceedings. The queen appeared to be signaling her approval of the impeachment by this swift Whig appointment, but the Tories were proceeding more effectively in the court of public opinion. The printer Henry Clements had just produced a two-penny pamphlet containing the text of Sacheverell's speech in the impeachment proceedings, in which Sacheverell presented himself as humble and loyal. Since postal delivery left London on Tuesday, Thursday, and Saturday evenings, the pamphlet would have allowed Sacheverell's uncharacteristically lucid and humble speech (which he probably had not written himself) to resonate around the country, with no opportunity for a reply from the other side. The Whigs, in a panic, issued a government order to break open every letter going out of town that evening, and all copies of the speech were removed from the post.[8]

Sacheverell's printed speech, even if unceremoniously removed from sealed letters on 16 March, nevertheless continued to circulate in the pamphlet printed by Clements and in an almost identical version printed by J. Baker. Whig printers meanwhile swiftly issued a rebuttal in the form of a pamphlet titled *A True Answer; or, Remarks upon Dr. Sacheverell's Speech, March 7th, 1710,* which included, according to the title page, "a Modest and Reasonable Comparison betwixt his sermon at St. *Paul's* and that at *Westminster.*"[9] Another, more substantial work appeared as well, which seemed from the title to be just another version of the speech: *Dr. Sacheverell's Speech Upon His Impeachment*. The subtitle, however, gives the full detail: *With REFLECTIONS thereupon Paragraph by Paragraph Wherein the Charge of the COMMONS against Him is fully justify'd.* This eighty-page tract also included copies of

Sacheverell's most incendiary sermons and pamphlets, "out of which," the editor tells us in the preface, "there are large Quotations here inserted to prove the Truth of the Charge against him." In other words, even if there was no prosecutable language in the sermons for which Sacheverell was impeached, this editor points out that there was plenty of other evidence in his other sermons. Moreover, in the preface, addressed "to all True Protestants," the editor reminds his readers that there is "no other Distinction heard of among us, but of those who are for the Protestant Religion and the present Establishment, and of those who are for a Popish Prince and a French Government." Sacheverell, he implies, for all of his fine words about defending the Church of England, was clearly of the latter "restless Faction."[10]

The Whigs were on the defensive in public in having to respond to the Tory scheme for publishing Sacheverell's speech, even as powerful Whigs in the House of Lords continued to debate in favor of impeachment and to fend off various procedural maneuvers that might have given the Tories an advantage. Queen Anne attended most of the deliberations in the House of Lords as a silent observer, only occasionally standing up and walking out if she felt that a speech was going on too long, straying too far from the topic, or undermining the Revolution of 1688 that had brought her to the throne. At 9 p.m. on the final day of deliberations in the Lords Chamber, the Tory Lord Guernsey began "clearing himself of the Revolution." The queen abruptly "riss & left them, which so confounded him that [he] had much ado to proceed." When the Duke of Somerset offered to escort her back to St. James's Palace, the queen refused to obstruct the proceedings. She replied, "No, not without he brought a lord of the other party [with him], for she would not have a vote lost on any score."[11]

The vote as to whether the House of Lords agreed with the House of Commons on the first article did not take place Thursday evening, although there was a vote on whether the vote should take place in the Lords Chamber or in the public venue of Westminster Hall. The Whigs won that vote, 68 to 51, so that the process of casting a vote would not be swayed or impeded by the presence of spectators. The debates on the individual articles of impeachment continued on Friday and Saturday, and the Whigs carried them all. Just before a vote on the whole on Saturday, the Tories yet again offered a procedural change that might have worked in their favor—voting separately on the individual articles of impeachment—with the hope that Sacheverell might not be found guilty of high crimes on every article. The Whigs fended that off, and finally a vote was taken, finding him guilty of high crimes and misdemeanors by a vote of 69 to 52. As one observer put it, "The Whig Lords knew how to make their court," and they achieved the guilty verdict they needed.[12] The lords sent a messenger to the House of Commons indicating that their decision would be announced in Westminster Hall on Monday morning. Rather than the ending the matter, however, this decision, which came almost a full month after the proceedings began, was only the beginning of the political fallout.

On Monday at 11 a.m., just when the lords were scheduled to announce their vote in Westminster Hall, the oak benches reserved for the lords remained unexpectedly empty, once again raising the suspense for the public. The peers were still in the Lords Chamber debating whether or not Sacheverell should be present at the bar while the votes were being announced. Finally, at two in the afternoon, a messenger arrived in the hall instructing Sacheverell to remove himself from the court. The lords then slowly filed in and took their places at the benches slightly before 3 p.m. One by one, starting with the most junior member of the House of Lords, the question was put to each of them: "Is Doctor *Henry Sacheverell* guilty of high Crimes and Misdemeanours charged upon him by the impeachment of the House of Commons?"[13] Each replied, guilty or not guilty, returning the same votes they had given in the Lords Chamber on Saturday. These very public returns not only resonated in the hall at the time; they were also printed and included with the printed versions of the proceedings now being typeset in the press. Every member of the House of Lords would continue to be known and judged for the rest of his political career on whether he had voted for or against "the Doctor." Some of the savvier peers, aware of the way public opinion was tending, decided to absent themselves so that there would be no record of how they might have voted. Lord Somerset, who had been so keen to curry favor with the queen by offering to escort her to the palace during one evening of debate, was one of those who deliberately avoided voting.

Sacheverell was then brought in and his guilty verdict was read to him. Appearing unsurprised and untroubled by it (suggesting he had discussed it with his legal counsel in advance), he then returned to the Tories' earlier objection that there were no words in his sermons cited in his indictment. He also said that the judgment against him was invalid because "he was impeached in the name of the knights, citizens, and burgesses of the parliament of Great Britain," but that he "humbly conceived it should have been in the name of the knights, citizens, and burgesses, and *commissioners* of shires and burghs." Once again, the lords filed out to the Lords Chamber, only to return to announce that "commissioners of shires and burgs were synonymous terms, implying the same thing as knights, citizens, and burgesses; therefore they saw no cause to arrest the judgment."[14]

Sidney Godolphin wrote to the Duke of Marlborough, busy with diplomacy and battle preparations in The Hague, informing him that Sacheverell had "at last" been convicted, but that the "Duke of Somerset did not vote." Godolphin cynically pointed out that even though Somerset's friends said he was ill, it was probably "only his profound wisdom that kept him from the House." Godolphin was also skeptical an adequate punishment would be assessed against the clergyman, knowing that without a lighter sentence than is "reasonable" they would lose some of the margin of seventeen by which they had won his conviction. Godolphin predicted, with cynical accuracy, that "things may run on very disagreeably for six months longer."[15] In fact, the political backlash against this trial, and those who had managed it, would last for the next four years.

■

In Britain at the time, the range of possible punishments was broad.[16] In Sacheverell's case, the Whigs in the House of Commons had hoped for a punishment to send a message to other Church of England clergymen to think twice before preaching against the government. The guilty verdict in Sacheverell's case, no matter how difficult it was to achieve, would mean little to the Whigs without a strong enough sentence—including a fine and imprisonment—to serve as a deterrent to other clergymen. Yet Queen Anne, just as she had made clear that she wanted a conviction in order to protect the principles of 1688 that guaranteed her right to the throne, was also dropping hints that she would prefer a light sentence.

In March, the queen told her doctor, David Hamilton, that "there ought to be a punishment but a mild one, least the mob appearing of his side, shoud occasion great commotions." She was already beginning to think that "his Impeachment had been better let alone."[17] The courtier Peter Wentworth wrote to his brother on the Continent that he had heard that the queen had told the Earl of Kent that "the Commons had reason to be sattisfied that they had made their allegations good, and the mildest punishment inflicted upon the Doctor she thought the best."[18] Whether through gossip from Hamilton or Kent, the rumor quickly circulated in the House of Lords that "the queen desired it might be mild," and some were concerned about an outbreak of "popular fury, if the censure was severe."[19]

Robert Harley had been actively making use of these rumors of the queen's preferences to the Tories' advantage, even before the vote on the impeachment itself. He had been corresponding and gossiping with MPs and lords, trying to use this to the best political advantage. As an ally of his reported the opinion of the Duke of Argyll, another moderate Tory, in a letter to him: "An absolute acquittal would rather tend to promote a high Tory scheme than to ruin the interest of the [Whig] Junto. . . . However, he thinks he may fairly oppose any excessive punishment that shall be proposed."[20] With Harley working behind the scenes and rumors circulating about the queen's own preference, the Whigs realized that they would not get a sentence harsh enough to set an example.

At the start of the proceedings, "no self-respecting Whig would have settled for anything less than a life ban on the Doctor's preaching, a bar on further preferment [no promotion, for example, to dean or bishop], a stiff term of imprisonment and a fine."[21] By the end of the third week of the trial, the Whigs were considering a seven-year ban on preaching, an imprisonment for no more than three months, and a public burning of the sermon. In the angry debate in the House of Lords, however, someone (whose name was not noted in the acrimony) proposed reducing the preaching ban to only one year. Finally, on Monday, 21 March, a compromise emerged for a three-year ban on preaching and a three-month prison term, but that proposal failed by one vote, meaning the Whigs would have to compromise still further. In the end, Sacheverell was not fined or given a prison sentence; he was merely barred from preaching for three years. Moreover, while he was not permitted to preach a sermon, Sacheverell was still allowed to collect his parish salaries, read prayers, and otherwise officiate during Church of England services. In being allowed to officiate, he could still greet his enthusiastic parishioners and raise his mellifluous voice in public prayers. His Guy Fawkes Day sermon of 5 November would be ceremoniously burned in public, but copies of it would be included in most printed accounts of the trial currently being typeset for publication.

Bishop Burnet rose in the House of Lords and announced that the punishment was "equivalent to returning the Doctor thanks."[22] Another eighteenth-century historian points out, "Nothing could possibly have given the doctor greater pleasure than to be relieved from the discharge of his duty, and at the same time to reap the benefit of a rich living [a salaried position as clergyman], and of all the valuable presents which were made to him by his party."[23] Others were furious that since the start of the trial, one month earlier, the populace had been roiled into a ferment, businesses had been neglected, and stocks had fallen. With the costs of lawyers, construction in Westminster Hall, militia to protect against the mob, and numerous other expenses, it was estimated that £60,000 had been spent on the trial, in addition to "the terrible animosities that are raised throughout the kingdom," as Robert Harley's sister reported.[24] The Whigs in the House of Commons were livid, but they had no recourse. On Thursday, 23 March, Sacheverell appeared at the bar of justice in Westminster Hall one final time, and Lord Chancellor Cowper pronounced the sentence on the clergyman, noting as he did: "You cannot but observe an extream Tenderness toward your character, as a Minister of the Church of *England*."[25] Although Sacheverell's impeachment trial had at last ended, "His triumph had barely begun."[26]

With the mild sentence, Sacheverell's supporters immediately expressed their "inconceivable gladness, as if they had got a victory; bonfires, illuminations, and other marks of joy appeared, not only in London, but over the whole kingdom."[27] The Whigs were cynical and disappointed. Godolphin described the outcome to Marlborough with frustration: "So all this bustle and fatigue ends in no more but a suspension for 3 years from the pulpit, and burning his sermons at the old Exchange." When the bad news about the outcome reached

Marlborough in The Hague, he observed cynically that he would never depart from the Whig interest and that he recognized that the "incincerity" of the Queen is such that neither he nor the duchess "should expect any other behavior than that of ingretude."[28]

Although the queen had initially approved the impeachment, the proceedings did not put the Whigs in their best light, with their need to force impeachment of a clergyman on mere suggestion and insinuation. Linking Anne's right to the throne to an act of resistance was also confusing to a populace that largely still accepted the tradition of obedience to the sovereign and to the established church. Many had understood the Glorious Revolution as a triumph over Catholicism rather than a philosophical defense of political resistance. Many, including Queen Anne, had also justified excluding Anne's Catholic half-brother from the throne because of the widely circulated (if dubious) rumor that he was not a legitimate son but an imposter infant that had been snuck into the birthing room in a warming pan in June 1688. Anne fully appreciated the Revolution principle of the right to resist, but she was also probably cautious about provoking further unrest with a harsh sentence for Sacheverell.

The queen's preference for a lenient sentence was further evidence of how the Whigs had tried her patience. Meanwhile, the Tories at court were thrilled at the possibility that they could leverage an electoral victory from this. Many in Parliament used Sacheverell's impeachment to pressure the queen to dissolve her current Parliament and call new elections.[29]

■

BETWEEN 1694 AND 1716, the Triennial Act required general Parliamentary elections to be held at a minimum of every three years, but if the monarch dissolved Parliament then elections could be held even more frequently. Since this system had led to excessive party factionalism, nowhere more evident than in the Sacheverell impeachment, a new law, the Septennial Act, would be passed in 1716, requiring that elections be held at a minimum of only every seven years, greatly reducing party strife.[30] Since Anne took the throne in 1702, there had been parliamentary elections in 1705 and 1708. The 1708 election brought in a Whig majority, and the ouster of Harley from Anne's cabinet earlier that year had helped shape a Whig majority in her cabinet. Another election might not have been held until 1711 had the Whig majority retained the confidence of the population. However, the anger at the Whigs over Sacheverell's impeachment appeared to justify calling a new Parliament.

Tories and even Jacobite supporters of Anne's Catholic half-brother in France flocked to court "to compliment the queen on her liberation from the thralldom in which she had been held." The Duke of Beaufort, the Tory and Jacobite sympathizer to whom Delarivier Manley had dedicated her *New Atalantis,* congratulated Anne by telling her "Your majesty is now queen indeed."[31] Even before these fawning courtiers arrived at Kensington Palace in late March, Anne had almost certainly been mulling over the possibility of dissolving Parliament as she sat through the weeks of debate over Sacheverell's guilt and punishment.

On 5 April, Queen Anne prorogued Parliament, thus ending the current session but not dissolving it.[32] The next day she gave royal assent to the Copyright Act, a piece of legislation that had passed the House of Commons in February, two days before the start of the impeachment proceedings. This law, which granted authors and their designated publishers ownership of their own works for a period of fourteen years, was much sought after by journalists, pamphleteers, and other writers. With the lapse of prior censorship legislation in 1695, there was no monopoly on printing through the Stationers' Company; nor were there requirements for government licenses. However, neither did authors yet have any rights or recourse against the practice of pirating editions of their work until Queen Anne signed this act into law. The Copyright Act came just in time for those printers and publishers planning to sell transcripts of the Sacheverell trial. Both Whig and Tory publishers were hoping to profit from their printed versions.

Jacob Tonson, a Whig printer, had secured the official printing contract from Parliament for *The Tryal of Dr Henry Sacheverell,* the complete version of the proceedings. The House of Commons passed a resolution in late February, just before the trial began, forbidding any portion of the proceedings from being printed or published "without leave of this House."[33] Tonson probably paid £1,000 to £1,500 for the copyright of the trial text. In exchange he was to supply bound copies to the members, but he was also hoping to make a profit by also selling them publicly before cheaper pirated editions—which were anticipated even if they were now illegal—cut into his profits. Tonson's difficulty was timing. Although he had likely begun the typesetting process even while the trial was in process, the average speed for typesetting at that time was one folio per day. The speeches had been so long and the trial so protracted that there would be 335 pages of densely printed text for the folio version (the largest, the most expensive, and the most profitable). Even to produce the work by June, Tonson would have had to produce the work at a rate of about five pages per day, paying other printers to work with him one the project.[34] He registered his copyright with the Stationers' Company (no longer a monopoly but now the agency that kept the records of authorial copyrights) on May 15 under a provisional title. He registered his final title on June 3, and the volumes were released for sale on June 15.

The Whigs were hoping that this official record of the trial, with the eloquent speeches by the best Whig lawyers, would help shape public opinion of Sacheverell, already being manipulated by shorter Tory pamphlets and continued sales of the mezzotint prints of Sacheverell's portrait. Sacheverell's printed sermon had been burned as soon as the trial was concluded, and the House of Lords issued a warrant for the arrest of the publisher Henry Clements for its unauthorized printing, but rumors of Sacheverell's sympathetic performance were still generating positive sentiment toward him. In the first week of April a concerned Whig wrote to Thomas Jervoise, the MP from Hampshire, expressing his hope that the printed trial could be produced as swiftly as possible, since "our enemy is all this while getting ground, and it is incredible to think they shooed be able to prepossess the ordinary people so much as they do in the Dr.'s fav[ou]r."[35]

One of those "enemies" of the Whigs was Delarivier Manley, who swiftly brought out the first volume of *Memoirs of Europe, Towards the Close of the Eighth Century,* a sequel to her *New Atalantis.* This publication, which featured Sacheverell as Plato the Patriarch, appeared in May 1710, about one month before Tonson produced his official *Tryal of Dr Sachverell.* The first volume of *Memoirs of Europe* was 380 pages, although each page in a quarto volume (one quarter the size of a folio) contained about 250 words per page, compared to the almost 500 words per page in Tonson's folio typesetting of the *Tryal,* which was taking much longer to typeset. Manley registered her new work of political satire with the Stationers' Office, signing her name as author, on 11 May 1710, and she sent an unsolicited copy of it to Robert Harley the following day. If the team of printers for *Memoirs of Europe,* were producing ten pages a day (twice the rate of Tonson's *Tryal,* since the pages contain half as many words), they would still have needed thirty-eight days to produce this work.[36] It is likely, then, that some of the printing may have been started as soon as Manley's libel trial was over in late February, just as the Sacheverell trial was commencing.

The printer John Barber, with whom Manley was living, almost certainly funded production of *Memoirs of Europe,* although his name was not on the title page (just as it had not been on the title page for *The New Atalantis*). As a successful businessman, one who had no doubt made a tidy profit from *The New Atalantis,* he would not have felt there was much financial risk in beginning to pay trade publishers to produce portions of Manley's next work two months before the entire first volume would be available for sale. He knew the sequel to *The New Atalantis* would sell well. The printer John Morphew, whose name was listed on the title page for *The New Atalantis,* was the trade publisher for her *Memoirs of Europe* as well, meaning he would again put his name on the title page and accept the risks of a libel suit. Even though he, like Manley and Barber and a third printer (John Woodward), had been forced to pay legal costs in preparing for the libel trial for *The New Atalantis,* Morphew must have been paid well enough by Barber that he was happy to print another politically risky work. This time, however, the author and printers were probably not as worried about the legal consequences of printing the volume since they could see how the Whigs were swiftly losing power in Queen Anne's cabinet. Recognizing that the Sacheverell trial was becoming a public relations fiasco for the Whigs, the printers would have surmised that the Earl of Sunderland would not have dared again harass Manley, who was clearly attempting to curry favor in high places through her glowing depictions of Abigail Masham, Robert Harley, and other prominent court Tories.

Unlike *The New Atalantis,* which is not typeset with any chapter or section breaks in either of the two volumes, each volume of *Memoirs of Europe* is divided into three books. This division would have facilitated the process of typesetting, printing, and even stitching the first sections in signatures (the sections or gatherings of pages bound together for each volume) as soon as Manley's libel case was dismissed in late February. In light of how swiftly the publication of the second volume of *The New Atalantis* in October had followed Manley's description of the Battle of Malplaquet in early September 1709, it is likely that she had also been finishing that work while the typesetting was taking place. The open-ended plotline of Manley's secret histories, in which she could leave off each volume at the end of almost any anecdote, allowed her to end a narrative in midstream, knowing she could continue her satiric account in a subsequent volume or in a sequel. For *Memoirs of Europe*, the division into books facilitated a swift publication, so Manley could publish a satire of Sacheverell's impeachment even before the official account of the trial was released. Book I (about 140 pages, or half the length of the first volume) depicts the Earl of Peterborough, a maverick military commander who had been censured by the Whigs and had been taken up as a martyr by the Tories. Book II concerns religious strife; toward the end of that book, there is a scene with Plato the Patriarch being excommunicated from the church, in a trial that serves as an obvious parallel to Sacheverell's impeachment proceedings.

Manley herself would have been too busy to have attended Sacheverell's trial even if she had managed to secure a ticket. She would have been in her apartment at John Barber's printing house, south of St. Paul's Cathedral, furiously scribbling away. She was fully aware of the daily events of the trial and knew the key details of Sacheverell's speech in Westminster Hall. In describing Plato the Patriarch's words in front of the judges and the auditors, Manley was clearly depicting the scene of Sacheverell's public defense: "He acquitted himself to the Applause of all his impartial Hearers: His Defense was so holy, so moving, so humble, so unaffectedly natural, so free from Ostentation or Vanity, that it drew Tears from the Eyes of the Spectators; who reflected, how he had been persecuted, imprison'd ruin'd in Property, abandon'd to the Friendship of the Faithful, and every way an Object both of Admiration and Pity."[37] This sympathetic portrayal of Plato the Patriarch brings to a close Book II. In Book III of this volume, Manley depicts the indolent and negligent Emperor Constantine (Queen Anne) beginning to rouse herself and wrest control of her nation from Irene (the Duchess of Marlborough) and Stauracius (the Duke of Marlborough).

By producing the first volume of *Memoirs of Europe* with such speed, Manley and her printers were assured of strong sales among a reading public eager to be reading political gossip and impatient for the appearance of published accounts of the trial. By mocking the Marlboroughs, encouraging the queen to break from their tyranny, and offering a sympathetic portrait of Sacheverell, Manley was producing a satirical riff on the events of the day even before the official printed version of the trial appeared.

■

JACOB TONSON, meanwhile, was still furiously managing his printing team for the official printed account of the trial. He wanted his account to be as complete and correct as possible, and he was probably granted access to the shorthand notes taken by the two official shorthand recorders, but he was still rushing. There would be no time to produce an index, and he omitted some of the speeches made by the bishops in the House of Lords during the trial, some of which were already being printed and sold as separate pamphlets. Tonson would produce an accurate and largely neutral account of the trial. His printed text was "scrupulously officious, and usefully laconic, when it came to the debates and divisions among the lords themselves with regard to the conviction and sentencing of Dr Sacheverell." He thus "managed to cover up, and paper over, the partisan divisions that had erupted during the deliberations among the lords themselves."[38] Despite this veneer of neutrality, however, Tonson inserted on the flyleaf the Whig seal of approval in the imprimatur of Lord Chancellor William Cowper: "I do Appoint *Jacob Tonson* to Print the Tryal of Doctor *Henry Sacheverell,* and do Forbid any other Person to Print the same."[39] Tonson's authorized version of the trial contains no portrait of Sacheverell, since the Whigs were trying to circumvent the sympathy so many readers felt when looking at the mezzotint prints of him already in circulation.

Three days before Tonson's magnificent folio volume appeared, however, a much shorter publication appeared with Jacob Tonson's name listed (falsely) as the publisher on the title page: *An Impartial Account of What Pass'd most Remarkable in the Last Session of Parliament, Relating to the Case of Dr Henry Sacheverell.* Several London printers and publishers were involved in producing this brief unauthorized Tory account, including Abel Roper, publisher of the *Post Boy,* and John Morphew, the same trade publisher who had just produced the first volume of Manley's *Memoirs of Europe.*[40] Although it was not a full version of the trial, this Tory abridgment scooped the Whig version and skimmed off the first few days of sales. Moreover, Tonson was not successful in blocking future sales even though he owned the sole right to publish the account of the trial because this other account was published as if it were his.

In fact, the shorter Tory account did not include the bulk of the speeches, but only summaries of the charges and the verdict. It contains Sergeant-at-Law Parker's eloquent speech in justifying the impeachment, but it also includes a summary of the discussion held in the House of Commons on 21 March as to whether or not to bring a vote of thanks to the managers of the House, a scornful conversation that was not included in Tonson's authorized *Tryal.* This brief account includes the sneering remark by one (Tory) Gentleman: "tho' he was against giving them [the managers of the House] the Thanks of the House, yet he could not forbear mentioning one Reason for it, that had been omitted by others, but was, in his Opinion, stronger than any the offer'd; and that was, because he was sure they would have Thanks no where else." This *Impartial Account* also includes Tory complaints that the proceedings "included railing and reviling language to the Doctor" and were full of "Bitterness" and "Inconsistency."[41]

Many printed versions of *An Impartial Account* also included, or were bound with, a printed image of Sachverell from the mezzotint engraving that made him appear so sympathetic to readers. The image was important to Tories but anathema to Whigs, who looked distastefully on those who treated it almost as a visual idol. Before the trial had even begun, a Whig newspaper complained that "*Sacheverell's* Picture is not more hugg'd and admir'd than any that we have in the late Editions of our Common-Prayer-Books."[42] The Tory *Impartial Account* also indicated on its title page that it was suitable to "be bound up with the *Tryal* of the said Doctor." In other words, this was a Tory pamphlet intended to be inserted as a somewhat ironical preface to the official Whig version of the proceedings, reminding readers before they began plowing through the more than 300 pages of Tonson's account that a vote of thanks was given with great scorn for what the managers of the House had accomplished.

Though we have become accustomed in the twenty-first century to the political power of populations easily and swiftly manipulated by electronic media via online social networks, in 1710 Britain was only just learning the power of media-influenced public opinion. Pamphlet wars had surged with the lapse of the licensing laws in 1695, the gradual decreases in costs of paper and printing, and the increasingly proactive role of booksellers in expanding readership.[43] The pamphlets for and against Sachverell had fanned and exacerbated political divides between Whig and Tory, between Dissenting Protestants and high church Anglicans, just as social media today magnify and exacerbate divisions between Republicans and Democrats in the United States and between Leavers and Remainers in the UK.

As soon as it was available, on 15 June, Tonson's authorized version of the *Tryal* "was quickly snapped up by an eager buying public."[44] Moreover, readers not only read it but scribbled in it and annotated it. Some readers, diligently reading through every speech and decision, constructed handwritten indexes so that the work would be more user-friendly for themselves, their family members and friends who read the book, and their progeny, who would inherit the book along with the family library. Some readers went much further, underlining key passages and writing opinions and commentary in the margins next to speeches. One reader filled the blank space on the flyleaf (surrounding Cowper's authorization to print) with first an elegantly phrased "Morall" at the top, followed by several paragraphs of neatly inked prose, in fine clear handwriting. The "morall" blames the provocateur of violence for that violence: "He that provokes & invites mischief, is the doer of it. Tis the man that kills, the bullet is only a passive instrument to serve his end and that directs it." In the handwritten reflections, the owner of this book continued: "This is to reprove those (according to the old morall) that stir up men in power to doe publick mischief which is much worse than any man's doing a private mischief himself and only a safer way of committing greater outrages."[45]

Not only did readers annotate and moralize avidly but many, buying an unbound copy, had it bound with other tracts, either Whig or

Tory. Tories might combine it with an engraving of Sacheverell's portrait and Roper's *Impartial Account.* Whigs might include with it Arthur Maynwaring's pamphlet *Four Letters to a Friend in North Briton,* which offered commentary, in the form of letters to a friend, on key Whig speeches. In that pamphlet, Maynwaring explains in an inviting conversational style the threat that Sacheverell's ideas posed to the foundations of the Protestant monarchy of Britain, post 1688. After summing up Lord Chancellor Cowper's argument about Sacheverell's sermon, the letter writer invites his friend to consider his own reply: "Pray let me know, in your next Letter, if you do not think this was Preaching her Majesty out of the Government; or, which is the same thing, preaching the Pretender into it." On the title page is an epigraph from John Tillotson, former archbishop of Canterbury, that sums up the Whig view of Sacheverell's behavior: "Tis not a controversy of Reason against Reason, but of Downright Impudence against all the Sense and Reason of Mankind."[46]

The printed versions of Sacheverell's trial, particularly Tonson's, became valued documents cherished by readers for how they portrayed their partisan views of the current government and of the political events that had brought it to power.[47] This was a document read and referred to by Whigs and Tories for several generations. Although by the mid-nineteenth century, the Sacheverell affair, would seem dull and irrelevant to most readers, Tonson's *Tryal* continued to sell briskly through the eighteenth century. The bookseller Michael Johnson (1657–1731), father to the writer Samuel Johnson, told his son that Sacheverell's *Tryal* had been one of his best-selling titles.[48] Because of its wide sales, this account became "the main compendium of political arguments for and against the Revolution of 1688."[49] Attitudes toward Sacheverell's trial would distinguish those who supported the ideological right to resist from those more comfortable with passive obedience to monarchy. This divide represented the central cultural and political difference in how Britons viewed their own nation during this era.[50]

■

Maynwaring's *Four Letters to a Friend in North Briton* signaled the strongly partisan sense of the word "friendship" at this time. The word conveyed friendship in the ordinary personal sense, but it also conveyed partisan allegiances, as when Queen Anne advised Marlborough in January (over the crisis about military appointments) to consult his friends. Anne also often told others at court that she was working with advice from her "friends." For several decades, those friends could only have meant three people: the Duke and Duchess of Marlborough and Sidney Godolphin. Even before she ascended to the throne, those had been her closest advisers—the future duke and duchess particularly, in 1688, when the duchess (then Lady Churchill) led Princess Anne from Whitehall Palace, assisting her in defecting from her father's cause. For the next three decades Anne relied on the advice and counsel of the Marlboroughs and Sidney Godolphin in making most political, economic, and military decisions, though she tended to resist their advice in matters of ecclesiastical appointments. When she began taking advice from Robert Harley, counsel usually facilitated and echoed by her bedchamber woman Abigail Masham, the Marlboroughs began accusing her of being influenced by others. Anne naturally became defensive, responding to Marlborough in October that "what I said was my own thoughts."[51]

The Marlboroughs and the Whigs were concerned that Anne was taking political advice from new "friends," but Sarah was also struggling emotionally with the realization that her behavior had already destroyed her prior emotional bond with the queen. Sarah had understood at some level that her nasty insinuating letters to Anne would make "her hate me," even if she mistakenly calculated that they would make it "easier for the ministers to govern her."[52] Sarah was not fully prepared, however, for how Anne would express that hatred. She was not prepared for silence, despite her own regular use of it to express her own displeasure with friends or family members. Yet Anne had already begun giving Sarah the silent treatment since their argument over the jewels Anne was wearing to the military victory service at St. Paul's in August 1708. After Sarah had whispered sharply to Anne to "be quiet," Anne had several times referred to "the commands" Sarah had given "on the Thanksgiving day of not answering you," when she chose not to respond to one of Sarah's insinuating letters.[53] In November, Anne had responded tersely to Sarah's lengthy letter merely by indicating that she had not "not yet had leisure to read all your paypers."[54] Anne was shutting Sarah down and shutting her out, but Sarah had not yet recognized the finality of this behavior. Somehow she felt she would be able yet again to mend their relationship. For Anne, however, things had gone past the point of repair.

Perhaps feeling buoyed by the support of Tory courtiers flocking to congratulate her after Sacheverell's light sentencing, or perhaps feeling confident in her decision to prorogue Parliament in early April 1710 as a step toward dissolving it, Anne also found the confidence to make a more thorough break with Sarah. She did not dismiss her from her court positions, although Sarah had not been performing her daily duties as groom of the stole at court for more than a year. Queen Anne did endure one final emotional meeting with the Duchess of Marlborough on 6 April 1710, the day after she prorogued Parliament. Sarah had written several times asking to meet Anne, to respond to unflattering rumors she suspected the Duke and Duchess of Somerset were spreading about her, but Anne had put her off, saying they should communicate by letter. Then Anne made an appointment for them to meet at St. James's Palace on 6 August but abruptly crossed town to Kensington Palace, canceling the appointment. Sarah wrote to Anne that she would follow her to Kensington and wait until Anne saw her, even offering that Anne need make no answer to whatever she would say. Even before the queen could open the letter, which was sent by a speedy messenger, Sarah had arrived at Kensington. The page sent to inform the queen of the duchess's arrival "stayed longer than usual" before returning to let her enter. "Long enough," Sarah wrote subsequently in her memoirs, "to give time to deliberate whether the favour of admission should be granted." Eventually, she recalled, "he came out and told me I might go in."[55]

They met in the Queen's Closet, a small wood-paneled sitting room with windows along one side. The walls of this room are elegantly decorated in blue silk damask edged with gold Indian embroidery, and furnished with lacquer furniture and adorned with many of the blue-and-white porcelain vases that Anne's sister, Queen Mary II, had collected.[56] Sarah had many things to say, but mostly she wanted the chance to defend herself against false rumors she felt were being spread about her by, for example, the Duke and Duchess of Somerset, or others at court gossiping with what she feared were "a thousand lies" about her and about what she had said about the queen.[57] Before she could defend herself, she wanted to find out from the queen who had said what. Anne, however, was determined to say nothing at all, and was prepared to repeat a certain phrase over and over, to avoid further conversation: "Whatever you have to say you may put it in writing." As soon as Sarah entered the room, she recalls, "the Queen said she was just going to write to me. And, when I began to speak, she interrupted me four or five times with these repeated words: 'Whatever you have to say, you may put it in writing.'" Sarah felt certain that Anne had been scripted by her "new counsellors" and had been "carefully provided with those words, as a shield to defend her against every reason I could offer."[58]

Sarah recalls saying, "I could not possibly rest, till I had cleared myself from some particular calumnies with which I had been loaded." In reply, "The Queen said, without doubt there were many lies told." This response, rich with double meaning, was not satisfactory to Sarah, and she begged to know "the particulars of which I have been accused." Anne returned "that she would give me no answer, laying hold on a word in my letter." The queen persisted in this reply, even as Sarah protested that she needed to know "the particular things" said against her so she could clear herself. Upon hearing this plea, "the Queen offered to go out of the room." Sarah followed, only to hear "the Queen repeating over and over again: "You desired no answer, and shall have none." Sarah felt "streams of tears" flowing "down against [her] will" which "prevented [her] speaking for some time."[59]

When at last she recovered, Sarah explained that she had heard from a "credible person about the Court" the false stories spread about her. Then, "with a fresh flood of tears, and a concern sufficient to move compassion even where all love was absent," she "begged to know" what had been said of her. "But still the Queen's only return was 'You desired no answer, and you shall have none.'" In her memoirs, Sarah next confesses to saying "the most disrespectful thing" she "ever spoke to the Queen" when she said that she was "confident her Majesty would suffer for such an instance of inhumanity." Allowing Sarah no credibility when weighing in on matters of morality and religion, Anne merely replied, "That will be to myself." The duchess observed decades later in her memoir, "Thus ended this remarkable conversation, the last I ever had with her Majesty."[60]

Sarah's memoir was published in 1742, three decades after Anne's death and two years before Sarah's own. In that memoir, Sarah acknowledged, "The Queen always meant well, how much soever she might be blinded or misguided."[61] Here, Sarah gives credit to the queen's good intentions only by stripping the monarch of her own capacity to think or act on her own by asserting that she was "blinded" or guided by others. Certainly, Anne was cautious of engaging in a full-on debate with someone who was much more verbally adept, more emotionally demonstrative, and quicker to respond. Yet by suggesting Anne was "blinded or misguided" by her current confidants and ministers, Sarah rejects the notion that Anne was choosing to change her advisers because she desired a change in policy.

Despite Sarah's assumption that Anne was being manipulated, the queen was actively resisting control by any one person. She had stopped listening to Sarah. She listened to Abigail, who often conveyed opinions that Harley had written to her, but she also listened to the Duke and Duchess of Somerset and to her medical doctor. Abigail herself found that the queen was resisting her attempts to advise or control her. Abigail tried to convey Harley's views about the best candidate for fill a vacant bishop's position, yet she was rebuffed. She wrote in early March to Harley that the queen was angry with her and told her that when she was "in a passion," she spoke "a little too warm." Abigail defended the warmth of her tone to Harley: "who can help that when one sees plainly she is giving her best friends up to the rage of their enemies."[62] Here she is echoing the Duchess of Marlborough in her frustration that the queen had stopped listening to her.

As Jonathan Swift later observed, "There was not, perhaps, in all England a person who understood more artificially to disguise her passions than the late queen."[63] Although Queen Anne was sometimes frustrated at Abigail's persistence in conveying Harley's advice, she did feel as if she needed advice from someone who was also seeking a moderate approach to party politics and to ending the war in Europe. Godolphin had at one point in 1709 confronted the queen for privately seeking advice from Harley, causing the queen temporarily to stop his visits. Anne did not want either of the Marlboroughs' daughters, Henrietta or Anne, who were still ladies-in-waiting to her, to know she was seeking Harley's advice. At some point that spring, Swift recalls, Anne sent Harley a letter surreptitiously, "all dirty, and by the hand of a very ordinary messenger," who said it had been delivered to him "by an under-gardener." She was writing to urge him to speak to her "with more freedom" and to offer his political assistance. At this point, he began again to advise the queen more regularly, visiting the palace surreptitiously, since he was not yet returned to her cabinet, under the pretense of visiting his cousin Abigail, then conveyed through hidden corridors to visit the queen. According to Jonathan Swift, Harley again "began to have entire credit with the Queen," helping her "lessen the exorbitant power of the Duke and Duchess of Marlborough." Following Harley's advice, Queen Anne embarked on a "moderating scheme" to gradually diminish the power of the Whigs in her government.[64]

Through Harley, Anne once again attempted to pursue her own preferred policy of political moderation—a view that included imeaching Sacheverell but not imprisoning him or banning him from preaching for life. She likewise sought a moderate foreign policy that saw the need to rein in Louis XIV's expansionist military policy but did not insist on the increasingly infeasible goal of "No Peace Without Spain," as the slogan had it. Even though Delarivier Manley was not directly taking suggestions from Harley (as were Swift and Defoe), she was knowingly promoting his policies in her *Memoirs of Europe* by supporting Sacheverell and mocking the Marlboroughs for being motivated by avarice and self-interest. She also offered another glowing depiction of Harley himself, as she had in *The New Atalantis.* When Manley sent Harley an unsolicited copy of the first volume of *Memoirs of Europe* on 12 May 1710, she explained that she "attempted some faint Representations . . . of the heads of That party who has mislead Thousands." In case there might have been something in her allegorical depiction of those Whigs that was not clear, she offered, "if any thing" should move his "Curiosity" that she would "explain what you desire."[65]

■

Though Manley offered to wait on Harley and explain it to him, *Memoirs of Europe* was fairly easy to decode. It begins with Horatio (the Earl of Peterborough), who has won victories in Spain (capturing Barcelona in 1705) but has not correctly followed orders from the Allied commanders aligned against France and Spain in the War of Spanish Succession. In Manley's secret history, the action takes place during the reign of Charlemagne. The work is ostensibly written by

"*Eginardus,* Secretary and Favourite to *Charlemagne*" and translated into English by the "Translator of The New *Atalantis.*" All the characters and places appear in easily recognizable pseudonyms: Constantinople is London; Iberia is Spain. For Tories impatient with the Whig slogan of "No Peace Without Spain" (meaning the war should continue until Spain was no longer ruled by a grandson of Louis XIV of France), the Whigs' dismissal of Peterborough, who had been successful in Spain, appeared to mean they were not serious about victory in Spain and therefore must have wanted to continue the war for their own personal gain and profit. Manley depicts Peterborough traveling around northern Europe, after his dismissal from his military command, and meeting an English courtier, who tells tales of how Marlborough (Stauracius) had prevented Peterborough from fully conquering Spain (here, Iberia), which would have been "the finishing Stroak" for the war, but Marlborough would not share the glory because it would have meant sharing "that stupendious Reputation he has acquir'd."[66] In Manley's version of the story, Marlborough is the aloof military leader, collecting his victories and monuments, concerned only with how posterity will view him.

Meanwhile, Herminius (Harley) is the romantic hero of *Memoirs of Europe,* who will eventually, at the end of the second volume, help rouse Queen Anne from the enchanting spell of her ministers and finally seize for herself the reins of government. Manley depicts Queen Anne as Caesar Constantine, as "indolent by Nature, easy of Temper, soft in his Humour, and generally Obliging," easily controlled by the avaricious Irene (Duchess of Marlborough).[67]

Queen Anne herself did not have a particular taste for satire, but Manley was not writing for the queen directly. Manley was writing for the public more generally, and also specifically to curry favor with Harley and Abigail Masham, expressing opinions about the war and the Marlboroughs that were sympathetic to Harley's views. She also continues the partisan feud between Whig and Tory pamphleteers by her mocking dedication of the first volume to Isaac Bickerstaff, the pen name of her former friend Richard Steele, as "editor" of *The Tatler* (Steele had borrowed the publication's name from Jonathan Swift's earlier use of it). Manley complains of the disparaging comment about *The New Atalantis,* in two issues of *The Tatler,* "levell'd directly at humble *Me.*"[68]

One month before the Whig account of Sacheverell's trial was published, helping to broadcast Whig principles, Manley's *Memoirs of Europe* would have encouraged criticism of the Marlboroughs, increasing public mockery of them and making it easier for the queen eventually to dismiss some of the powerful Whigs in her cabinet, call new elections, and pursue a different military policy. By emphasizing the Duke of Marlborough's pride in his own reputation, Manley was describing the resentment among soldiers and military officers, including the Earl of Peterborough, who resented Marlborough's power, his control over military strategy, and his financial gain from his years as Queen Anne's captain-general. She also described the resentment against the Duchess of Marlborough (Irene) for amassing wealth and building the "Superbe and Costly" palace at "*Elutherium*"—that is, Blenheim. Though Blenheim was neither finished nor furnished by the spring of 1710, Manley imagines it as a storehouse where Irene and Stauracius (Marlborough) "laid up an immense Treasure, which *Caesar* [Anne] out of his Sweetness of Temper suffer'd her [Irene] to enjoy."[69]

Manley also appealed to populist concerns about the Church of England. While today we look back at the religious Toleration Act of 1689 as a turning point in human history, one that paved the way for even greater religious toleration in many portions of the globe today, many citizens living in England in the aftermath of that remarkable piece of legislation were resentful of the increasing power and financial influence of Dissenting Protestants, especially those wealthy merchants who helped fund the construction of impressive Presbyterian meetinghouses, such as the ones destroyed in the riots during the Sacheverell trial. Manley alludes to this anger as she describes "the Citizens of *Constantinople,* when they found there was no other way to preserve the Purity of their Religion," became furious, and "their Rage, animated by their Fears, turn'd into Fury." This fury, in Manley's satire, becomes the reason why Constantine (Anne) "re-instated" Plato (Sacheverell) in "the Patriarch's Seat, and permitted the Return of his own Friends," that is, Anne's own "Friends"—in Manley's view, the Tories.[70]

Manley was accurate in depicting the Tories flocking to congratulate Anne after the trial. She was also correct about Sacheverell's return to public life as soon as his trial was over. Since his lenient sentence allowed him to read prayers, but not to preach, at Church of England services, he attracted mobs of supporters wherever he appeared. Moreover, almost immediately after his trial concluded, his supporters celebrated with bonfires and riots in the streets. In the days after Sacheverell's sentence was announced on 23 March, "there was scarcely a major street in Westminster or in the western suburbs of London, which did not have its bonfire, its illuminated windows or its crowd of people drinking the Doctor's health and blessing the Queen." Orderly and boisterous celebrations turned into more dangerous riots. Some of this mob included apprentices, who may have been literate and may have been familiar with Sacheverell's printed sermons or his speech in Westminster Hall or other publications in support of him. Other participants were likely drawn to his cause for other reasons, including resentment of Presbyterians, cash handouts by wealthy Sacheverell supporters, or simply a desire to participate in the violent euphoria of the day.

Queen Anne had been concerned about the rioting since the start of Sacheverell's trial. By Tuesday, 28 March, five days after his sentencing, she had written to the Lord Mayor of London complaining of the "disorderly tumults occasioned by bonefires [sic], &c., requiring him for the future to suppresse all such proceedings." The queen also made the military available to him, if needed, and a government committee ordered "4 companies of the trained bands to keep guard every night."[71] On 30 March the Queen had to request the lord mayor of London to order all magistrates, constables, and church wardens to restore order.

Order was restored in London, but the good news for Sacheverell quickly spread to the rest of the country. A parson in the midlands wrote, "His enemies . . . have had their turn. Now, his friends have theirs."[72] In Oxford, a high church Tory stronghold, the lenient sentence was celebrated with new displays of violence toward Dissenting Protestants. A tub with an effigy of the Presbyterian minister Daniel Burgess was ceremonially burned, in an echo of the London bonfire in which his pulpit (scorned by Tories as a "Tub") was burned. In the market town of Sherborne, in Dorset, the Dissenting pastor John England described how "Dr. *Sacheverell's* Health was publicly drank in our *Town-Hall*" and "as for us that are *Dissenters,* we were . . . forced to keep our *Doors fast;* and this was scarce sufficient to keep us from the Rabble, who Curs'd the *Presbyterians* to the pit of *Hell,* beat a drum about the town." These rioters threatened to pull down Dissenting meetinghouses and fired guns at some, including John England's own, "to the affrightement" of his family.[73]

Queen Anne would not have wanted to fan the flames of intolerance toward Presbyterians, Quakers, or any other members of Dissenting religious sects. She wanted to change the makeup of her cabinet, but she was not ready to dissolve Parliament. While some would have her dismiss the Duchess of Marlborough, she feared that both Godolphin and the Duke of Marlborough would immediately resign. She would not have wanted to dismiss the most talented military leader in Europe just at the start of the spring military campaign. Nor did she dare rattle the financial markets of London by dismissing Godolphin, whose experience and stability gave confidence in the government's taxing and borrowing schemes for the war. The cabinet minister who was the most expendable, in her eyes, was the Marlboroughs' son-in-law, the Earl of Sunderland.

The queen had never liked Sunderland and had resisted bringing him into her cabinet for the first four years of her reign. She knew he was brilliant and a tireless administrator, but he was also an outspoken Whig, impatient with the nicety of the queen's personal preferences and feelings. She resented the fact that he had voted against a measure, early in her reign, to allow a royal allowance to her husband, in case she predeceased him. Although it was Marlborough's decision to remove the Earl of Peterborough from his military command, it fell to Sunderland to write the official letter of dismissal. Sunderland's precipitous decision to arrest Delarivier Manley and to urge the Whigs to impeach Sacheverell may have accounted for Manley's depiction of him as "Furious *Cethegus!*" punctuated with an exclamation mark.[74] Bishop Burnet reported that "the queen said lord Sunderland always treated her with great rudeness and neglect."[75] She considered him "obnoxious to all people, except a few."[76] If the Tories were going to begin removing members of Queen Anne's cabinet, Sunderland would be the logical first target for the queen's rebuttal. Rumors about this possibility began circulating at court.

On the Continent, the Duke of Marlborough was strategizing with the Allied commanders and planning the first battle of the spring military campaign between Douai and Arras, in northern France. Catching the

French off guard in preparations, and having dug trenches to divert the Sensé river to inundate Douai, Marlborough marched forward with his battalions over dry riverbeds in late April, taking forty miles of territory in just a few days and laying siege to the town of Douai. He wrote to Sarah that he hoped "this happy beginning will produce such success this campaign as must put an end to the war."[77] He explained to Godolphin that he hoped "God will so bless" the negotiations that even if "the Queen should not be so happy as to have a prospect of peace, before the opening of the next sessions of Parliament," he would at least be able to demonstrate to her "that we do our best here in the army to put a speedy and good period to this bloody war."[78]

By May, however, as the Allied and French troops were lined up to face off again at near the town of Arras, Marlborough expressed caution. The French were trying, as in past years, to avoid a direct battle—and Marlborough was cautious about taking too large a risk, given the political threat at home that would follow another fiasco like Malplaquet. He wrote to Godolphin, "What I hear from your side [of] the watter gives me so much uneasiness, that I am not so fully possessed with those sanguine thoughts as formerly, that God would protect and bless us."[79] In late May the Allies took the fortress of Douai, but they did not engage in an all-out battle that might have brought the French to their knees and leveraged a peace treaty that would have ended the war with honor for the Allies. Marlborough grumbled to Sarah that it was hard to see why he was "every day in danger of exposing my life, for those who are seeking my ruin?"[80] Ten days later, again writing to his wife, after his birthday on 26 May, he acknowledged that he felt old at age sixty: "Now that I have the misfortune of having passed three score, I may own freely my being weary of the war. However, I hope to find strength and resolution for . . . this campaign."[81]

Sunderland himself, though he certainly would have heard the rumors that his own departure was imminent, remained diligent, writing letter after administrative letter to ensure that funding, troops, and supplies flowed as smoothly as ever to the Allies on the Continent. Until 9 June, he was still regularly writing to speed on the next embarkment of troops to battles in Catalonia.[82] He was also taken with a bad cold about this time, and Queen Anne, always attentive to medical ailments, sent him some medicine.[83] Despite her personal concern for his health, the monarch was determined to carry out her change in cabinet ministers. The Duke of Marlborough, who had heard a rumor of her intentions, wrote from the Continent, beseeching the queen to reconsider. "For God's sake, Madam," he protested, "what has Ld. Sunderland done, or rather what have I done, to deserve so great a mortification[?]," an insult he interpreted as "a stroke rather aimed at me than him."[84] As he told Godolphin in a letter that he encouraged Godolphin to show to the queen, he argued for deferring the dismissal until the end of the summer military campaign, insisting that at stake was not only "the welfare of England, but of all Europe."[85] The queen, however, felt he was overstating the case. She acknowledged that Marlborough would have felt the dismissal was a "mortification," but, she queried mockingly, "must the fate of Europe depend on that?"[86]

On 13 June, one month after Manley's *Memoirs of Europe* appeared in print, the queen asked Henry Boyle, Sunderland's friend and fellow secretary of state, to collect his seal of office (for sealing and authenticating official documents). Tacitly acknowledging that she was dismissing him for no act of misconduct or mismanagement, she offered Sunderland an annual pension of £3,000, knowing he needed the income. He refused it, insisting that "if he could not have the Honour to serve his Country, he would not plunder it."[87]

Marlborough and Godolphin both saw the writing on the wall for themselves and for the war, knowing that without Sunderland—assiduous in all correspondence about the war and military supplies—the Allies would suffer. Marlborough wrote to Godolphin that Sunderland's "being at this time singled out, has no other reason but that of being my son-in-law."[88] Meanwhile, there would be no great decisive battle or victory on the Continent that season. Rather than a successful victory against the French on the battlegrounds of Europe, followed by a celebratory sermon in St. Paul's Cathedral, the only victory celebration that summer would be Sacheverell's progress through the countryside, savoring his victory against the Whigs.

8

A Tory Victory Lap and Parliamentary Elections

PART OF SACHEVERELL'S impeachment sentence involved a public burning of his two offending sermons, yet the lord mayor of London, who had invited Sacheverell to preach on Guy Fawkes Day and who was in charge of burning his sermons on 27 March, seems to have skipped the event. According to one account, the sermons "were burnt by the hangman before the Royal Exchange, in the presence of the sheriffs, the lord mayor not present."[1] This brief conflagration of printed pages did nothing to bring to closure the public divisions stirred up by his impeachment. As a contemporary observer pointed out, although the "Business of Doctor *Sacheverell,* which had made so much Noise, both at home and abroad, seem'd to terminate with these *Small Flames;* yet it new-kindled old Animosities."[2] Some of the victory bonfires in the weeks after his lenient sentencing had turned into riots, particularly in Sacheverell's parish of Southwark. While Queen Anne and the Earl of Sunderland (when he was still her secretary of state) issued orders to quell the tumults, there is no record of Sacheverell himself making any efforts to quell the violent enthusiasms of his supporters, who were aroused into intolerant anti-Dissenting mobs. Meanwhile, Dissenting Protestants throughout Britain feared for their own safety.

Even as his supporters provoked unrest in London and in Tory strongholds across England and eastern Wales, Sacheverell was being repeatedly fêted by supporters in London. Despite Church of England canon law forbidding ministers going to taverns "other than for their honest Necessities," twelve of his staunchest supporters celebrated Sacheverell's "Deliverance" in a "Thanksgiving Supper" at the Queen's Arms Tavern, at the west end of St. Paul's Cathedral, "with Plenty of Wine, and a Consort of Musick."[3] In subsequent weeks, thrilled with his own success "and thus inflated with pride, he went from house to house" among the peers who had voted for him "to congratulate them all on his and their common safety." As he attended these dinners in his honor, he was "followed by a train of link-boys and blackguards" and on every street where he was seen, "he was huzzaed by the mob like a prize-fighter."[4]

A set of playing cards offering a Tory spin on the impeachment includes a card (the two of Diamonds) of "Sacheverell's Triumph," showing Sacheverell, visible through his carriage window, being cheered by a crowd of supporters of all ranks, including one carrying a basket of potatoes. The caption refutes the Whig perception of his narcissism, asserting, "Others would swell with Pride if thus cares'd. But he bears his humble Thoughts within his Breast."[5]

Meanwhile, Sacheverell regularly read prayers at the Sunday afternoon services at St. Saviour's Church in Southwark, which was packed with admirers. His wealthy supporters donated generously to cover his legal fees, generating a surplus of more than £1,000. However, not every Tory peer was delighted with his behavior. As the Duke of Argyll responded, when "hearing that the doctor was coming to return him thanks, commanded a servant to check him." The duke ordered the servant to tell him "what I did in parliament was not at all done for his sake."[6]

While some Tories found Sacheverell's vain behavior distasteful, even if they had voted in his favor, many Tories were happy to use him as a propaganda tool. Their goal was to pressure Queen Anne to dissolve Parliament swiftly so that they could call elections while the backlash against the Whigs was powerful enough to boost the Tory's chances in Parliament. Queen Anne herself still favored a policy of moderation. In her speech on 5 April when proroguing Parliament for the summer, Anne offered tacit approval of the impeachment proceedings, acknowledging to the MPs the necessity of taking up "so much of their time" and refuting the notion, so prevalent in Tory propaganda, that the Church was in any danger.[7] Her moderate language appeared to signal that she was in no rush to dissolve Parliament or call elections, and the Tories realized that "they and their friends could not hope to sustain indefinitely the massive impetus which the Sacheverell affair had given their cause."[8]

The Tories might not be able to sustain the public backlash against the Whigs until the next scheduled elections in 1711, but they were doing everything they could to rally local towns, counties, and parishes throughout summer of 1710, hoping to pressure the queen to call elections one year early. One of Sacheverell's former students at Oxford made him the present of a living in eastern Wales, close to the English border. While it might seem surprising today that clergymen in the Church of England could hold several positions simultaneously, this practice of accepting multiple livings, and then subcontracting with curates to perform the parish duties at a lower salary, was still standard in Britain. In rewarding his former Oxford tutor with the rectory of Selattyn, Robert Lloyd was not only presenting Sacheverell with a salary of £200 per year (with no expectation that he would live in Wales or interact in any regular fashion with his parishioners there), he was also giving him an opportunity to travel in ceremony across the expanse of southern England, from London to the Welsh border.

William Fleetwood, bishop of St. Asaph in Wales, was in charge of approving this position for Sacheverell. As an erudite Whig, Bishop Fleetwood hesitated for a few weeks, but ultimately found no grounds to forbid the appointment. Before the leisurely summer trip to Wales began, Sacheverell had already traveled with the Duke of Atterbury to Devon, where he was fêted in early April, and to Oxford on 15 April. He returned to Oxford again on 15 June, just two days after the queen dismissed the Earl of Sunderland, on the first stop on his very public journey to Wales. Sixty-six horsemen, many of them his parishioners from Southwark, accompanied him as far as Uxbridge, about twenty miles northwest of London. One of the members of his traveling party insists, somewhat implausibly, that this group of well-wishers had made plans to meet him "without his Knowledge," since the ostensibly modest doctor "was always averse to such Cavalcades." At Uxbridge, his London well-wishers returned to town, but he was joined by "a Convoy of at least 300 Able bodied Men, who were come from all Parts to see him." This convoy, continuing to swell as it traveled, took him as far as West Wickham. When these well-wishers turned back, another crowd formed the next convoy. At Wheatley, six miles east of Oxford, Sacheverell was welcomed and accompanied into town by the Earl of Abingdon, one of the MPs for Oxford, along with "most of the noblemen, Heads of Houses, both the Proctors, most of the Fellows of Colleges, gentlemen, commoners, etc." This noble procession echoed the traditional pageant of a royal progress—the formal entry of a monarch into a city. Sacheverell dined with the earl and then retired to his chambers in Magdalen College, "which were crouded the next Morning by Visitors of the first Rank and Quality; who distinguish'd themselves, by giving him Invitations to their several Colleges."[9] Sacheverell and his companions then spent the next few weeks in a circuit of celebratory dinners and church services, at which the doctor was regularly invited to read prayers.

From Oxford, Sacheverell proceeded across England, making about a dozen stops across the counties of Oxfordshire, Warwickshire, Staffordshire, Cheshire, Denbighshire, and Flintshire, visiting welcoming towns or villages sometimes for a few hours, sometimes for several days. It took him more than two weeks to arrive in Selattyn, a journey he could have made in as little as three days. Once there, he spent only two days with his new parishioners. He was inducted on 1 July and read prayers in his church the next day. He would spend almost no time in this parish during the three years that he held the living. Alluding to the Tory slogan "the Church in Danger," the twentieth-century historian Geoffrey Holmes ironically observes that apparently, "the Church, whatever its other perils, was not in danger from pluralists and non-residents," that is, clergymen (like Sacheverell) holding multiple salaried positions in parishes where they did not reside.[10]

At most towns where he stopped, Sacheverell was wined and dined by the local gentry in their finest garments. The eighteenth-century Whig historian John Oldmixon reports that at Banbury, for example, "the Doctor was waited upon by that Worshipful Body, in Scarlet Gowns, and Black Gowns," and was presented a "Hamper of the best Wine in *Banbury:* The Night concluded with Bonfires, and ringing of Bells." He then proceeded to "the County of Warwickshire, doing it "the Honour," as Oldmixon ironically observes, "to stay some Days in it, to make Riots, and assemble the Populace together, to receive his Instructions against the next Elections." Oldmixon emphasizes how Sacheverell was being used by the Tories as an electoral tool. He points out that the Doctor "was never weary of speaking well of Mr. *Harley,* Mr. *Harcourt,* and Mr. *St John,* all like himself, Champions and Pillars of the Church."[11] The queen had not yet dissolved Parliament, but the Tories were laying the groundwork for their candidates, hoping she would soon dissolve it and call elections for a new Parliament that autumn.

Not everywhere was the Doctor greeted with enthusiasm. In Worcester, Sacheverell was offered only a "cold treat" at the Bush Inn, since the Common Council was not unanimous in its support of him and allocated only £20 toward his reception.[12] These dismissive accounts of the visit were countered by a contradictory *Letter from a Citizen of Worcester,* insisting that these were all "Whiggish Lies, and our *Whole Town* so highly resent their Proceedings, that the Doctor's Foes are hiss'd as they pass through our Streets."[13] Sacheverell's traveling companion's glowing description of his reception in the pamphlet *Dr Sacheverel's Progress* was motivated in part as a response to more satirical accounts of their journey, including *The Banb—y Apes: or, The Monkeys Chattering to the Magpye,* a mocking account of their visit to Banbury, in which the "High-Ch—ch IDOL [*in Garments as black as his Deeds*] on a Sorrel Horse" is depicted arriving in a train of attendants, being greeted by "the Bellman and Sexton of the Town, with Staves," then "Two Pursivants, bearing Pendants, with the D—r's Crest (Pope *Clement* the XI's Head) and his Motto in these Words, *Unlimited Passive Obedience.*" This idol is greeted by the town sergeant, the mayor, carrying a printed copy of Sacheverell's sermon, and followed by "a vast Mob, hollowing, hooping and playing the Devil." He was then "conducted to his Inn, where he was again Congratulated, and presented with Wine."[14] The anonymous satirist here suggests not only that Sacheverell was being worshipped like an idol but also that his real high church Tory aim was to return the country to Catholicism.

The pamphleteer likens this whole pageant to a fabled visitation of the royal ape during the reign of Elizabeth I, during which a "Fellow" with a feather in his hat, "got a License to make a Show of a great *APE* about the Country." In a town that the author believes might have been *Banbury,* the "Towns-People, being poor, thought it not worth their while to see this sight." The ape's showmaster than sends a warrant demanding that the mayor and the important persons in town show their respect to the "*Queen's Ape, who is a Person of Rank and Quality . . . having been bred at an University.*" Although many assert the ape is a mere "Knave," others insist that it would be "*Treason*" not to greet the queen's ape. Thus the town grandees duly attend him at a local inn, but it was "the Mob" that was most "taken with this new Raree-Show." At the next town, Coventry, there were only a few "Butchers and Barbers" who took up an offering, not for a hamper of wine but for "Two Hogsheads of Ale, which were set in the Publick Street, where the Rabble got shamefully drunk in Toasting a Health to their beloved IDOL."[15]

The sympathetic insider's account of the journey in *Dr Sacheverel's Progress* was written partly in response to the satirical treatment of his stop in Banbury. Its author, identified only as J. K., insists, "Our Reception here was so very different from the *Account* that is handed about by the disaffected Party, in a Libel, call'd *the Banbury Apes.*" This witness explains that "the Entertainment prepar'd for us, and the Decency that was us'd at it, were such as was altogether answerable to the Character of a Loyal Corporation." Moreover, Bunbury well understood "the Merit of a Person, who had so openly Espous'd the Rights of the Church Establish'd."[16]

Sacheverell's supporters might emphasize the Doctor's love for the established church, but the seven weeks of his tour from Oxford to Wales and back again were also marked by acts of hatred. An effigy of the Whig Bishop Hoadly was burned in Wrexham, in north Wales, just twelve miles from Selattyn. Hoadly's books had previously been burned in public in Sherborne.[17] Sometimes the high church and Dissenting protesters were side by side, without constabulary protection to reduce the possibility of conflict. In late June in Bridgnorth, "both parties" were "making bonfires where about one they drink Dr Sacheverell's health and the other his confusion." On 30 June the bishop of Worcester wrote in response to the high Tory speeches that the "danger is so great that I cannot but tremble to think of it, if her Majesty should dissolve the present Parliament and change her ministry."[18]

After the ceremony in Selattyn, Sacheverell and his entourage took a different, but equally leisurely route on their return journey. They arrived in Oxford on 19 July, where he was again greeted with enthusiastic revelry. Sacheverell's progress had accomplished precisely what the Tories had hoped: a swelling expression of support for a Tory government and almost daily epistles and formal Tory "addresses," formal letters, sent to the queen from parishes, villages, dioceses, and counties from all over England. Groups of clergymen had been sending addresses to Queen Anne since the start of Sacheverell's impeachment. Sacheverell's progress across the country only encouraged these formal epistles, some of which were handed to a local peer to deliver directly to the queen at court. Most of these elegant letters expressed concern about anti-monarchical sentiment. An address on 26 June to "the Queen's most Excellent Majesty" from "the High-Sheriff, Deputy-Lieutenant, Justices of the Peace, Gentlemen, Clergy and Freeholders, of the County of Derby" is typical. The writers describe their amazement at "such Abominable, Blasphemous, and Antimonarchical Principles, as are daily publish'd, and industriously spread about." They therefore "humbly presume to assure Your Majesty" that they will at "the utmost Hazard" of their "Lives and Fortunes" work to "maintain Your Majesty's undoubted Title to Your Crown, and support the Church of *England*, as by Law establish'd."[19]

That same week the County of Denbigh, in north Wales, sent an address, penned at the Midsummer quarter-session meeting of court (in late June) complaining of "Republican and Factious Spirits, the implacable Enemies of Your Majesty's Family and Government," which are "reviving and maintaining those pernicious and fatal Doctrines that "pav'd the Way to the Execrable Murder of Your Majesty's Royal Grandfather [Charles I]."[20] While some of the addresses were from Whigs expressing gratitude for her support of Revolution principles, the vast majority were Tory; by early August, Anne had received ninety-seven Tory addresses from counties and dioceses around the country.[21] The queen herself probably did not appreciate this barrage of Tory epistles, many of them implicitly undermining the Revolution principles that had brought her to the throne. She commented to her doctor in September that "*Sacheverel* was a foolish man, for going into the Countrey."[22]

Robert Harley, who favored political moderation rather than reactionary high church Toryism, would not have been sympathetic to this populist anti-Dissenting rioting or these Tory addresses to the queen. However, as a politician, he saw the advantage of these crowds for gaining a Tory victory in the elections that were growing ever more likely as the summer advanced. His eventual concern, however, as the populist uprisings continued, even after Sacheverell's summer progress ended, was that the Tories might succeed too well, bringing in a "new Parliament as violently High Tory as its predecessor had been violently Whig."[23]

■

WHEN QUEEN ANNE dismissed the Earl of Sunderland in June, she signaled her willingness to change her cabinet from Whig to Tory. Rumors were circulating that Godolphin, lord treasurer, would be the next minister to be asked to resign, and these rumors were throwing the bankers of London into a panic. Godolphin had served in the Treasury under every monarch since Charles II and was trusted for his financial acumen by Whigs and Tories alike. Although he had authorized borrowing immense sums to finance the War of Spanish Succession, the Bank of England, as well as the bankers and moneylenders in the City of London, had great trust in his judgment.

Godolphin's skill in leveraging national credit allowed the British and their Protestant Allies to curtail French and Catholic hegemony in continental Europe. He had been pivotal to passing the Act of Union in 1707 that joined England with Scotland, forming Great Britain. His diligence in weeding out corruption in the Treasury was crucial to the stability of the financial systems. He was both tireless as an administrator and proactive in how he proceeded. For example, encountering difficulty in raising credit in 1708, after so many years at war, he mediated a union between the Tory-controlled East India Company with the Whig-controlled New East India Company. This merger not only secured government funding for the 1708 military campaign, it also greatly improved Britain's trading position in India, establishing India as a central financial piece of Britain's future empire, "the jewel in the crown," as it would be known in Queen Victoria's era. From today's postcolonial perspective, we may critique the ethical foundation of that empire, but Godolphin's measures to secure the credit markets in early eighteenth-century Britain nevertheless marked his centrality to the nation's military and economic development for the next two centuries.[24]

In June 1710, the mere rumor that Anne might replace Godolphin as lord treasurer was threatening financial credit markets, in particular foreign holders of bank stock. On 15 June, two days after Sunderland was dismissed, four directors of the Bank of England sought an audience with the queen to underscore the dangers to national credit if

Godolphin were to be replaced. While Anne appreciated the gravity of the situation, Robert Harley was critical of what he saw as political interference on the part of the Bank of England. First of all, he felt that everyone lobbying the queen about Godolphin's importance was overplaying, with "tragical expressions," the possibility that stocks would fall and "the Bank be ruined," leading to the "ruin of the nation." Second, he was concerned that four of the bank's directors were acting as "private gentlemen" not officially deputized to speak on behalf of the bank. Referencing the debate Sacheverell's sermon reignited over passive obedience to the monarch, Harley ironically observed, "Let us swear allegiance to these four men and give them a right to our passive obedience without reserve."[25]

Queen Anne was greatly concerned about riots and tumults and would not have been directly persuaded, for example, to dismiss Godolphin because any mob mocked him as "Volpone." But the Tories, as they returned to their home constituencies over the summer, recognized the anger toward the Whigs who had managed the impeachment. These Tory MPs and lords, further emboldened by satirical treatments of Whigs by writers such as Delarivier Manley, actively lobbied the queen at court to dissolve Parliament and call elections. They also actively lobbied Robert Harley behind the scenes, believing him again to have the queen's confidence and her ear. By late July, influential Tories were expressing increasing confidence that Anne would dissolve Parliament. Lord Weymouth wrote to Harley, "I believe there shall be a new parliament." Two days later Viscount Dupplin, Harley's son-in-law, wrote to Harley, expressing hope that the queen would act soon. He let Harley know that his own father, the Earl of Kinnoul (in Scotland), would be happy to help in any way needed: "My father is impatiently waiting to hear that the Parliament is dissolved and wishing that all good designs may be speedily effectuated. He says, if you'll let him know how matters stand, he'll be very ready to use his utmost endeavours to serve you." Possibly conveying the mindset of friends near his father's seat, near Perth, in Scotland, Dupplin added, "I'm glad to find the generality in this country so much pleased with the expectations of a new Parliament."[26]

In late July the writer Daniel Defoe also wrote to Harley, with a suggestion for fixing the public credit problem. Defoe, whom we know today as a novelist (after the publication of *Robinson Crusoe* in 1719 and *Moll Flanders* in 1722), was better known in his own time as a political journalist, pamphleteer, and policy wonk. In 1697 he published *An Essay Upon Projects,* in which he offered schemes to improve many aspects of society, from trade to female education, highway safety, pensions, and insurance. In light of Defoe's wide-ranging views on public policy, it is not surprising that he had conceived of a scheme that might "prevent the ruin of the public credit." Defoe, who had written propaganda for Harley since 1704, had also been critical of the Tories' treatment of Dissenters, though in July 1710 he once more promised his loyalty to Harley.[27]

In his letter to Harley Defoe also refers to his own anecdotal opinion polling about a potential change from a Whig to a Tory majority through parliamentary elections. He reports that, according to his conversations, such a change would be popular if it brought in a balanced election result rather than reversion to extreme Toryism: "I find, that acquainting some people they are not all to be devoured, and eaten up—will have the effect upon them [as] could be wished for; assuring them that moderate counsels are at the bottom of all these things; that the old mad party are not coming in . . . that toleration, succession or union are not struck at, and they may be easy as to the nation's liberties."[28] This style of moderation may have made good political propaganda in favor of dissolving Parliament, but with Sacheverell whipping up anti-Whig sentiment around the country, such a balanced, moderate government was not likely to be the outcome.

Whether or not Defoe's talking points helped Harley persuade Queen Anne, she was certainly aware of his new pamphlet, *An Essay Upon Publick Credit,* which she mentioned to her doctor in September 1710.[29] Perhaps with the help of Defoe's analysis, she eventually reached the decision that she could dispense with her lord treasurer. Godolphin himself had seen this coming in mid-July and had expressed his concern to Marlborough that the country's "affairs here are more and more in disorder every day," with credit continuing "to sink." He warned Marlborough not to be surprised if he shortly learned that he (Godolphin) would "no longer" be "in a capacity of doing him any farther service," even while promising that he was in the meantime "willing to bear the greatest uneasynesses of all kinds" in order to be "of the least use to him."[30] Ever industrious to the last, Godolphin was still writing to Marlborough at the end of July, promising the gunpowder and provisions Marlborough had requested. At the same time, he was predicting the dissolution of Parliament and the boost it would give to the French in the war, but pointing out that the queen "seems to bee deaf to all reasonings of that nature."[31] Godolphin's pessimism and frustration made him "increasingly strident in his criticism of the Queen and more disrespectful of her in person."[32] Robert Harley wrote to a friend that "every day" Godolphin "grows souer and indeed ruder to the Queen. . . . It is impossible he can continue many days."[33]

Although he had been half expecting to be dismissed all that summer, on 7 August, in the second of two meetings with Anne, he asked whether it was "the will of your Majesty that I should go on?" He was heartened to hear her respond immediately, "Yes."[34] But she was not telling the truth. The next morning she sent him a brief note complaining of his recent treatment of her and "the many unkind returns" he had lately given her. Rather than having him return the long thin wooden staff that was the symbol of the lord treasurer's position, she asks him simply to "break it, which I believe will be easier to us both."[35]

The way that Anne handled the dismissal of a public servant who had served so loyally for so many decades and who had served her as de facto prime minister when he was lord treasurer was nothing less than insulting. As the Duchess of Marlborough would write in her memoirs, Godolphin had patiently nurtured and mentored Anne at the very start of her monarchy, offering "the care and tenderness of a father or a guardian through a state of helpless ignorance."[36] On receiving the queen's letter of dismissal, Godolphin replied immediately to let her know that he had "the honour" of her letter with the "commands in it to break my staff." He explained that he did this "with the same duty and satisfaction as when I had the honour to receive it from yr Matys hand." He also added in his own defense, "I should never bee able to forgive myself if I had not always served yr Maty with the most particular respect & duty, as well as with the greatest zeal & integrity."[37]

Godolphin wrote to Marlborough immediately, enclosing copies of the queen's letter to him and his reply to her; anticipating the dissolution of Parliament, he enclosed a letter from a candidate in Scotland he hoped Marlborough would endorse. The next day Godolphin reiterated his diligence, resolving "to continue to take the same pains and care he did before" to support Marlborough "to the end of this campagne." Even if Godolphin was no longer lord treasurer, he was still a member of the House of Lords, and he would work tirelessly behind the scenes supporting the alliance between Britain and the Allies in the war. As Bishop Gilbert Burnet wrote of him, "He was the man of the clearest mind, the calmest temper, and the most uncorrupt of all the ministers of state I have ever known."[38]

Godolphin and Marlborough continued their regular correspondence, much of it now concerning the meetings Godolphin was having with others in government and at court. Marlborough himself wrote to his wife that now that Godolphin had been dropped, it would not be long before the two of them also lost their positions. Marlborough also anticipated an imminent dissolution of Parliament and elections, and he warned Sarah to stay away from their estate at St. Albans during the election period rather than attempt to help the local Whig MP with his reelection. He was worried by the anti-Whig violence around the country and feared she "might meet with some insult." He ended that letter by expressing his concern that the queen and her current advisers "have no resentment but to" the Marlboroughs, Godolphin, "and their children." He adds, "God know[s] how litle I have deserved this. May He grant me pastience, and His will be done." He concludes to his wife, "You shall ever find me with much tenderness yours."[39]

When she asked Godolphin to break his staff of office on 8 August, Queen Anne did not appoint another lord treasurer; instead she established a commission to manage the Treasury. She appointed Harley to be chancellor of the exchequer, and then brought him, along with two other Tories, into her cabinet (although the chancellor of the exchequer was not usually a cabinet member), making him in essence first minister. As the Whigs predicted, Bank of England stock fell as soon as news spread of Godolphin's dismissal, dropping from a value of 113 on 8 August to 108 ¾ three days later.[40] Stock values in the Bank of England, the East India Company, and other public funds "continued sinking all the remainder of the year."[41] However, Harley soon located sources of financing other than the Bank of England, finding a consortium of financiers that loaned the government £350,000 to solve the immediate crisis. But Harley was not able to function with the current Whig Parliament. Prominent Whigs had refused to serve on the Treasury commission, and the Dukes of Somerset and Devonshire complained that their access to the queen was greatly diminished since Harley returned to power. Harley believed he would not be able to achieve the moderate power sharing that he desired unless there were elections and a new parliament.

In her cabinet meeting on 21 September, Anne had the clerk read out a proclamation stating that Parliament was to be dissolved. Before Lord Chancellor William Cowper could begin to protest, Anne "rose up, and would admit of no debate, and ordered the writs for a new parliament to be prepared."[42] At this news, most of the Whigs promptly resigned from Anne's cabinet. Anne then brought in as one of her lord lieutenants the Duke of Beaufort, the Jacobite sympathizer to whom Manley had dedicated her *New Atalantis*. She appointed as lord president of the Privy Council her uncle, the Earl of Rochester, a staunch Tory who opposed any military operations on the Continent and viewed the Whigs as "republicans, atheists, war-mongers, war-usurers, and friends of the Dissenters."[43] Bishop Burnet observes in his history of this era, "So sudden and so entire a change of the ministry [i.e., cabinet] is scarce to be found in our history, especially where men of great abilities had served, both with zeal and success." Anne was reportedly dismayed at the loss of Lord Chancellor Cowper and Secretary of State Boyle, but she was nevertheless reported to be relieved to be "freed from the chains the old ministry held her in."[44] On 28 September the Queen sent out a proclamation for a new Parliament, to be opened on 25 November.[45]

■

THE PROCLAMATION for a new parliament required the elections that many people had been anticipating all summer. In eighteenth-century Britain parliamentary elections were local affairs, taking place at different times in different counties and districts. Insofar as Sacheverell's progress across the country had aroused mobs, there was concern that local elections would be riotous events, with mob pressure exerted by the Tories. The Duke of Marlborough had already warned his wife to stay away from St. Albans during its election. And indeed, there was good reason to be concerned. In Woodstock, near the building site at

Blenheim, where angry laborers were still awaiting their pay, the Duke of Marlborough's estate agent borrowed £300 (on his personal credit) to distribute among those in distress, thus turning the tide in favor of the Whigs and ensuring the reelection of Marlborough's preferred candidates, one of whom was his trusted lieutenant-general, William Cadogan.[46] In other places there was no such straightforward measure to calm the scene of the election. As Bishop Burnet observes, "In London, and in all the parts of England, but more remarkably in the great cities, there was a vast concourse of rude multitudes brought together, who behaved themselves in so boisterous a manner, that it was not safe." In "many places," he adds, it was "not possible, for those who had a right to vote, to come and give their votes for a whig; open violence was used in several parts."[47]

By modern standards, there were very few eligible voters. Fewer than 3 percent of the population could actually vote, since voting depended on owning land valued at forty shillings or more, and most of the population consisted of rural peasant tenant farmers. Even many wealthy merchants and professionals did not own, as freeholders, the land on which they lived or worked. The tiny total number of voters meant that every single vote mattered, and for the Tories who felt the Church was in danger, emotions were running high. Burnet, a bishop himself, blames the Tory clergy, at least in part, for the role they played for having roused sentiments "for some months," with "inflaming sermons." Burnet describes clergymen during the elections, going "from house to house, pressing their people to shew, on this great occasion, their zeal for the church, and now or never to save it."[48]

Robert Harley worked hard to prevent the impression that he was hoping the elections would bring in a lopsidedly Tory government. He masterminded a pamphlet titled *Faults on Both Sides* (published anonymously) to appeal to Whig Dissenters, merchants, and others concerned about the elections and the new cabinet. He promoted the idea that "the Difference . . . of Opinions" between "Honest *Whigs* and *Honest* Tories" is "not so great as they are made to believe."[49] But as the elections played out, there was "never so apparent a fury," Marlborough's master-general of the ordnance wrote to him, "as the people of England show against the Whigs and for High Church."[50] Daniel Defoe reported that there was fighting "with swords and staves at Coventry, with stones and brickbats as at other places." He observed, "Even our civil war . . . was not carried on with such a spirit of fury as is now to be seen."[51] Along with weariness of war, the public response to Sacheverell was at the heart of the fury. Printed lists of which MPs had voted for or against impeaching the Doctor circulated widely, and those who voted against impeachment fared badly in the elections. Several managers of the impeachment proceedings dared not even stand for reelection. Tory candidates boldly allied themselves with Sacheverell by marching in processions with his portrait, which became "the favourite emblem on the rallying standards of the Tories."[52]

As the elections ended on 16 November and results were gradually tallied across the country, 270 Whig MPs found they had lost their seats. In the new Parliament, the Tories would claim 332 seats to the Whigs' 181, thus outnumbering their opponents by almost two to one. The Tory backlash of 1710 was resounding. But the stunning electoral victory came at a cost. Many of the high church Tories also harbored Jacobite sympathies, meaning they wished Anne's successor to be Anne's Catholic half-brother, rather than the Protestant Elector of Hanover. As the queen's doctor informed her after she dismissed Godolphin, the talk at court was "of her Majesty's Inclinations to the Pretender."[53] The new government would need propaganda writers to rally support for it.

Anticipating the Tory victory, and keen to support the new government, Delarivier Manley had finished the second volume of *Memoirs of Europe* in time for it to appear on bookseller stalls on 16 November, during the very week that the elections were being concluded. As MPs returned to Westminster from their home constituencies, they would be met by a populace already devouring Manley's newest Tory secret history, in which Robert Harley appears as the romance hero, Herminius, in time to save the Caesar (Queen Anne) from him(her-)self. Deploying a metaphor for Anne escaping the persistent hold of the Marlboroughs and Godolphin, Manley describes Herminius watching "the lazy vapour of Indolence breaking from around the easier Emperor [Queen Anne]," which "left him at length—strengthen'd—confirm'd—all bright—and all himself." Seeing "his Sovereign Lord returning to his native Vertue," Herminius "fell at his sacred Feet in Raptures that bespoke his Loyalty; and Transports." In the second volume of

Memoirs of Europe, Abigail Masham is depicted as Leonidas, a brave young man who, "with a becoming Boldness," refused to let AEmilius (Godolphin) through the door—thus representing Godolphin's loss of position and place in Anne's cabinet. Meanwhile, Manley describes the time "drawing nigh for the Election of new Magistrates," pointing out that the "People were for *Caesar* [Anne] whom they doated on, as well as on the *Orthodox* [Church of England] Religion."[54]

In this volume, which is dedicated to Louisa of Savoy, Countess of Angoulesm (another pseudonym for Abigail Masham), Manley describes the change in sentiment toward the war after the election. The newly elected "have no Interests but that of the Empire; nor need the People scruple to lend their Aid to the continuation of the War." That "Aid" will not "be employ'd to no other Use but to bring the Enemy to advantageous Terms." Manley notes that Stauracius (Marlborough) "still continu'd" in his position of captain-general, but that Caesar (Anne) continued to hope that "Time and Reason wou'd awaken him from the Golden Dream of Lawless Power."[55]

As Manley predicted in the final section of *Memoirs of Europe,* Queen Anne kept Marlborough as her captain-general, but he hardly felt that he held unlimited or "Lawless Power" over the military or the Allies' strategy in the war. The difficulty for the Allies at this moment of Tory triumph was that the war was not yet over, nor was there an easy path to peace, given the different competing interests among the Allies. Every country involved was suffering from the costs, but the Allies as a whole had not reached consensus about their demands or their strategy to bring Louis XIV to the negotiating table. It was tempting for some individual countries to attempt to negotiate a separate peace, and some in Anne's ministry were keen for Britain to do just that.

Under Marlborough's command, the Allies continued to win strategic victories through successful sieges at Béthune, St. Venant, then Aire in the months leading up to the parliamentary elections, but these territorial gains did not bring the French any closer to the negotiating table. Meanwhile, Harley had engaged Jonathan Swift, newly arrived from Ireland, to edit the Tory weekly paper *The Examiner.* In the 23 November issue, Swift satirically attacked the Duke of Marlborough for the lavish rewards given him, comparing his thousands of pounds in lands, gifts, and employments to those perks of "*Gratitude*" usual for war heroes in Roman times, including frankincense (£4 10), a crown of laurel (two pennies), and a triumphal arch (£500). In that same issue Swift also described a certain lady's woman who had appropriated £22 for herself out of the £26 from which she was to pay the expenses for her "Lady." Making clear that he was referring to Queen Anne's £26,000 annual budget for the privy purse and Sarah's having borrowed £22,000 to construct Marlborough House, Swift concludes: "It is but supposing instead of twenty six Pounds, twenty six thousand; and by that you may judge what the Pretensions of *Modern Merit* are, where it happens to be its own Paymaster."[56]

Having seen this satire, the duchess immediately wrote to Anne's doctor, David Hamilton (to whom she wrote whenever she wanted to communicate something to the queen), complaining about being depicted as "a common cheat and a pickpocket" in a publication "printed and cried out." She threatened again that it was in her "power to publish other papers" that would "give people a very different notion."[57] Anne's only response to Hamilton when he read the letter to her was that the duchess "wrote free."[58] Sarah's threat was to publish an account she referred to as the "History of Mrs. Morley," using the former nickname for Anne they had taken in their early correspondence, between "Mrs. Freeman and Mrs. Morley." She never carried out this threat, but it shows that her response to a published attack would not be to request a government charge of libel but to publish a counterattack. She had fully accepted the new rules of the game in which, since 1695, "the power of the press, so hated by many, was hijacked by whigs and tories, who used it to attack each other remorselessly."[59] In later years, as Dowager Duchess of Marlborough, Sarah even acknowledged her admiration for Jonathan Swift's satirical talents. In 1736, as she was rallying opponents to then prime minister Robert Walpole, she "could not help wishing that we had his assistance in the opposition," even volunteering that she would "easily forgive all the slaps he has given me and the Duke of Marlborough, and have thanked him heartily whenever he would please to do good."[60]

When the queen gave her opening speech to Parliament on 27 November, she acknowledged "what my People suffer by this Long and Expensive War," but expressed her support for continuing it "with the utmost Vigour" as "the likeliest Means, to procure a Safe and

Honourable Peace for Us, and all Our Allies."[61] Parliament would vote £6 million for the next season of war, but Harley's propaganda assault against Marlborough undermined the Allies even as they planned for the military campaign for the spring of 1711.

Anne wanted to retain Marlborough for one more campaign season, but she was determined to dismiss the duchess and her daughters from their court positions. Although Sarah wrote a letter of apology, which her husband delivered to the monarch on 17 January, the queen was insistent. While for years Anne had assumed that if she dismissed Sarah, John would resign, she now recognized, as she told her doctor, that Marlborough was "ambitious and wont go out" from his command even if she dismissed his wife.[62] When the duke presented Sarah's letter of apology to the queen, she informed him that she needed him to return to her within three days Sarah's gold key of office. There are different accounts of what happened when John asked Sarah for it, some suggesting that Sarah flung it on the floor and demanded that her husband, "the victor of Blenheim and Ramillies," pick it up and return it to the queen.[63] Other accounts merely suggest that the duke having conveyed the queen's demand when they were in bed together, the duchess demanded he get up, get dressed, and return it to the queen that same night.[64]

■

THE QUEEN had won the standoff with the Duchess of Marlborough and made Abigail keeper of the privy purse and the Duchess of Somerset groom of the stole. This change inspired a printed playing card (in the pack of cards with scenes from the Sacheverell proceedings) depicting a kneeling Duchess of Somerset accepting her new office with respectful humility, with the caption: "Upon her Knees fam'd Somerset receives an Office which another D——ss leaves."[65] Although Sarah seems to have returned the money from the privy purse that she had borrowed for building Marlborough House, she decided to pay herself a final sum of £18,000, based on nine years of ostensible arrears of a supplemental salary of £2,000 a year, which the queen had once offered her (before Parliament granted her husband a permanent supplemental payment of £5000 per year, once he was granted the dukedom). This appears not to have been the only irregularity in the Duchess of Marlborough's bookkeeping, but the queen nevertheless signed off on Sarah's privy purse accounts, after hesitating for two weeks.[66] She probably signed with the tacit understanding that Sarah would never carry out her threat of publishing Anne's early passionate letters to her.[67]

The Duke of Marlborough returned to the Continent, still hoping to pull off a decisive victory but knowing that his negotiating position was weak because the Tory Parliament clearly wanted a swift peace. The 1711 campaign was slowed by the death of the Holy Roman emperor Joseph I. His brother, the king of Spain, became emperor on his death, completely changing the power balance among France, Spain, and the Allies and negating one of the initial rationales for the war, the contest over who should rule Spain.

The French, meanwhile, were emboldened by the sense that "the whole Alliance might collapse." With their position weakened, the British relied on the poet and diplomat Matthew Prior to enter into secret peace negotiations with the French, a negotiation that the French clearly saw for what it was: "a separate peace for its own special advantage behind the backs and at the expense of its allies."[68] While Anne's Tory cabinet approved this peace measure, the Tory backlash appeared to have diminished Britain's position: previously seen as a major player in the European balance of power, the nation was now acting more narrowly in its own interests.

Jonathan Swift, at the request of Robert Harley, spent several months penning a lengthy satirical pamphlet, *The Conduct of the Allies,* justifying the need to end the war with France. Swift, who had become friendly with John Barber and Delarivier Manley that spring, asked Manley to take his place in writing *The Examiner* and some shorter pamphlets while he finished his pamphlet. Manley spent the summer anonymously writing as the voice of *The Examiner,* in a sparring contest with the Whig paper *The Medley,* written by the Whig MP Arthur Maynwaring. Manley also wrote a pamphlet in late September in response to Marlborough's victory at Bouchain in early September 1711, in honor of which Whig pamphleteers had written odes in praise of Marlborough.

In *The Duke of Marlborough's Vindication,* Manley counters Whig concerns that "*the Fruits of all his Victories*" would be "*thrown all away at once, by a shameful and scandalous Peace.*" Manley retorts "No!" Such a peace, as she viewed it, was what "our People" supported unanimously.

It would also not "un-Prince" or "un-Duke" Marlborough. Nor would it take from him "all those immense Riches of which himself and his Lady, as good an Accomptant as she is, do not yet know the Extent of," as Manley points out, with a sly nod to Sarah's borrowing from the privy purse. Nor would it leave him with nothing to show for his efforts but Blenheim, "that Edifice of *Memento* of a Subject's Ambition" still being underwritten by the public, while "his gracious Benefactress [Queen Anne]" resides in an "old patch-up Palace . . . without once desiring to rebuild *Whitehall*" after the fire of 1698. For Manley, "the generality of the People" would easily "be brought to agree" that a separate peace, negotiated without the other Allies, would be "better than no Peace at all."[69] Manley's pamphlet was so effective that Jonathan Swift included a copy in a batch of publications he sent to his friend Stella in Ireland, describing it as "the best" of what he enclosed.[70]

Meanwhile, after Sarah sent Marlborough a copy of Manley's anonymously published pamphlet, he described his "real concern . . . on the account of this barbarous libel, when I am emparing [impairing] my health, and venturing every thing for the good of my Country."[71] The captain-general also wrote to Robert Harley with the same concerns, pointing out that the "authors of these papers . . . are not only my enemies, but yours too," and also "enemies to the Queen, and a poison to her subjects." Apparently not sharing his wife's (or her friend Arthur Maynwaring's) Whig belief in press freedom (in which a libelous Tory pamphlet should be answered with a scathing Whig reply), Marlborough expressed his hope that "a strict search" will be made "after them" and that "the punishment they deserve may be inflicted upon them." Harley, rather disingenuously (given that Swift was writing pamphlets at his suggestion, and passing some of the suggestions to Manley), replied that his own "sentiments" on that subject were "fully known." He pointed out that when he was "Secretary of State" (until his fall from power in 1708), he "did, by an impartial prosecution, silence most of them, until a party of men [i.e. Whigs], for their own ends, supported them against the laws and my prosecution."[72]

Swift's own pamphlet, *The Conduct of the Allies,* appeared in November, offering a justification for peace and a scathing satire of the Marlboroughs. He asserted that "the true Spring or Motive" for the entire war "was the aggrandizing of a particular Family." It was, he asserted, "a War of the *General* [Marlborough] and the *Ministry* [the Whigs], and not of the *Prince* or *People*."[73] He also repeated a now familiar charge, that Marlborough was skimming a profit from the Allied bread contracts. The tide had turned against Marlborough in the Tory-dominated Parliament, and Swift's scathing satire prompted an investigation into the 2.5 percent Marlborough routinely took from the bread contracts. Marlborough never denied taking this percentage, but he argued that it was a traditional prerequisite to a commander-in-chief and that the funds were used for espionage operations and secret correspondence. He defended himself in the House of Lords and promised that he "should always be ready to serve" his queen and country "if he could but crawl along, to obtain an honourable and lasting peace."[74] Before Parliament had finished gathering evidence, "her majesty thought fit to dismiss him from all his employments, that the matter might undergo an impartial investigation."[75]

On 24 January 1712, shortly after Queen Anne had dismissed him from his military command, Parliament voted 265 to 155 that Marlborough's conduct was "unwarranted and illegal," but it did not pursue further prosecution or impeachment, probably because Anne's cabinet ministers allowed the same percentage of the bread contract to the Duke of Ormonde, Marlborough's successor as captain-general.[76] Meanwhile, with Marlborough's dismissal, the French felt they had the upper hand in peace negotiations. As Louis XIV of France remarked, "The affair of displacing the Duke of Marlborough will do for us all we desire."[77] At the same time, the soldiers on the front lines complained that the quality of the provisions had greatly diminished since Marlborough's departure. For all the complaints about the percentage of bread contracts taken for espionage, Marlborough (with the financial and administrative assistance of Godolphin and Sunderland) had been assiduous in feeding his troops. While at court or in London he may have been mocked for considering himself "King John," on the battlefields he had been known as the "Old Corporal" for his hands-on care and concern for his men. The new military commanders were so careless in nourishing the troops that Allied soldiers were close to mutinying.[78]

Although Marlborough House in London was finally complete, the Marlboroughs had little inclination to reside in London during the height of the public outcry against them. They left for Holywell House in St. Albans in June. Sidney Godolphin joined them there for a visit, and in September he died there of kidney failure. Following the death of his oldest friend, Marlborough requested permission from Harley to travel abroad. He left Britain at the end of November 1712, settling in Frankfurt. The Duchess of Marlborough joined her husband on the Continent in January 1713, following the death of Arthur Maynwaring, who died of consumption in November. Although not there on any officially sanctioned diplomatic missions, Marlborough nevertheless cultivated contacts with Allied military commanders and George of Hanover to guarantee their military support for the Protestant succession in British, in case Queen Anne's Catholic half-brother made any attempt to take the throne on Anne's death.

Meanwhile, Viscount Bolingbroke, was so determined to bring the war to a close that in May 1712 he ordered the Duke of Ormonde to withdraw his forces before the Battle of Denain, informing the French but not the Allies. The French commander de Torcy subsequently congratulated Ormonde on the French victory. The French went on to recapture several of the towns won by the Allies in previous campaigns, and the British, with a weaker hand than they held in 1709, began negotiating a peace treaty with France. The Dutch, almost bankrupt from the costs of the war, were also ready to negotiate, as were Portugal, Prussia, and Savoy.

The war finally came to an end in 1713 for Britain and the other Allied powers (except the Holy Roman Empire) when they signed a series of treaties at Utrecht with France in April 1713 and with Spain in July. The emperor Charles kept fighting the French but struggled without the other Allies, and eventually signed a peace treaty at Rastatt in March 1714. As Winston Churchill points out, had the Tories not allowed the "military disasters in the autumn of 1712, the united Allies could have forced France into far more satisfactory arrangements for the Dutch, the Germanic states, and the Holy Roman Empire than were in fact achieved."[79] Although the final agreement was no better than what France had offered during peace negotiations in 1709, Britain probably benefited more than any other country in future economic prospects. While the Dutch gained a protective barrier and a right to half the trade with the Spanish Netherlands, Britain gained extensive territories in North America and the West Indies, including Hudson Bay, Newfoundland, Nova Scotia, and St. Christopher Island in the British West Indies. Britain also retained Minorca and Gibraltar and earned the rights to the Asiento slave trade for thirty years. France agreed to recognize the Protestant line of succession in Britain through the House of Hanover and expel Anne's half-brother (known to history as the "Old Pretender") and his family, including his son, Charles Edward Stuart (the "Young Pretender" or "Bonnie Prince Charlie"), who would make his own attempt to claim the English throne in 1745. France and Spain agreed that their two countries would never again be ruled by the same monarch.

Although all the nations involved suffered financially from the war, Britain's Whig system of financing debt through the Bank of England, however fraught at some moments, established the mechanism for future mercantile and manufacturing growth—with the ensuing advantages and disadvantages to future civilizations defined by the dream of growth.[80] For some historians, the most important aspect of the Treaty of Utrecht was that it included, in the articles signed between Britain and Spain in July, language asserting that peace could only be preserved if a balance of power was maintained.[81] While wars would be fought between European nations for another two and a half centuries, this language nevertheless inaugurated an idea of European cooperation that is now central to the modern European Union.

■

In October and November 1713, Parliamentary elections were held as required according to the Triennial Act, which required elections every three years. Rather than returning any advantage to the Whigs, the elections brought in an even greater Tory majority than had been elected in 1710, indicating the continued power of the Tory propaganda campaign tarnishing the Marlboroughs and the Whigs. However, not all was smooth sailing for Robert Harley, now Earl of Oxford, who was competing for power with Henry, Viscount Bolingbroke. By May, Oxford had lost the queen's confidence, and Anne dismissed him on 27 July 1714. Queen Anne had been extremely ill all winter, and the Marlboroughs were impatient to return home from the Continent. They set sail for England on 28 July, hitting stormy weather, which delayed the crossing. On 1 August, as their ship was approaching Dover, Queen Anne died.

When the Marlboroughs reached London on 4 August 1714, politicians and courtiers began scrambling for the duke's favor, recognizing that he would once again wield power under the new monarch. Indeed, when George of Hanover arrived in September to be crowned George I, he immediately made Marlborough captain-general of the land forces, master of the ordnance, and a privy councillor. When the Earl of Mar launched a Jacobite rising in Scotland in 1715 aimed at putting Anne's Catholic half-brother on the throne, resulting in the Battle of Preston, the last Jacobite battle on English soil, Marlborough's leadership helped suppress the attempt and ensure the stability of the Protestant succession, for which he had fought initially in 1688.

The Tory backlash to the Revolution of 1688 that had begun with the reaction to Sacheverell's impeachment trial in 1710, followed by the Tory victory in the fall elections, ended abruptly with the death of Queen Anne in August 1714. Under George I, Anne's Protestant successor and a Whig sympathizer, the Whigs regained control of Parliament in the election of 1715 and regained public approbation as the country rallied once again to fight off the Catholic Pretender to the throne. The Earl of Oxford, Viscount Bolingbroke, and the Earl of Strafford were impeached in 1715 for giving "pernicious" advice to the former queen to agree to the terms of the Treaty of Utrecht. But Parliament sought few impeachments during the rest of the eighteenth century; the final impeachment ever attempted in Britain was in 1848.[82]

The Tory backlash against the Whigs in the Parliamentary elections of 1710 did not lead to a return of the Catholic line of Stuart monarchs or to Britain's loss of its liberty to France. For the Whigs who had seen a reversal of government twice in their lifetimes already (with the return of the Stuart monarchs in 1660 and the deposition of the Catholic James II in 1688), the fear of a third reversal certainly seemed justified. Nevertheless, there was no violent overthrow of Britain's Protestant monarchical line in 1710, nor were the achievements of the 1688 Glorious Revolution reversed. Power sharing continued in Britain's system of parliamentary monarchy, and Britain saw its political disagreements play out through normal election cycles.

As moderate Whig governments were elected over the course of the next century, the Whigs in Parliament sought to placate the Tories in a variety of ways. Under George I and the first minister Robert Walpole in the 1720s, the Tories were appeased with a reduction in the land tax. Parliament also retained traditional limits on the civil rights of Dissenters: by reinstating the practice of occasional conformity (outlawed by the Tories in 1711 to reduce the number of Whigs in Parliament), the Whigs permitted Dissenters once again the limited right to hold government office if they took communion in the Church of England at least once per year.[83]

With the change from triennial to septennial elections in 1716, the vehement propaganda wars between Whig and Tory gradually diminished. While the rallying cry of "the Church in Danger" had animated Tories in 1709, it was "rarely heard after 1720." Because of real or perceived threats from the poor to the landed gentry, by 1760 there was a closing of ranks among property owners, and "a divided elite" became "a ruling class" in a "stable social order," but not a radical or progressive one.[84] In the nineteenth century this social order would be challenged as the working classes sought remedies to their lack of parliamentary representation through repeated petitions to Parliament and organized public protests. Gradually these efforts saw increased democratic representation and expanded suffrage following the Reform Acts of 1832 and 1867 and the Representation of the People Acts of 1918 and 1928, which expanded suffrage to include women.

■

None of the participants in the backlash of 1710, not even the staunchest Whigs, would have foreseen, or necessarily desired, the incremental legislative reforms over the course of the next two centuries, reforms that would lead to an increasingly representative government. Moreover, most of the central political players in 1710 faded from public view once George I came to the throne in 1714.

After Anne's death, the Duke of Marlborough did not long enjoy the fruits of his reestablishment at court. In 1716 his favorite daughter, Anne, Countess of Sunderland, died unexpectedly at age thirty-two. Shortly thereafter Marlborough suffered a stroke. Construction resumed on Blenheim Palace that year, but not until 1719 was it complete enough for the duke (incapacitated after two more strokes) and duchess to take up residence there. The duke would die in 1722, the same year his stately home, the nation's monument to victory in the Battle of Blenheim, was finally finished.

Following his year of fame, Henry Sacheverell found himself relatively ignored, once he was no longer needed as an electioneering tool for the Tories. He never rose in the church hierarchy beyond the level of parish clergyman, although he would add the rectory of St. Andrew's, Holborn, to his list of salaried positions. When the ban against his preaching was lifted in 1713, he preached a sermon on Palm Sunday at his parish of St. Saviour's in Southwark on the verse in Luke asking God to "forgive them for they know not what they do," implicitly linking his own sufferings to those of Jesus. Henry Clements, his printer in 1710, paid him £100 for the right to print the sermon, but of the 30,000 copies printed, only half that number were sold. When Sacheverell subsequently preached at St. Paul's, invited by the Corporation for the Sons of the Clergy, his procession was hissed as it passed by the Royal Exchange. After inheriting a cousin's estate in Derbyshire and marrying his cousin's widow, Sacheverell spent the rest of his life "living high," continuing to enjoy the material comforts of wealth.[85] In 1724 he slipped and broke two ribs, then died of medical complications at age forty-nine.

While Queen Anne was ill and believed to be dying, in the spring of 2014, Delarivier Manley produced her self-flattering memoir, *The Adventures of Rivella,* which appeared just six weeks before Anne's death. Knowing that the Whigs would return to power as soon as George of Hanover took the throne, Manley, who had written a begging letter to Harley, by then Earl of Oxford, in early June, coyly pointed out in the memoir that her Tory patrons had never paid her for her best-selling satires. She observed that "as to Gratitude or Generosity, the *Tories* did not come up to the *Whigs.*"[86] Perhaps seeing this as a veiled threat from a satirist to whom he had never sent any reward, a satirist, moreover, who was perfectly capable of mocking him as he was falling out of favor with Queen Anne, Oxford promptly sent Manley £50. She wrote back later that summer with suggestions of a pamphlet she could write to bolster his reputation, but no such pamphlet could have saved him.[87] In July 1715 he was impeached by the Whig Parliament for high crimes and misdemeanors and spent two years imprisoned in the Tower. He was eventually acquitted of those charges and returned to the House of Lords but took little part in public affairs during the last decade of his life. He died in early June 1724, just two weeks after Henry Sacheverell and seven weeks before Delarivier Manley, who died in late July that year.

Sarah, who became Dowager Duchess of Marlborough after her husband's death, lived for two more decades, surviving not only her husband and sons (who had died young) but also three of her four daughters. She was estranged from Henrietta, Duchess of Marlborough, until the latter's death in 1733, and from Mary, Duchess of Montagu, for many decades. Her third daughter, Elizabeth, had died of smallpox while the Marlboroughs were living abroad in 1714. Sarah was reconciled with Mary only near the end of her life. She remained close to Henrietta's daughter, Lady Diana Spencer. Sarah also eventually established a warm relationship with Henrietta's younger daughter Mary, likely fathered by Congreve.

Sarah remained active in politics her entire life. Although always a Whig in principle, she joined the opposition Whigs against Robert Walpole as he rose to power in the 1720s and served George I and George II as first minister until 1742. Sarah managed her investments and estates with an eagle eye, but she offered generous dowries to her marriageable granddaughters, particularly Lady Diana Spencer, whom she had hoped to marry into the Hanoverian royal family. Walpole intervened to prevent the match between Diana and Frederick, Prince of Wales, despite the rumored dowry of £100,000. Only in subsequent generations would female heirs of the Marlboroughs rise to political prominence: Georgianna, Duchess of Devonshire, as a political hostess and active campaigner for the Whigs in the late eighteenth century (the heroine of the film *The Duchess*), and, of course, in the twentieth century Lady Diana Spencer, who married Prince Charles in 1981 and whose sons, William and Henry, are second and sixth in line to the British throne.

The Duchess of Marlborough's memoirs, her *Account of the Conduct of the Dowager Duchess of Marlborough*, helped secure the depiction of Queen Anne as childlike and not very bright, a reputation reiterated by other Whig historians, including Gilbert Burnet and Oliver Goldsmith—one reason why Anne's real accomplishments, as one of the last British monarchs to take a fully active role in running the country, have been largely overlooked. Even on the tourist circuits at Kensington Palace and Hampton Court Palace, evidence about Anne's years as monarch must be teased out in period rooms dedicated to William and Mary's reign.

The reputations of the Marlboroughs themselves, tarnished by accusations of greed and self-serving ambition, were such that in the twentieth century Winston Churchill felt obliged to write a four-volume biography of the first Duke of Marlborough, to assert the duke's genius as a military commander and reestablish his legacy. In that work Churchill dismisses Delarivier Manley, who so boldly satirized the Marlboroughs, as a woman of "disreputable character."[88] She is now, in academic circles, recognized as a brilliant literary innovator. Henry Sacheverell, meanwhile, remains of interest mostly to small number of historians interested in early eighteenth-century British political and religious history.[89]

■

THE TORY BACKLASH to the progressive changes in government brought about by the Glorious Revolution did not ultimately reverse the increased power of Parliament over the monarch, nor did it reverse the basic tenets of the Toleration Act. The effect of the Sacheverell trial and the Tory backlash of 1710 did not so much change the course of history as change the way that history was narrated. The historian Steve Pincus has pointed out that when the Whigs were defending the Glorious Revolution during Sacheverell's impeachment trial, they "asserted with one voice that the revolution was fundamentally transformative" and that it was "ushering in a new age of civil and religious liberty buttressed by a new social agenda." Yet the Tory electoral triumph of 1710 ultimately "severed the connection between the Whig establishment and the radical interpretation of the revolution." As Pincus explains, the young MP Robert Walpole had been an eloquent proponent of "the radical reading of the revolution" during Sacheverell's trial, yet when Walpole rose to power as England's first minister in 1720, he spoke of the revolution as having brought about "parliamentary rather than popular sovereignty and that it had established a constitution rather than a blueprint for further reform."[90]

Although resulting from a political backlash, this moderated way of referring to the revolutionary power of the Glorious Revolution may actually have been beneficial to long-term social reform. It is possible that the practice, after 1710, of describing the events of 1688 as less radical than they really were facilitated gradual legislative reform, under the guise of moderation rather than revolution. Britain did not suffer the bloodshed of the French Revolution in 1789, nor did it experience the mass revolutionary uprisings across Europe in 1848. The Tory backlash of 1710, in tempering the language of revolutionary change, may in fact have enabled long-term change without another revolution. If that is the case, then perhaps we have reason to hope that the current moment of reactionary cultural backlash in the United States and the United Kingdom could lead politicians to articulate their goals for societal improvements and global cooperation in ways that are palatable to voters across the political spectrum.[91] Under this scenario, Western democracy could survive the current backlashes, international institutions could flourish, and humans could work together around the world to address urgent global problems, such as the climate crisis and the increased frequency of global pandemics predicted in a warming world.

EPILOGUE

Why the Backlash of 1710 Matters Today

THE BACKLASH against the Whigs in 1710 lasted only four years, but it offers an important historical precedent for the 2016 electoral political backlash in the United States and the United Kindom. The lessons of 1710 and its aftermath demonstrate that even in a period of political backlash, it is possible to preserve a balance of power between legislative and executive branches, support a free press, respond with some empathy to an immigration crisis, develop functioning international agreements, and aim for long-term poltical progress that will address the most urgent challenges facing humanity. Doing so, however, requires leaders willing to unite a nation by speaking across cultural and political divides, rather than playing to a single partisan base.

Queen Anne would have prefered to balance Whigs and Tories in her cabinet, even in the midst of the Tory backlash. Subsequent politicians, including the first minister Robert Walpole, learned to speak in moderate rather than radical terms about the Glorious Revolution, a savvy political strategy. In the face of the global pandemic that emerged in 2020, in the wake of the political backlash of 2016, it remains to be seen whether leaders who came to power through the partisan force of that backlash will pivot and learn to speak across the cultural chasms that divided us before we were struck by a virus that has no concern for partisan allegiance.

The backlash of 1710, like the political backlash in the United States and United Kingdom today, was as much political as cultural. The distinctions between conservatives and progressives, then as now, were not always rigidly ideological but local and cultural. For example, Sacheverell's conservative supporters in 1710 were culturally biased against religious Dissenters and sympathetic to a Church of England clergyman expressing loyalty to his queen. These supporters apparently were not necessarily opposed to the system of parliamentary monarchy put in place by the Glorious Revolution of 1688. In fact, through their populist disruptions in the name of "passive obedience" to the monarch, these protesters were paradoxically enacting an implicit right to protest government policies, a right consistent with the experience of the Glorious Revolution, during which members of Parliament convened themselves in February 1689 to declare that James II had abdicated and to offer the crown to William and Mary. Today we may identify similar paradoxes in how reactionary political players are enacting their protests against the status quo. In the United States, a political party that has traditionally aligned itself with respect for law, law enforcement, and the military defends a president who often demonstrates little respect for the rule of law, military expertise, or checks and balances in government. As in 1710, when populist protesters were apparently motivated by anti-Presbyterian sentiment rather than a philosophical objections to the Glorious Revolution, so today American's political alignments often correlate with religious affiliation.[1] Meanwhile, in the modern UK, attitudes toward Brexit appear to have been as much determined by cultural attitudes and local affiliations as by objective analysis of an exit proposal for which few details existed at the time of the 2016 referendum.[2]

At the start of the COVID-19 pandemic, both Donald Trump and Boris Johnson rallied their science-skeptical political bases by cavalierly disregarding the advice of scientists and experts to stop public gatherings. Both leaders eventually acknowledged the need for social distancing, but Trump continued to express skepticism toward scientists and medical experts. Even while announcing recommendations to the American public to wear non-medical-grade masks in public on 4 April 2020, President Trump refused to set an example by wearing one himself. Once Prime Minister Johnson was himself infected with the virus, he changed his tone. When he was hospitalized in early April, he tweeted his appreciation of the NHS, but he nevertheless left it to the monarch to speak across the partisan divide and address the nation as a whole, in a televised address on 5 April 2020.

Queen Elizabeth II's speech to the UK and the Commonwealth, at the height of the COVID-19 crisis in April, was a model of appreciation, inclusion, and unity. She thanked both front-line medical workers for their extraordinary sacrifice and ordinary citizens for staying at home. She spoke to people "people of all faiths, and of none," following the spirit of the Toleration Act of 1689. She also helped articulate a sense of identity for the UK and the entire Commonwealth, through attributes that exclude no one: "attributes of self-discipline, of quiet good-humoured resolve and of fellow-feeling."[3] In citing the UK's current monarch, I do not mean to suggest that our political future would best be protected by a reactionary return to monarchy. I refer to Elizabeth II's recent speech in the same spirit that I refer to Queen Anne's respect for parliamentary procedure and a balanced royal cabinet. Both these queens, reigning in dfferent eras of a parliamentary monarchy, have articulated, sometimes better than elected politicians, a deep respect for the procedures and protocols of governmental institutions and for a balance of power between the branches of government.

■

As I SUGGESTED in the last chapter, one significant feature of the backlash of 1710 was that it changed the way the Glorious Revolution would be spoken about in future decades, but it did not roll back the basic premises or the radical move toward democracy that that revoltion enacted. It remains to be seen whether in the United States and the United Kingdom today the current backlash movements will permanently degrade norms of shared power between different branches of government or permanently undermine public support for a free press, religious tolerance, and international institutions.

A central premise of American democracy and its balance of power between branches of government is the impeachment clause. In fact, the framers of the US Constitution agreed to create the office of president only if the person holding that office could be impeached for abuse of power.[4] The backlash of 1710, while apparently offering a cautionary tale about impeachment as a process that could backfire politically, does not represent a direct parallel to the US impeachment of President Trump in 2019 and his trial in the Senate in 2020. Sacheverell was impeached because there was not enough printed evidence to pursue a charge of libel. His prosecution was designed to set an example for outspoken Tory clergymen, whereas the members of

Congress in 2019 who voted for impeachment were trying to prevent a president from soliciting foreign interference in US elections. Those senators who voted in February 2020 to convict the president were likewise attempting to uphold the Constitution and their oaths of office, regardless of any potential political risk to themselves in the 2020 elections. Meanwhile, President Trump took advantage of the news overload surrounding the COVID-19 crisis in April 2020 to launch a further attack on our democratic system of checks and balances by terminating Inspector General Michael Atkinson, the person who was responsible for allowing a whistleblower to come forward to Congress, ultimately triggering Trump's impeachment. In the same week, he removed as the Pentagon's inspector general Glenn Fine, who had been appointed by Congress to oversee the trillions of dollas authorized in crisis-response spending, thus undermining the power of Congress to do its duty in overseeing governmental expenditure.

Threats to properly functioning government can arise either at home or emerge from abroad. The British in 1710 were justifiably concerned about the French monarch's schemes to interfere in British domestic politics through his continued political and financial support for Queen Anne's Catholic half-brother. The Duke of Marlborough had come to understand corruption as a young soldier at court, watching Charles II accept bribes from Louis XIV to reconvert England to Catholicism. It was because he understood this existential risk to his country and its national religion that he continued to put his life on the line leading the Protestant Allies in the War of Spanish Succession. Marlborough was determined to resist Louis XIV's expansionist tendencies and maintain a balance between Catholic and Protestant powers in Europe. Even the Duchess of Marlborough, for all her rudeness to Queen Anne between 1708 and 1710, was insulting to the monarch only because she felt the queen did not always understand the risks to the nation and the Church of England in not giving her full political support to the Whigs. In 1710, both the queen and the majority in Parliament understood the threat to the nation of French expansionism and foreign interference in British politics. The queen's and the Tories' decision to seek a swift, peaceful conclusion to the War of Spanish Succession ultimately did not fundamentally change the peace treaty France signed with Britain, despite Whig fears that it might. By contrast, President Trump's supporters seem to believe that "soliciting help from a foreign government for personal political gain is just not that bad."[5] President Trump, moreover, has never ceased promulgating Russian-perpetrated lies about Ukrainian interference in the 2016 US elections.

During the last four years of Queen Anne's reign, the structural foundations of Britain's parliamentary monarchy did not suffer any permanent damage because of the backlash against the Whigs. The nation's respect for the rule of law and parliamentary procedure, its increasingly unfettered press, and increasing religious toleration since 1689 all withstood the Whigs' electoral defeats in 1710 and 1713. The practice of occasional conformity was reinstated in 1714, once again allowing a loophole for Dissenters to participate in government, and more complete religious toleration eventually became the law of the land. The backlash of 1710 meant that future political leaders would refer to the Glorious Revolution of 1688 as brief, necessary, and peaceful, yet its radical long-term implications were not rolled back. Furthermore, the Treaty of Utrecht, while it did not put an end to military conflicts with other European powers, nevertheless pointed the way toward a continued international appreciation for a balance of power in Europe.

Queen Anne, whose grandfather was executed and whose father was deposed by Parliament, fully appreciated the value of checks and balances between monarchical and parliamentary power. Her respect for parliamentary procedure and the rule of law stands in contrast to the inclinations of President Trump, who often acts as if he were a monarch with more power than Anne would have dared assert. The impeachment of Sacheverell was a model of fair process, in contrast to the impeachment proceedings against President Trump, which were undermined by his blocking crucial witnesses. In 1710, the queen, members of the Houses of Parliament, and the spectators listened attentively and respectfully to eloquent legal scholars speaking on both sides of the case. In 2020 Senate Republicans prominently exhibited their boredom by playing with fidget spinners during the impeachment trial of President Trump. Furthermore, Queen Anne attempted to defuse the ensuing mob riots, whereas President Trump often encourages his supporters to demonize his political opponents. Queen Anne understood that the rhetorical tone of moderation was essential to maintaining her throne. Even when proroguing Parliament in April

1710, in the height of the Tory backlash, she reached out to Whigs in acknowledging that impeachment had been necessary.[6]

Today, President Trump frequently refers to his impeachment as a partisan "hoax," refusing the language of moderation or partisan unity. Given his indifference to Constitutional limits on his power, it remains to be seen whether the precedents of governmental checks and balances in the United States will survive his disruptive behavior, now accepted by most Republican politicians and cheered by his political base. Trump's lack of cooperation in the impeachment process and the Senate majority's resistance to taking the trial seriously threaten the future of that foundational check on the executive branch. While the modern UK has developed other kinds of checks and balances on federal officeholders, impeachment is still a core tenet of the US Constitution. If that core tenet is no longer taken seriously by a majority of elected officials, then the power of the US Constitution to maintain the integrity of our three co-equal and independent branches of government is at risk.

■

NOT ONLY DID the participants and spectators in 1710 respect the impeachment process, they also demonstrated an interest in the written transcript of Sacheverell's trial. His impeachment in 1710 became an opportunity for public speeches outlining and reiterating the fundamental principle of British government that the monarch is not above the law. The printed transcript of the trial, which remained a bestselling volume for the first half of the eighteenth century, became a public record of Revolution principles, one in which individuals and families could record their individual agreements and disagreements in marginal annotations. While interested US citizens today are still buying transcripts of President Nixon's 1972 and Bill Clinton's 1992 impeachment hearings (sales no doubt spurred by President Trump's impeachment), it is hard to predict who will want to purchase and review the transcript from the Senate impeachment trial of President Trump, a transcript lacking the testimony of key witnesses, since the Senate chose not to call any.

The political pamphlet wars of 1710 not only foreshadowed the virulent partisan political divides in many countries today, they also anticipated the ever-increasing pace of the news cycle. While the official printed version of the trial would remain in print for decades, ephemeral pamphlets and broadsheets were being printed and distributed almost daily. Every time a pamphleteer offered "A True Account" of some aspect of the Sacheverell trial, he or she inevitably suggested that a prior pamphlet had offered merely misleading information (or fake news) about the same event. The speed and frequency of these partisan publications were fueled by the rise of the popular press after the expiration of the last Licensing Act in 1695, as well as by the gradually decreasing costs of paper and print production.

Whereas today one result of the barrage of unverifiable posts on social media is an overall distrust of the media, the pamphlet wars over Sacheverell often demonstrated a level of public appreciation of the newly liberated press. The Duchess of Marlborough embraced the value of an unfettered press in her impulse to counter Tory pamphlets with Whig ones, rather than prosecuting satirists for libel. She admired the talent of the satirist Jonathan Swift even when he was writing for the Tories. This type of public support for press freedom continues today, despite attacks on the press by some political leaders, including President Trump in the United States, who regularly asserts that it should be easier to sue news organizations for defamation.[7] The best cure for fake news will not be government censorship but better real-time fact-checking systems, with continued efforts taken to protect against foreign and computer-generated interference.[8]

■

THE PERSONAL attacks against the Marlboroughs—who were devoted to what they felt was best for the future of the country, even if they also felt comfortable profiting handsomely from royal favor—show the political costs of tone-deaf elitism, a charge sometimes leveled today against Democratic leaders in the United States or Labour leaders in the UK.[9] Whereas many "liberal elites" today espouse genuinely progressive policies, the Marlboroughs, like other Whigs in the landed gentry and nobility, did not necessarily embrace the fully democratizing potential of the Revolution principles of 1688. Although Whig attitudes toward Protestantism and Parliament were liberal, the Whig powerbrokers of the early eighteenth century were not radical progressives.

Worried about the dangerous populist mobs during the elections of 1710, most Whigs during the reign of Queen Anne also did not believe that the social contract between subject and sovereign implied by the Glorious Revolution should lead the country to fully representative government. After the Tories passed an act in 1711 requiring minimum landholdings for anyone elected to Parliament (thus giving an electoral advantage to traditional Tory landowners over Whig merchant classes), the Whigs did not repeal this rule when they regained power in 1714 but sought workarounds for property requirements for wealthy merchants, thus keeping government offices in the hands of the wealthy (whether old landed wealth or new merchant money). The act would not be repealed until 1858, as part of the mid-nineteenth-century electoral reforms, including the Reform Acts of 1832 and 1867.[10] However, even if the Whigs during the reign of Queen Anne had not envisioned a more fully democratic government, their insistence on upholding the principles of a parliamentary monarchy meant that Parliament could and would incrementally pass laws that would lead the country gradually to a more inclusive democracy.

One positive result of the virulent party strife of Queen Anne's reign was a slight change to the election system with the passage of the Septennial Act in 1716. Less frequent elections meant fewer seasons of the sort of politicking and mob behavior seen in the autumn of 1710. That structural reform suggests that slight structural reforms today (for example, retooling partisan electoral districting systems to reduce the polarizing forces of gerrymandering) might likewise help temper partisan factionalism in the United States. It is also possible that President Trump's pattern of refusing to submit to Congress or the courts documents requested in investigations will eventually result in Congress passing new legislation that spells out more specific checks over a future president. Depending on the partisan makeup of Congress and the Senate after the 2020 elections, laws could be passed requiring release of tax returns and financial documents for all elected officials that could elucidate corrupt presidential dealings with foreign or domestic entities. More stringent penalties could also be instated (and enforced) against officeholders who refuse to cooperate in investigations. The best-case scenario for a post-Trump United States would be reinvigorated participation in our democracy, as well as increased government transparency, accountability, and respect for the rule of law.

■

THE BACKLASH of 1710, insofar as it was abetted by the crisis of the "Palatine" refugees, also predicts the political unease today generated by immigrants seeking political asylum or relief from climate-change-induced poverty. The experience of 1710 does not offer an obvious solution, since many of the German-speaking refugees, initially welcomed by the government and the queen, were simply parceled off elsewhere, to rural England, to America, or back to the Continent, thus ending the complaints about the newcomers in London but not offering a viable model for resolving twenty-first-century immigration crises. The anti-immigrant sentiment, then as now, only demonstrates that politicians around the world will need to develop new ways of approaching the challenges of displaced persons, especially as that displacement increases as the planet continues to warm. At the same time, attitudes toward immigrants may also change, depending on the language used to refer to them. As the world is discovering during the COVID-19 crisis, seasonal workers from eastern Europe, blocked by border closures, are essential to harvesting crops in western Europe.[11] In the United States, immigrant field workers, often undocumented, were receiving letters from the Department of Homeland Security in early spring 2020 designating them "critical to the food supply chain."[12] While this is not a permanent change to the status of these workers, politically it may become more feasible eventually to grant such works legal status when they are viewed as "essential workers" rather than "illegal aliens."

Domestic political backlashes can also inflect foreign policy. Queen Anne understood the value of the Act of Union, which in 1707 joined Scotland with England and Wales (which had become part of the Kingdom of England under Henry VIII, in the 1540s) to form the nation of Great Britain. That union may not withstand the jolt of Brexit, which may potentially reduce England and Wales without Scotland to the status of a little Britain, greatly diminished in national and international importance. While this dissolution may offer some advantages to the individual nations of Scotland, Ireland, England, and Wales, it may not be a change that improves the lives of the inhabitants of those countries.[13] The Union of 1707, now at risk today, was initially a model for future political unions, including the United States. John Jay, in defending the necessity of a unified federal government in *The Federalist Papers,* cited from Queen Anne's letter to the Scottish Parliament in 1706, in which the queen described it as "the solid foundation of lasting peace."[14] The Union of 1707, by extension, may be understood as something of a precursor to the European Union itself, a union that demonstrates the advantages for peace and prosperity when groups of nations voluntarily establish forms of shared governance.

Although it was not popular in Scotland when first instituted, the Union of 1707 gradually increased in popularity because of the economic advantages to both countries of opening markets to each other. Incremental changes in the precise political structure of the Union have gradually addressed the concerns of Scotland and Wales (which experienced secondary status to Britain in the initial years of the Union), including most recently the institution of Scottish and Welsh national parliaments. Britain could have followed that model of seeking incremental changes to the EU as a member nation, rather than exposing itself to the economic risk and uncertainty posed by Brexit. Meanwhile, a weakend EU post-Brexit has been further challenged by the international border closures necessitated by the COVID-19 pandemic.

■

While the Whigs in 1710 felt that the future of Protestant Britain and Europe was at stake in their war against an autocratic French Catholic monarch, today we face an even greater and more existential crisis. With the onset of climate change of such severity and pace as to threaten the future of the human race, we find ourselves hobbled by partisan politics so virulent that Republicans in the United States today deny the scientific basis of climate change more strongly than they did in 1979, a denial that threatens the very existence of our species—and many more.[15] Certain innovative climate protestors in Britain articulated the urgency of this threat, in contrast to the stalemates in government institutions, in presenting themselves naked in the viewing galleries of Parliament during a debate about Brexit in April 2019. This protest was quickly shut down by security guards, while the political tribes for and against Brexit remained in a stalemate in their partisan blinders, much as the response to the climate crisis has been paralyzed by partisan politics in the United States.[16] Meanwhile, in a post-Brexit world, the fate of the most prominent such international body, the EU, appears likewise to be at the mercy of political partisanship, both at the national level and at the level of international institutions.

Current psychological research suggests that humans are hard-wired for tribal loyalty, as Ezra Klein has detailed in *Why We're Polarized.* Moreover, our tribal loyalties are frequently signaled by our cultural identities—including our religion, our educational background, and even our choice of neighborhood. Despite the way partisan difference appears to be baked into our cultural differences, Klein suggests that there are concrete things we can do to work against it. In the United States, we could reinvigorate democracy in presidential elections by abolishing the Electoral College and in congressional elections level through systems of either proportional representation or ranked-choice voting. In the United States, the UK, and around the world, we might also learn to develop what Klein terms "identity mindfulness," in which we practice being "mindful of which of our identities are being activated, so that we can become intentional about which identities we work to activate."[17]

Suggesting that we respond to a partisan political crisis by being more mindful may seem naïve, but becoming aware and alert to the way we perceive and categorize others is a necessary part of any cultural change.[18] In 1991 Susan Faludi opened the world's eyes to the cultural backlash against feminism in her groundbreaking book *Backlash: The Undeclared War against Women,* and feminists have been responding to that backlash in innovative ways ever since. While there is still a long way to go for women, the world has now experienced the power of the #MeToo movement and seen a female presidential candidate win the popular vote, if not the presidency, in the United States. Even at the worst moment of disappointment after that electoral loss in 2016 (in part explained by a continued backlash against women seeking power), there was a spontaneous cultural outpouring of energy against that backlash, prompting the Women's March and the political movements stemming from it. Those movements demonstrate how the progressive response to a reactionary backlash can become an opportunity for positive progress. As Cass Sunstein has documented, changes in cultural norms can sometimes occur swiftly in "norm cascades."[19]

While the backlash of 1710 was over by 1714, with the succession of George I and the election of a Whig majority in Parliament, we cannot yet tell whether we will address the current political backlash and partisan stalemates in the United States, the UK, or many other countries around the world in time to effectively take up pressing global problems, from climate change to new global pandemics (predicted to increase in frequency with global warming) that require not only functioning national governments but functioning international institutions.[20] As COVID-19 spreads around the globe in 2020, democracy faces further risk as some national leaders exert increasingly autocratic power in their attempts to control the spread of the virus. Yet research on whether democracies or autocracies are better positioned to respond to a pandemic suggests that democracies "hold a clear advantage" in such a response because of "the flow of information and public give-and-take" of ideas.[21] In considering the importance of this free flow of information, we will need to be vigilant to protect against fake news and misleading pronouncements. The first several months of the COVID-19 crisis unfortunately demonstrated the dangers to humanity of reactionary leaders with a disregard for expertise in science, medicine, and logistics management.

It remains to be seen whether democracy as we know it, currently incapacitated by stalemate between opposing political parties, will be adequate to elect national leaders who are able to resist the forces of authoritarianism, maintain a public exchange of ideas, and address humanity's future from a global perspective. One possible outcome of the unfolding tragedy of COVID-19 is the rise of authoritarianism and the suppression of democracy in the name of necessity. Another possibility is, as John Ikenberry suggests, that "over the longer term, the democracies will come out of their shells to find a new type of pragmatic and protective internationalism."[22] Daily we watch citizens rally together across party lines to address basic human needs in life-or-death situations. Inasmuch as we and our elected representatives in government can cross party lines to address the current medical and economic crises, we may become more inclined to work together to rebuild national and international institutions and infrastructures that leave us better prepared for future crises. Our elected leaders must also inspire us to build that future in language that speaks to citizens on both sides of a partisan divide. Nothing less than the future of humanity depends on it.

NOTES

Introduction

1. In *The Favourite,* Anne is portrayed as overweight, petulant, and not very bright. Director Yorgos Lanthimos depicts an infantilized monarch caught between two scheming lovers—Sarah, Duchess of Marlborough, and her cousin, the bedchamber woman Abigail Masham, each a caricature of power-hungry ambition. While beautifully acted and filmed, *The Favourite* does not do justice to what really occurred that year in history, the winter of 1709–10, or to the monarch who was on the throne.
2. Steve Pincus argues that the standard centrist Whig version of history emphasizes the brief and unradical nature of the Revolution of 1688–89 while he recognizes its radical nature, suggesting that it "was an inspiration for late-eighteenth-century revolutionaries in France, in North America, and elsewhere." See Pincus, *1688,* 21, 477.
3. See Pincus, *1688,* 21. He is taking the reevaluation of history further than Herbert Butterfield did in *The Whig Interpretation of History.*
4. Bruno Latour points out that "to reject modernization is also to *resist courageously* by refusing to trade one's own province for another—Wall Street, Beijing, or Brussels—that is even narrower and above all infinitely remote, thus much more indifferent to local interests." See Latour, *Down to Earth,* 15.
5. Churchill, *Marlborough,* 1:53.

1. A "Very Murdering" Battle and a Salacious Court Memoir

1. Malplaquet today is on the French side of the Franco-Belgian border. At the time, Belgium didn't exist.
2. Pointon, "Material Manouvres," 485–515.
3. Duke of Marlborough to the Duchess of Marlborough, 10 Sept. 1709, in Churchill, *Marlborough,* 2:600.
4. Duchess of Marlborough to Queen Anne, 24 July 1708: British Library (BL) Add. MS 61417, f. 153v.
5. Duchess of Marlborough to [Sir David Hamilton], 6 Dec. [1710]: BL Add. MS 61423 f. 36. See also Carnell, "The 'Lye' of Queen Anne's Lesbianism," 565–67.

6. There were three groups of personal servants to female royalty: ten ladies of the bedchamber, all peeresses; four to six bedchamber women, responsible for services such as dressing the queen; and maids of honor, who worked in the drawing room. Frances Harris, "The Honourable Sisterhood: Queen Anne's Maids of Honour," *Electronic British Library Journal,* 1993, 181–98, https://www.bl.uk/eblj/1993articles/pdf/article13.pdf.
7. The significance of Sarah's lack of adornment was of much greater magnitude than, for example, the possible meaning of Queen Elizabeth II's choice of brooch during President Trump's visit to the UK in July 2018. Freeman, "Was the Queen Sending Coded Messages to Donald Trump via Her Brooches?"
8. Churchill, *Marlborough,* 2:417.
9. Duke of Marlborough to Duchess of Marlborough, [29–31 Aug. 1709], in *The Marlborough-Godolphin Correspondence,* ed. Snyder, 3:1359.
10. Duke of Marlborough to Earl of Godolphin, [31 Aug. 1709], in *The Marlborough-Godolphin Correspondence,* ed. Snyder, 3:1360.
11. Anquetil, *Histoire de France depuis les Gaulois jusqu'à la mort de Louis XVI,* 10:164. My translation.
12. Manley, *The New Atalantis,* in *Selected Works,* 2:238.
13. Ibid., 2:238.
14. Ibid., 2:20.
15. Duchess of Marlborough to Mr. Malet, cited in Field, *The Favourite,* 15; Francis Hare to Duchess of Marlborough 24 Sept. 1726: BL Add. MS 61464, f. 84.
16. Hamilton, *Memoirs of Count de Grammont,* 351.
17. See [Brémond], *Hattige,* 80. This work is regularly misattributed to Gabriel Brémond. E. P. Grobe establishes that Sébastien, not Gabriel, Brémond wrote *Hattigé.* Grobe, "Gabriel and Sébastien Brémond," 132–35.
18. Nye, "Pounds Sterling to Dollars."
19. Evelyn, *The Diary of Sir John Evelyn,* 744.
20. Harris, *A Passion for Government,* 14.
21. Lady Chaworth to Lord Roos, 23 Nov. [1676], in Rutland, *Manuscripts of his Grace the Duke of Rutland* (HMC *Rutland MSS*), 2:32.
22. Sarah Jenyns to John Churchill [n.d.]: BL Add. MS 61427, f. 30.
23. Marvell, *An Account of the Growth of Popery,* 1.
24. The example of Charles II taking bribes from Louis XIV would be one reason why, just over a century later, American delegates to the Constitutional Convention of 1787 would draft the emolument clause, forbidding federal officeholders from accepting "any present, Emolument,

Office, or Title, or any kind whatever, from any King, Prince, or foreign state."

25. Tribe and Matz, *To End a Presidency,* 5, 2.
26. Hoffer and Hull, *Impeachment in America,* 4. See also Bowman, *High Crimes and Misdemeanors,* 22–39.
27. American delegates to the Constitutional Convention in 1787 would give Congress the power to impeach a president (or other federal officeholder) so as to avoid the "tumults & insurrections" that would be the only other option against a sitting ruler guilty of "high Crimes and Misdemeanors." Tribe and Matz, *To End a Presidency,* 6, ii; Sunstein, *Impeachment,* 149.
28. Queen Anne to Sarah Churchill, [1683], cited in Field, *The Favourite,* 43.
29. Queen Anne to Sarah Churchill, 1685, cited in Field, *The Favourite,* 44.
30. Somerset, *Queen Anne,* 53.
31. Marlborough, *Memoirs of Sarah, Duchess of Marlborough,* 255.
32. Pincus, *1688,* 6–7.
33. Churchill, *Marlborough,* 1:240.
34. John Churchill to William of Orange, 4 Aug. 1688, facsimile reprint in Churchill, *Marlborough,* 1:240.
35. Pincus refutes the standard model of the Glorious Revolution (promoted by nineteenth-century historians) as "bloodless, consensual, aristocratic, and above all sensible." See Pincus, *1688,* 5.
36. Speck, "James II and VII."
37. Narrative by Duchess of Marlborough for Elizabeth Burnet: BL Add. MS 61421, f. 72.
38. Pincus, *1688,* 6–7.
39. Churchill, *Marlborough,* 1:309.
40. Princess Anne to Countess of Marlborough: BL Add. MS 61415 f. 37, cited in Somerset, *Queen Anne,* 143.
41. [Defoe], *The True Born Englishman,* 20.
42. Field, *The Favourite,* 49.
43. Manley, *The New Atalantis,* in *Selected Works,* 2:239.
44. Duchess of Marlborough to Queen Anne, [27 Aug. 1706]: BL Add. MS 61417, f. 20r–v.
45. Field, *The Favourite,* 171.
46. Marlborough, *Memoirs of Sarah, Duchess of Marlborough,* 156.
47. Hearne, *Remarks and Collections,* 2:265.
48. Manley, *The New Atalantis,* in *Selected Works,* 2:234.
49. Earl of Sunderland to Duchess of Marlborough, 4 Nov. 1709: BL Add. MS 61443, f. 35.

2. Secret History and Seditious Libel

1. Secretaries of State, State Papers, Criminal Correspondence and Warrents: Sunderland, arrest warrant signed 28 Oct. 1709: TNA SP 44/78:64.
2. See Hamburger, "The Development of the Law of Seditious Libel and the Control of the Press," 735.
3. Ibid.
4. Earl of Sunderland to Duchess of Marlborough, 4 Nov. 1709: BL Add. MS 61443, f. 35.
5. Sarah, Duchess of Marlborough, to Queen Anne, [Nov.] 1709, cited in Marlborough, *Private Correspondence of Sarah, Duchess of Marlborough,* 1:244.
6. Manley, *The Adventures of Rivella,* in *Selected Works,* 4:55
7. Ibid., 4:13.
8. Manley, *The New Atalantis,* in *Selected Works,* 2:254
9. Manley, *The Adventures of Rivella,* in *Selected Works,* 4:12, 4:10. Manley herself does not liken her own hair to the Duchess of Marlborough's, but the latter was known for her abundant, beautiful ash-colored (i.e., reddish gold) hair.
10. Manley, *The New Atalantis,* in *Selected Works,* 2:256.
11. Carnell, *A Political Biography of Delarivier Manley,* 11, 72.
12. Manley, *The New Atalantis,* in *Selected Works,* 2:255–56.
13. Carnell, *A Political Biography of Delarivier Manley,* 75.
14. Churchill, *Marlborough,* 1:53.
15. Manley, *The Adventures of Rivella,* in *Selected Works,* 4:10.
16. Manley, *The New Atalantis,* in *Selected Works,* 2:257–58.
17. Ibid., 2:257.
18. Manley, *The Adventures of Rivella,* in *Selected Works,* 4:21.
19. Ibid., 4:21.
20. Ibid., 4:20.
21. Ibid., 4:21.
22. Ibid., 4:11, 4:10.
23. W. M., *The Female Wits,* 22.
24. Carnell, *A Political Biography of Delarivier Manley,* 115, 134.
25. Summary of a letter from "Dela Manley" to [the Duke of Montagu], n.d., in Buccleuch and Queensberry, *Report on the Manuscripts of The Duke of Buccleuch and Queensberry* (HMC *Buccleur and Queensberry MSS*), 1:357.
26. *Life and Character of John Barber,* 12.
27. Ibid., 10.
28. Manley, *The Adventures of Rivella,* in *Selected Works,* 4:58.

29. Manley, *The New Atalantis,* in *Selected Works,* 2:18.
30. Ibid., 2:3.
31. Lady Mary Pierrepont to Mrs. Frances Hewet, [Oct. 1709], in Montagu, ed. Halsbad, *The Complete Letters of Lady Mary Wortley Montagu,* 1:17.
32. Manley, *The New Atalantis,* in *Selected Works,* 2:120.
33. Hawkins, *A Treatise of the Pleas of the Crown,* 1:194; see also Carnell, *A Political Biography of Manley,* 182.
34. Manley, *The New Atalantis,* in *Selected Works,* 2:20.
35. Ibid., 2:21.
36. Manley, *The Adventures of Rivella,* in *Selected Works,* 4:21.
37. Manley, *The New Atalantis,* in *Selected Works,* 2:21.
38. Ibid., 2:22.
39. Ibid., 2:219.
40. Ibid., 2:33.
41. Ibid., 2:42.
42. Ibid., 2:44. In fact, Machievelli makes a somewhat different point in book I, chapter 27, of his *Discourses:* "No man can be exquisitely wicked, no more than good in perfection." See Machiavelli, *The Works of the Famous Nicholas Machiavel,* 297.
43. Anne to Sarah, Duchess of Marlborough, [22 May 1703], in Brown, *The Letters and Diplomatic Instructions of Queen Anne,* 125.
44. Harris, *A Passion for Government,* 92.
45. This work was once presumed to have been written by Manley but has subsequently been attributed to Browne. See Downie, "'What If Delarivier Manley Did *Not* Write *The Secret History of Queen Zarah?*,'" 247–64.
46. Manley, *New Atalantis,* in *Selected Works,* 2:226.
47. Ibid., 2:229.
48. Ibid., 2:230.
49. Diary of Lady Sarah Cowper, entry for 19 July 1709: Hertfordshire Archives: DE/P/F33:11,10.
50. Manley, *The New Atalantis,* in *Selected Works,* 2:233, 2:234.
51. Ibid., 2:234.
52. Ibid., 2:237.
53. Ibid., 2:238.
54. Ibid., 2:238.
55. Ibid., 2:238.
56. Ibid., 2:239.
57. Secretaries of State, State Papers, Criminal Correspondence and Warrents: Sunderland, arrest warrant signed 28 October 1709: TNA SP 44/78:64.
58. Manley, *The New Atalantis,* in *Selected Works,* 2:239, 2:240.

59. Arthur Maynwaring to the Duchess of Marlborough, [late Oct. 1709], in Marlborough, *Private Correspondence of Sarah, Duchess of Marlborough,* 1:236.
60. Swift, *Journal to Stella,* 28 Jan. 1712, 2:474
61. Manley, *The Adventures of Rivella,* in *Selected Works,* 4:54.
62. Ibid., 4:55.
63. Marlborough, *Memoirs of Sarah, Duchess of Marlborough,* 62.

3. A Provocative Tory Sermon

1. Holmes, *The Trial of Doctor Sacheverell,* 12.
2. Bisset, *The Modern Fanatick,* 1–2
3. Cited in Tinniswood, *His Invention So Fertile,* 31.
4. Sacheverell, *The Perils of False Brethren,* 3.
5. Ibid., 25.
6. Holmes, *The Trial of Dr. Sacheverell,* 81.
7. Sacheverell, *The Perils of False Brethren,* 37.
8. Holmes, *The Trial of Doctor Sacheverell,* 21.
9. Sacheverell, dedicatory preface to *The Perils of False Brethren,* sig. A3v, A4r.
10. Holmes, *The Trial of Doctor Sacheverell,* 50.
11. [Kennett], *A Visit to St Saviour's, Southwark,* 16, 9–10.
12. Holmes, *The Trial of Doctor Sacheverell,* 4n.
13. Katherine Hearst to Robert Cox, 1 Jan. 1711, in [King], *A Vindication of the Reverend Dr. Henry Sacheverell,* 15.
14. Holmes, *The Trial of Doctor Sacheverell,* 9; Bisset, *The Modern Fanatick,* 21.
15. Bisset, *The Modern Fanatick,* 19.
16. Comments by Lady Clobery, mother-in-law of Sir Charles Holt, whom Sacheverell served as curate, cited in a letter from William Wiston, in Bisset, *Modern Fanatick,* 2:20 (italics reversed).
17. Bisset, *The Modern Fanatick,* 27.
18. Geoffrey Holmes offers these two explanations for Sacheverell being granted a doctorate at an earlier age than more accomplished scholars. See Holmes, *The Trial of Doctor Sacheverell,* 16.
19. Hearne, *Remarks and Collections,* 2:229; the translation is by Geoffrey Holmes, *The Trial of Doctor Sachverell,* 13.
20. Bisset, *The Modern Fanatick,* 63.
21. [Defoe], *The Shortest way with the Dissenters,* 29.
22. Holmes, *The Trial of Doctor Sacheverell,* 58.
23. Sacheverell, *The Perils of False Brethren,* 31.

24. Ibid., 40.
25. Holmes, *The Trial of Doctor Sacheverell,* 63.
26. Cited in Bisset, *The Modern Fanatick,* 24.
27. Sundstrom, "Sidney Godolphin."
28. Papers of first Earl of Shaftesbury: TNA (PRO), 30/24/21:101–102.
29. Evelyn, *The Life of Mrs. Godolphin,* 48–49.
30. Godolphin to the Duchess of Marlborough, 19 Aug. 1709: BL Add. MS 61434, f. 85.
31. Manley, *The New Atalantis,* in *Selected Works,* 2:239.
32. Sacheverell, *The Perils of False Brethren,* 4.
33. Godolphin to Duchess, 5 Nov. [1709], in *The Marlborough-Godolphin Correspondence,* ed. Snyder, 3:1405.
34. Godolphin to Duchess, 5 Nov. 1709, ibid., 3:1405–6.
35. Godolphin to Marlborough, 14 Oct. 1709, ibid., 3:1399.
36. Godolphin to Marlborough, 18 Oct. 1709, ibid., 3:1400.
37. Manley, *The New Atalantis,* in *Selected Works,* 2:20.
38. Anne to Duchess of Marlborough, [24 Oct. 1702]: BL Add. MS 61416 f. 24.
39. Harris, *A Passion for Government,* 91, citing Marlborough, *Memoirs of Sarah, Duchess of Marlborough,* 255; Queen to Duchess, 21 Nov. [1704], in *The Letters and Diplomatic Instructions of Queen Anne,* ed. Brown, 100.
40. Anne to Countess of Marlborough, [June 1703]: BL Add. MS 61416, f. 95, f. 93.
41. Anne to Duchess of Marlborough, [16 Oct. 1703]: BL Add. MS 61416, f. 139v.
42. Lady Pye to Abigail Harley, 14 Apr. 1703, in Beuccleuch and Queensbury, *Report on the Manuscripts of the Duke of Buccleugh and Queensbury* (HMC *Buccleugh and Queensbury MSS*), 4:59.
43. Duchess of Marlborough to Queen Anne, 24 July 1708: BL Add. MS 61417, f. 153v.
44. Arthur Maynwaring refers to the Duchess of Marlborough's recounting of Anne's comment in a letter to her, Dec. 1709, in Marlborough, *Private Correspondence of Sarah, Duchess of Marlborough,* 1:264. See also Sarah's reference to Anne having said "you thought you might love who you please." Duchess to Queen, 24 July 1708: BL Add. MS 61417 f. 157r.
45. Princess of Denmark to Countess of Marlborough, [6 Sept. 1692]: BL Add. MS 61415 f. 17; see also Harris, *A Passion for Government,* 66.
46. Maynwaring to Duchess of Marlborough, [Apr.–May 1710]: BL Add. MS 61461, f. 30. For Montagu's ostensible compliment to Manley, see Manley, *The Adventures of Rivella,* in *Selected Works,* 4:49.
47. Hamilton, *Memoirs of Count de Grammont,* 312.

48. Duke of Marlborough to the Duchess, [20 Apr. 1708], in *The Marlborough-Godolphin Correspondence,* ed. Snyder, 2:951; Harris, *A Passion for Government,* 144.
49. Lady Wentworth to Lord Raby, 1 Aug. 1710, in Wentworth, *The Wentworth Papers, 1705–1739,* ed. Cartwright, 127.
50. Maynwaring to Duchess of Marlborough, [April 1708], in Marlborough, *Private Correspondence of Sarah, Duchess of Marlborough,* 1:127.
51. Harris, *A Passion for Government,* 144.
52. Narrative by the Duchess of Marlborough about her loss of favor, c. 1709–12: BL Add. MS 61425, f. 122v; narrative vindicating the Duchess of Marlborough's financial management, compiled by her chaplain, Dr. Wadcock Priest, [1713]: BL Add. MS 61422 f.15v.
53. Cited in Geary, *Royal Friendship,* 120.
54. Marlborough to the Duchess of Marlborough, 2 Aug. 1708, in *The Marlborough-Godolphin Correspondence,* ed. Snyder, 2:1049.
55. Maynwaring to Duchess of Marlborough, Apr. 1708, in Marlborough, *Private Correspondence of Sarah, Duchess of Marlborough,* 1:129.
56. Harris, *A Passion for Government,* 161.
57. Godolphin to the Duchess of Marlborough, [1 Nov. 1709], in *The Marlborough Godolphin Correspondence,* ed. Snyder, 3:1403.
58. Duchess to Queen 29 Oct. 1709: BL Add. MS 61418 ff. 20–32.
59. Harris, *A Passion for Government,* 161.
60. Marlborough, *Memoirs of Sarah, Duchess of Marlborough,* 187.
61. Queen Anne to Duchess of Marlborough, [7 Nov. 1709], in Gregg, *Queen Anne,* 295.
62. Maynwaring to Duchess of Marlborough, [late Oct. 1709], in Marlborough, *Private Correspondence of Sarah, Duchess of Marlborough,* 1:238.
63. Maynwaring to Duchess of Marlborough, [late Oct. 1709], ibid., 1:237–39.
64. Duchess of Marlborough to Queen Anne, [Oct. 1709], ibid., 1:244.
65. Queen Anne to Marlborough, 25 Oct. 1709, in Anne, *The Letters and Diplomatic Instructions of Queen Anne,* ed. Brown, 285–86.
66. Duchess of Marlborough to [David Hamilton], 22 Dec. 1710, citing Anne's letter of 26 Oct. 1709: BL Add. MS 61423, f. 65v-66r.
67. Duchess of Marlborough to Queen Anne, [1709], in Marlborough, *Private Correspondence of Sarah, Duchess of Marlborough,* 1:246.
68. Field, *The Favourite,* 46.
69. Narrative draft by Duchess of Marlborough relating to her relations with Queen Anne, c.1704–1730: Add. MS 61426 ff. 5, 7.
70. Somerset, *Queen Anne,* 364.

71. Duchess of Marlborough to [Sir David Hamilton], 6 Dec. [1710]: BL Add. MS 61423 f. 36. See also Carnell, "The Lye of Queen Anne's Lesbianism," 565.
72. Marlborough, *Memoirs of Sarah, Duchess of Marlborough,* 10.
73. Duke of Marlborough to the Duchess of Marlborough, 26 Aug. 1709, in *The Marlborough-Godolphin Correspondence,* ed. Snyder, 3:1345.
74. Burnet, *Bishop Burnet's History of His Own Time,* 5:440n.
75. Maynwaring to Duchess of Marlborough, 3 Nov. 1709: BL Add. MS 61460, ff. 74–75:
76. Hearne, *Remarks and Collections,* 2:304.
77. Ibid., 2:306.
78. Peter Wentworth to Thomas Wentworth, Lord Raby, 16 Dec. 1709, in Wentworth, *The Wentworth Papers, 1705–1739,* ed. Cartwright, 99.
79. Holmes, *The Trial of Doctor Sacheverell,* 74.
80. Ibid., 75.
81. Hearne, *Remarks and Collections,* 2:320.

4. The General Who Would Be King

1. James Brydges to Henry St. John, in Snyder, *The Marlborough-Godolphin Correspondence,* 3:1405 n2.
2. Queen Anne to Marlborough 25 Oct. 1709, in Anne, *The Letters and Diplomatic Instructions of Queen Anne,* ed. Brown, 286.
3. Churchill, *Marlborough,* 2:641.
4. Ibid., 2:643.
5. Snyder, "The Duke of Marlborough's Request of His Captain-Generalcy for Life," 75.
6. Hearne, *Remarks and Collections,* 2:265.
7. Churchill, *Marlborough,* 2:643.
8. Luttrell, *Brief Historical Relation of State Affairs from September 1678 to April 1714,* 6:511
9. Arthur Maynwaring to the Duchess of Marlborough, [latter part of 1709], in Marlborough, *Private Correspondence of Sarah, Duchess of Marlborough,* 1:270.
10. Bennett, *White Kennett, 1660–1728, Bishop of Peterborough,* 105.
11. Hearne, *Remarks and Collections,* 2:313.
12. John, Duke of Marlborough, to Comte Maffey, 25 Nov. 1709, in Marlborough, *The Letters and Dispatches of John Churchill, First Duke of Marlborough,* ed. Murray, 2:657.

13. Lady Mary Pierrepont to Mrs. Frances Hewet, 12 Nov. [1709], in Montagu, *The Complete Letters of Lady Mary Wortley Montagu,* ed. Halsbad, 1:18.
14. Ibid., 1:18.
15. Secretaries of State, State Papers, Criminal Correspondence and Warrents: Sunderland, arrest warrant for author and printers of *The Rehearsal,* 11 November 1709: TNA SP 44/78:63.
16. Steele, *Tatler,* 3 Sept. 1709, Steele, *The Tatler,* 1:439–40.
17. Montagu, *The Complete Letters of Lady Mary Wortley Montagu,* ed. Halsbad, 1:19.
18. Manley cites portions of this letter to her in her satirical dedicatory preface to *Memoirs of Europe,* in *Selected Works,* 3:8.
19. Steele, *Tatler* 92 (10 Nov. 1709), 2:74.
20. Avery, *The London Stage, 1660–1800,* 1:200.
21. Banks, *The Unhappy Favourite,* 35.
22. The line is known as the Godolphin Arabian. The progeny, including the renowned Seabiscuit, are still winning races today.
23. Congreve, *The Tears of Amaryllis for Amyntas,* 2, 6, 3.
24. Ibid., 7, 8.
25. *A Satyr against Love,* 3, 7, 9, 8.
26. Papers relating to the Duchess of Marlborough's "Green Book," where she narrated accounts of her quarrels with her children, [1722–44]: BL Add. MS 61451, f. 20.
27. Lady Strafford to Thomas, Earl of Strafford [formerly Lord Raby], 27 Nov. 1711, in Wentworth, *The Wentworth Papers, 1705–1739,* ed. Cartwright, 214.
28. Will of William Congreve, PRO (now TNA) B 11/677:139–141.
29. Marlborough, *Memoirs of Sarah, Duchess of Marlborough,* 10.
30. *A Satyr against Love,* 7.
31. Holmes, *The Trial of Doctor Sacheverell,* 86.
32. Walpole, *The Works of Horace Walpole,* 3:362. This often cited comment (e.g., in the entry on the Kit-Cat Club in the *Oxford Dictionary of National Biography* and elsewhere) is usually cited from Horace Walpole, *Memoirs of the Reign of King George II,* ed. J. Brooke, 3 vols. (New Haven, CT: Yale University Press, 1985), 1:186. However, it is not found on that page (or anywhere in that work) but rather in his comments about the Kit-Cat paintings of Godfrey Kneller, included in the 1798 edition of his works.
33. Holmes, *British Politics in the Age of Anne,* 298.
34. Holmes, *The Trial of Doctor Sacheverell,* 87.
35. Cunningham, *The History of Great Britain from the Revolution of 1688 to the Accession of George the First,* 2:276.

36. The procedure for trying holders of high office for crimes of high treason at the court of the King's (or Queen's) Bench, used only seventy times between 1376 and 1806, is obsolete in the modern UK, having "been superseded by other forms of accountability." Caird, *Impeachment,* 3.
37. Hoffer and Hull, *Impeachment in America,* 4.
38. Bowman, *High Crimes and Misdemeanors,* 22–33.
39. Caird, *Impeachment,* 6, 4.
40. The relative frequency of impeachment in Britain in the seventeenth century meant that it was familiar practice to American colonists, and would then be incorporated into many state constitutions after the American Revolution and adopted in 1787 as the legislative branch's ultimate check on misuses of power by the executive and judicial branches of the US government. Hoffer and Hull, *Impeachment in America,* 4.
41. Cunningham, *The History of Great Britain from the Revolution of 1688 to the Accession of George the First,* 2:277.
42. Hoffer and Hull, *Impeachment in America,* 7. In 2019, a similar judgment about giving bad advice was pronounced by the UK Supreme Court against Prime Minister Boris Johnson for his request to Queen Elizabeth to prorogue Parliament in the midst of debates about Brexit (before the withdrawal deadline of October 31, 2019). Since impeachment is no longer part of British parliamentary procedure today, it was up to the UK Supreme Court to determine that "the prime minister's advice to Her Majesty was unlawful, void and of no effect," as Lady Brenda Hale, president of the Supreme Court, announced in September 2019. Lady Brenda Hale, cited in Landler, "Brexit Turmoil Increases as Court Rebukes Boris Johnson."
43. Cunningham, *The History of Great Britain from the Revolution of 1688 to the Accession of George the First,* 2:278.
44. Ibid., 2:276.
45. The English process shaped the modern procedure in the United States, where a government official is impeached in the House of Representatives, then subsequently either convicted (and removed from office) or acquitted by the Senate. Hoffer and Hull, *Impeachment in America,* 27–106.
46. Ralph Bridges to Sir W. Trumbull, 14 Dec. 1709, cited in Holmes, *The Trial of Doctor Sacheverell,* 89.
47. Holmes, *The Trial of Doctor Sacheverell,* 90.
48. Ibid., 93.
49. Hearne, *Remarks and Collections,* 2:334.
50. Articles of Impeachment, included as appendix A in Holmes, *The Trial of Doctor Sacheverell,* 280–81.

51. Holmes, *The Trial of Doctor Sacheverell*, 101.
52. Cunningham, *The History of Great Britain from the Revolution of 1688 to the Accession of George the First*, 2:286.
53. Hearne, *Remarks and Collections*, 2:235, 234.
54. Holmes, *The Trial of Doctor Sacheverell*, 103.
55. Lansdowne MS 1024, f. 202, cited in Holmes, *The Trial of Doctor Sacheverell*, 104.
56. Holmes, *The Trial of Doctor Sacheverell*, 105.
57. Trevelyan, *England under Queen Ann*, 50.
58. Cunningham, *The History of Great Britain from the Revolution of 1688 to the Accession of George the First*, 2:278.
59. Holmes, *The Trial of Doctor Sacheverell*, 78–79.
60. Ibid., 97.
61. Churchill, *Marlborough*, 2:663.
62. Ibid, 2:664.
63. Marlborough, *Memoirs of Sarah, Duchess of Marlborough*, 164, 162.
64. Cited in Churchill, *Marlborough*, 2:665.
65. Cited in Coxe, *Memoirs of the Duke of Marlborough*, 5:131.
66. Gregg, *Queen Anne*, 303.
67. Cited in Holmes, *The Trial of Doctor Sacheverell*, 115.
68. Cited in Holmes, *British Politics in the Age of Anne*, 210.
69. Duchess of Marlborough to Arthur Maynwaring, Jan. 1710, in Marlborough, *Private Correspondence of Sarah, Duchess of Marlborough*, 1:296.
70. Churchill, *Marlborough*, 2:669.
71. Brown, introduction to Anne, *The Letters and Diplomatic Instructions of Queen Anne*, vii.
72. Anne [Princess of Denmark] to Mary [Princess of Orange], 20 Mar. 1688, in Anne, *The Letters and Diplomatic Instructions of Queen Anne*, ed. Brown, 36.
73. Swift, *Journal to Stella* (31 July 1711), 1:324.
74. Worsley and Souden, *Hampton Court Palace*, 84, 85.
75. Ibid., 85.
76. Cobbett, *Cobbett's Parliamentary History*, 6:893–94.

5. A Female Satirist in Court

1. Marlborough, *The Letters and Dispatches of John Churchill, First Duke of Markborough*, ed. Murray, 4:683, my translations.
2. Luttrell, *Brief Historical Relation of State Affairs from September 1678 to April 1714*, 6:535.

3. Hearne, *Remarks and Collections,* 2:337.
4. Hoadly, *The Works of Benjamin Hoadly, D.D.,* 2:108.
5. Ward, "The Early Influence of John Locke's Political Thought in England, 1689–1720," 90.
6. Luttrell, *Brief Historical Relation of State Affairs from September 1678 to April 1714,* 6:538.
7. [Toland], *High Church Display'd,* 11–12.
8. *Free Debates Betwixt the H——L——and the H—- C——on Doctor Sacheverell* (copy in Magdalen College Library), cited in Holmes, *The Trial of Doctor Sacheverell,* 108.
9. Ibid., 109.
10. Hearne, *Remarks and Collections,* 2:339.
11. Holmes, *The Trial of Doctor Sacheverell,* 106.
12. Sacheverell, *The Answer of Henry Sacheverll. D. D. to the Articles of Impeachment,* 8, 12–13.
13. Ibid., 14, 15, 21, emphasis added.
14. Holmes, *The Trial of Doctor Sacheverell,* 107; House of Lords, *Journal of the House of Lords: Vol. 19, 1709–1714,* 64.
15. Holmes, *The Trial of Doctor Sacheverell,* 106.
16. Cunningham, *The History of Great Britain from the Revolution of 1688 to the Accession of George the First,* 2:286.
17. Luttrell, *Brief Historical Relation of State Affairs from September 1678 to April 1714,* 6:540. See also Hearne, *Remarks and Collections,* 2:339.
18. Siebert, *Freedom of the Press in England 1476–1776,* 301.
19. Holmes, *The Trial of Doctor Sacheverell,* 110.
20. House of Lord, *Journal of the House of Lords: Vol. 19, 1709–1714,* 56.
21. Holmes, *The Trial of Doctor Sacheverell,* 112. Luttrell, *Historical Relation,* 6:542.
22. Peter Wentworth to Thomas Wentworth, Lord Raby, 17 Feb. 1710, in Wentworth, *The Wentworth Papers, 1705–1739,* ed. Cartwright, 111.
23. House of Lords, *Journal of the House of Lords: Vol. 19, 1709–1714,* 66.
24. Holmes, *The Trial of Doctor Sacheverell,* 98–99.
25. Marlborough, *Memoirs of Sarah, Duchess of Marlborough,* 167.
26. Holmes, *The Trial of Doctor Sacheverell,* 116.
27. That portrait is now owned by Magdalen College, Oxford. The disapproving scowl and rigid jaw are what modern scholars now associate with Sacheverell; the portrait that appears to capture what we know of his abrasiveness and self-importance. In the subsequent mezzotint print, his tight jaw has been softened, and the pursed lips hold the promise of a hopeful smile. Sacheverell does not appear attractive by modern chiseled

standards of masculinity, which prioritize a leaner visage with more defined cheekbones.

28. Bisset, *The Modern Fanatick,* 2
29. *Evening Post,* no. 85, 35–28 Feb., cited in Holmes, *The Trial of Doctor Sacheverell,* 119.
30. *The Officers Address to the Ladies.* 2.
31. This four-page tract outlined the connections between progressive national politics and progressive gender politics—a link not often articulated at this point in history. In fact, several of the most prominent voices in seventeenth- and eighteenth-century proto-feminism were those of high-church Tory women. Mary Astell, a high-church Tory with a deep knowledge of theology, complained that the Whigs who had engineered the Glorious Revolution may have wanted to overthrow divine-right monarchy in the nation, but they liked it well enough in the household
32. *The Officers Address to the Ladies,* 3, 2, 4.
33. Burnet, *Bishop Burnet's History of His Own Time,* 5:439.
34. Otterness, *Becoming German,* 27. As Otterness explains, a parliamentary investigation into the causes of the 1709 mass immigration identified an unnamed "golden book," believed to be by Joshua Kocherthal, whose title translated into English is *A Complete and Detailed Report of the Renowned District of Carolina Located in English America* (26).
35. Ibid., 43, citing PRO (now TNA) CO 388/76:64, 68, 69.
36. Ibid., 55
37. Ibid., 56.
38. Ibid., 61.
39. Ibid., 71, citing BL Add. MSS 61652 ff. 188, 194; 61649 ff. 102, 112.
40. Marlborough, *The Letters and Dispatches of John Churchill, First Duke of Marlborough,* ed. Snyder, 4:691.
41. Carnell, "Delarivier Manley and the Queen's Bench," 582–84.
42. Secretaries of State, State Papers, Criminal Correspondence and Warrents: Sunderland, arrest warrant signed 28 Oct. 1709: TNA SP 44/78:64.
43. Carnell, *A Political Biography of Delarivier Manley,* 164.
44. Herman, *The Business of a Woman,* 28.
45. Manley, *Letters Writen by Mrs. Manley,* in *Selected Works,* 1:59.
46. Manley, *The Adventures of Rivella,* in *Selected Works,* 4:55
47. Manley, *The New Atalantis,* in *Selected Works,* 2:152.
48. Ibid., 238.
49. Richard Steele, *Tatler* 1 (12 Apr. 1709), in Steele, *The Tatler,* 1:23.
50. Manley, *The New Atalantis,* in *Selected Works,* 2:152. Manley is paraphrasing here from Steele's *Tatler* 61 (30 Aug. 1709, in Steele, *The Tatler,* 1:421),

though in fact Steele does not specifically mention avarice in his discussion of satire.

51. Manley, *The Adventures of Rivella,* in *Selected Works,* 4:54, 53.
52. Secretaries of State, State Papers, Criminal Correspondence and Warrents: Sunderland, arrest warrant signed 28 October 1709: TNA SP 44/78:64–5.
53. Manley, *The Adventures of Rivella,* in *Selected Works,* 4:56.
54. For a discussion of the identity of this character given in published keys (John Tidcomb), see Carnell, *Political Biography,* 13–14, 63, 92.
55. Manley, *The Adventures of Rivella,* in *Selected Works,* 4:53, 53–54.
56. Lutrell, *Brief Historical Relation of State Affairs from September 1678 to April 1714,* 6:546.
57. Manley, *The Adventures of Rivella,* in *Selected Works,* 4:55.
58. Ibid., 4:55.
59. Cunningham, *The History of Great Britain from the Revolution of 1688 to the Accession of George the First,* 2:278–9, 280, 286.
60. Peter Wentworth to Lord Raby, 14 Feb. 1710, in Wentworth, *The Wentworth Papers, 1705–1739,* ed. Cartwright, 108.
61. Luttrell, *Brief Historical Relation of State Affairs from September 1678 to April 1714,* 6:546–47.

6. Impeachment and Public Opinion

1. Churchill, *Marlborough,* 2:670.
2. Manley, *The New Atalantis,* in *Selected Works,* 2:239.
3. Cited in Bradley and Pevsner, *London 6 Westminster,* 591.
4. Lady Wentworth to Peter Wentworth, 22 Aug. 1709, in Wentworth, *The Wentworth Papers, 1705–1739,* ed. Cartwright, 98.
5. Gregg, *Queen Anne,* 298.
6. Defoe, *A Tour through the Whole Island of Great Britain,* 1: 362.
7. Cited from a letter "in the possession of W. Tooke," in Society for the Diffusion of Useful Knowledge, *The Lives of Eminent Persons,* 27. The Duchess of Marlborough was writing this letter in trying to haggle down a surveyor's bill for Blenheim.
8. B[aldwin]., *A Letter to the Good People of Great Britain,* 4, 1, 2, 8.
9. Burnet, *Bishop Burnet's History of His Own Time,* 5:446.
10. [Abigail Masham to Robert Harley], [Feb. 1710], in Portland, *A Report on the Manuscripts of His Grace the Duke of Portland* (HMC *Portland MSS*), 4:532.
11. Shrewsbury to Harley, 20 Oct. 1710, citing Queen Anne, in Bath, *Calendar of the Manuscripts of the Marquis of Bath,* 5 vols. (London: Eyre & Spottiswoode, 1904) (HMC *Bath MSS*), 1:199.

12. Cited in Holmes, *The Trial of Doctor Sacheverell,* 122.
13. Hearne, *Remarks and Collections,* 2:350.
14. Cited in Holmes, *The Trial of Doctor Sacheverell,* 122.
15. Cunningham, *The History of Great Britain from the Revolution of 1688 to the Accession of George the First,* 2:290.
16. Diary of Sarah Cowper, entry for 19 July 1709: Hertfordshire Archives, DE/P/F33:11.
17. *The Tryal of Dr. Henry Sacheverell,* 1
18. Holmes, *The Trial of Doctor Sacheverell,* 129.
19. *Tryal of Dr. Henry Sacheverell,* 2.
20. Holmes, *The Trial of Doctor Sacheverell,* 129.
21. *Tryal of Dr. Henry Sacheverell,* 16, 17, 18.
22. Ibid., 21–23.
23. Hearne, *Remarks and Collections,* 2:350.
24. Lady Wentworth to Lord Raby, 6 Mar. 1710, in Wentworth, *The Wentworth Papers, 1705–1739,* ed. Cartwright, 113.
25. Boyer, *The History of the Reign of Queen Anne,* 8:265.
26. Holmes, *The Trial of Doctor Sacheverell,* 134.
27. Ibid., 134.
28. Burnet, *Bishop Burnet's History of His Own Time,* 5:426.
29. Holmes, *The Trial of Doctor Sacheverell,* 134.
30. Osborn MSS 21/2, 28 Feb. 1710, cited in Holmes, *The Trial of Doctor Sacheverell,* 135n.
31. Narrative by the Duchess of Marlborough, describing episodes in her own and her family's loss of royal favor, [c. 1709–12]: BL Add. MSS 61422 f. 63; 61425 f. 74r–v.
32. *Tryal of Dr. Henry Sacheverell,* 47–50.
33. Ibid., 57.
34. Holmes, *The Trial of Doctor Sacheverell,* 126.
35. *Tryal of Dr. Henry Sacheverell,* 62.
36. Ibid.
37. Ibid., 78, 77.
38. Ibid., 84, 86.
39. Cited in Holmes, *The Trial of Doctor Sacheverell,* 127.
40. *Tryal of Dr. Henry Sacheverell,* 88.
41. Ibid., 92.
42. Ibid., 93.
43. Holmes, *The Trial of Doctor Sacheverell,* 149.
44. *Tryal of Dr. Henry Sacheverell,* 105, 106.
45. Ibid., 107, 110, 114.

46. Holmes, *Thte Trial of Doctor Sacheverll,* 128
47. Ibid., 157.
48. Hearne, *Remarks and Collections,* 2:351.
49. Holmes, *The Trial of Doctor Sacheverell,* 156.
50. Ibid., 161
51. Abigail Harley (Robert Harley's sister, not his cousin, Abigail Masham) recounted this. Abigail Harley to Edward Harley, 2 Mar. 1710, in Portland, *Report on the Manuscripts of His Grace the Duke of Portland* (HMC *Portland MSS*), 4:532.
52. Holmes, *The Trial of Doctor Sacheverell,* 161.
53. From a deposition by Anne Newth, cited in Holmes, *The Trial of Doctor Sacheverell,* 161.
54. From a deposition by Sarah Sawery, cited in Holmes, *The Trial of Doctor Sacheverell,* 163.
55. Howell, *A Complete Collection of State Trials and Proceedings for High Treason and Other Misdemeanors,* 15:557–9; Sarah Sawery's deposition, cited in Holmes, *The Trial of Doctor Sacheverell,* 165; Boyer, *The History of the Reign of Queen Anne,* 8:265.
56. [Ward], *The Whigs Unmask'd,* 99. The engraving is reproduced on page 9 of the illustrations gallery.
57. Boyer, *The History of the Reign of Queen Anne,* 8:266.
58. Marlborough, *Memoirs,* 230.
59. Ibid., 232.
60. Boyer, *The History of the Reign of Queen Anne,* 8:266.
61. Holmes, *The Trial of Doctor Sacheverell,* 172.
62. Cited ibid., 174.
63. Luttrell, *Brief Historical Relation of State Affairs from September 1678 to April 1714,* 551–52.
64. *London Gazette* 4660, cited in Hearne, *Remarks and Collections,* 2:176.
65. Boyer, *The History of the Reign of Queen Anne,* 8:267.
66. *Tryal of Dr. Henry Sacheverell,* 117.
67. Luttrell, *Brief Historical Relation of State Affairs from September 1678 to April 1714,* 552.
68. Hearne, *Remarks and Collections,* 2:351.
69. Ibid., 2:351.
70. Boyer, *The History of the Reign of Queen Anne,* 8:267.
71. Holmes, *The Trial of Doctor Sacheverell,* 175.
72. Ibid., 178.
73. Especially with populism spurring large masses of people to vote for Brexit in England and for Donald Trump in the United States, the rise of populist

movements has spurred much recent research. Gelfand, "Here's the Science behind the Brexit Vote and Trump's Rise."

74. Gelfand, *Rule Makers, Rule Breakers,* 3.
75. Holmes, *The Trial of Doctor Sacheverell,* 177–8.
76. This anonymous pamphlet was likely a joint authorial effort to convey ideas Harley had drafted. See Downie, *Robert Harley and the Press,* 106–11.
77. Godolphin to Marlborough, 5 Mar. 1710, in *The Marlborough-Godolphin Correspondence,* ed. Snyder, 3:1428.
78. Abigail Harley to Edward Harley, [2 Mar. 1710], in Portland, *Report of the Manuscripts of His Grace the Duke of Portland* (HMC *Portland MSS*), 4:533.
79. Osborne MSS 21/22: 3 Mar., cited in Holmes, *The Trial of Doctor Sacheverell,* 180.
80. Ballard MSS 7, f.36, cited in Holmes, *The Trial of Doctor Sacheverell,* 181.
81. *Tryal of Dr. Henry Sacheverell,* 121, 131.
82. Marlborough, *Memoirs of Sarah, Duchess of Marlborough,* 252.
83. *Tryal,* 238.
84. Boyer, *The History of the Reign of Queen Anne,* 8:288–91.
85. Marlborough, *Memoirs of Sarah, Duchess of Marlborough,* 252.
86. Boyer, *The History of the Reign of Queen Anne,* 8:294.
87. This image appears in William Howett, *John Cassell's Illustrated History of England,* vol. 4, *From the Accession of William III to the Death of George II* (London: Cassell, Petter, and Galpin, n.d.) and is reproduced on page 7 of the illustrations gallery.
88. *Tryal of Dr. Henry Sacheverell,* 320.
89. Hearne, *Remarks and Collections,* 2:359.
90. Ibid., 2:352.

7. Impeached but Triumphant

1. *Tryal of Dr. Henry Sacheverell,* 320–21.
2. House of Lords, *Journal of the House of Lords: Vol. 19, 1709–1714,* 100.
3. Luttrell, *Brief Historical Relation of State Affairs from September 1678 to April 1714,* 6:555.
4. Peter Wentworth, for example, wrote to his brother Lord Raby, in Berlin about it on 7 April 1710. *Wentworth Papers,* 115.
5. Starr, *Communication from Kenneth W. Starr, Independent Counsel,* 24 n106.
6. Anne to James Clavering, 18 Mar. 1710, in Clavering, *Correspondence of Sir James Clavering,* ed. Dickinson, 70.
7. House of Lords, *Journal of the House of Lords: Vol. 19, 1709–1714,* 106.
8. Holmes, *The Trial of Doctor Sacheverell,* 215.

9. *A True Answer,* 1.
10. *Dr. Sacheverell's Speech Upon His Impeachment;* the subtitle, however, gives the full detail: *With* REFLECTIONS *thereupon Paragraph by Paragraph.* Citing i–v.
11. Anne to James Clavering, 18 Mar. 1710, in Clavering, *Correspondence of Sir James Clavering,* ed. Dickinson, 71.
12. Peter Wentworth to Lord Raby, 7 Apr. 1710, in Wentworth, *The Wentworth Papers, 1705–1739,* ed. Cartwright, 115.
13. House of Lords, *Journal of the House of Lords: Vol. 19, 1709–1714,* 115.
14. Luttrell, *Brief Historical Relation of State Affairs from September 1678 to April 1714,* 6:559. Emphasis added.
15. Godolphin to Marlborough, 20 Mar. 1709, in *The Marlborough Godolphin Correspondence,* ed. Snyder, 3:1440.
16. In the United States today, if the president or another federal officeholder is impeached by the House of Representatives, the only available punishment, if the Senate convicts by a two-thirds margin, is removal from office. (If the Senate acquits the officeholder, the person will still have been impeached, but will not be removed from office.)
17. Hamilton, *Diary of Sir David Hamilton,* 6.
18. Peter Wentworth to Lord Raby, [Sept. 1710?], in Wentworth, *The Wentworth Papers, 1705–1739,* ed. Cartwright, 146.
19. Burnet, *Bishop Burnet's History of His Own Time,* 5:435.
20. Earl of Orrery to Robert Harley, [14?] Mar. 1710, in Portland, *Report on the Manuscripts of His Grace the Duke of Portland* (HMC *Portland MSS*), 4:537.
21. Holmes, *The Trial of Doctor Sacheverell,* 228.
22. Cited ibid., 230
23. Cunningham, *The History of Great Britain from the Revolution of 1688 to the Accession of George the First,* 2:301.
24. [Abigail Harley] to Edward Harley, in Portland, *Report on the Manuscripts of His Grace the Duke of Portland* (HMC *Portland MSS*), 4:539.
25. *Tryal of Dr. Hencry Sacheverell,* 326.
26. Holmes, *The Trial of Doctor Sacheverll,* 232.
27. Burnet, *Bishop Burnet's History of His Own Time,* 5:436.
28. Marlborough to the Duchess, [4 Apr. 1710], in *The Marlborough-Godolphin Correspondence,* ed. Snyder, 3:1445.
29. Similarly, some members of Parliament in 2019 strategized in their various votes over Brexit with an eye toward triggering a general election.
30. In modern times in the UK, elections are held every five years unless they are called for by a vote of no confidence in the prime minister or a two-thirds vote in the House of Commons.

31. Coxe, *Memoirs of the Duke of Marlborough,* 5:278.
32. This prorogation caused no harm and produced no controversy, unlike Boris Johnson's request to prorogue Parliament in September 2019, which cut off crucial deliberations in the weeks before an October 31 Brexit deadline.
33. *Journal of the House of Commons* 16:337, cited in Cowan, "Introduction," in *The State Trial of Doctor Henry Sacheverell,* 9.
34. Cowan, "Introduction," in *The State Trial of Doctor Henry Sacheverell,* 10–11. Cowan bases his estimates on printing speeds estimated by James Raven in *The Business of Books,* 23.
35. E[dward] C[hute] to Thomas Jervoise, 4 Apr. 1710: Hampshire Archives, Jervoise Papers, 44M69/G2/179. cited in Cowan, "Introduction," in *The State Trial of Doctor Henry Sacheverell,* 12. Getting the first crack at the news cycle was as important in 1710 as it would be in the spring of 2019, when US Attorney General William Barr dominated the news cycle after Robert Mueller submitted his report (about the investigation of Russian interference in the 2016 election) by peremptorily releasing a misleading summary of Mueller's investigation. See, for example, *New York Times* Editorial Board, "Bob Mueller's Extraordinary Letter to Bill Barr," *New York Times,* May 1, 2019, https://www.nytimes.com/2019/05/01/opinion/barr-mueller-letter.html?searchResultPosition=1.
36. I am presuming that Barber and his trade printers, who put their names on the title page, would have employed about the same number of additional printers as Tonson did, but this is speculation on my part.
37. Manley, *Memoirs of Europe,* in *Selected Works,* 3:113.
38. Cowan, "Introduction," in *The State Trial of Doctor Henry Sacheverell,* 15.
39. *Tryal of Dr Henry Sacheverell,* flyleaf.
40. Cowan (17) refers to Madan's hypotheses about these publishers in BL Add. MS 88473–81.
41. *An Impartial Account of What Pass'd most Remarkable in the Last Session of Parliament, Relating to the Case of Dr Henry Sacheverell,* 31–32.
42. *Observator* 9, no. 12 (22–25 Feb. 1710): 1.
43. Raven, *The Business of Books,* 1–8, 40, 324.
44. Cowan, "Introduction," in *The State Trial of Doctor Henry Sacheverell,* 12.
45. Flyleaf, *The Tryal of Dr. Henry Sacheverell.* This page is reproduced in Cowan, *The State Trial of Doctor Henry Sacheverell,* 111.
46. [Maynwaring], *Four Letters to a Friend in North Briton,* 7, title page.
47. Although today we do not usually acquire books with the idea that they will be in a family library for generations, the desire to own a copy of a government investigation persists. The *Washington Post*'s published version (Scribner) of Robert Mueller's investigation was second on Amazon's best-seller

list three (May 9, 2019) just ten days after its publication date (April 30, 2019), according to Amazon's best-seller chart for the week of May 7, 2019.

48. Johnson, *Lives of the Most Eminent English Poets,* 2:101.
49. Clark, *English Society 1660–1832,* 45.
50. Similarly, the line between Brexiteers and Remainers represents a central cultural divide in the UK today.
51. Queen Anne to Marlborough, 25 Oct. 1709, in Anne, *The Letters and Diplomatic Instructions of Queen Anne,* ed. Brown, 286.
52. Maynwaring to S[arah] M[anley], 3 Nov, 1709, BL Add. MS 61460, ff. 74–75.
53. Marlborough, *Memoirs of Sarah, Duchess of Marlborough,* 156–56.
54. Queen Anne to Duchess of Marlborough, [7 Nov. 1709], cited in Gregg, *Queen Anne,* 295.
55. Marlborough, *Memoirs of Sarah, Duchess of Marlborough,* 170.
56. This room is currently part of the tourist circuit at Kensington Palace.
57. Narrative by the Duchess of Marlborough, describing episodes in her own and her family's loss of royal favour; [c.1709–12]: Add. MS 61422 f. 72v.
58. Marlborough, *Memoirs of Sarah, Duchess of Marlborough,* 170, 169, 171.
59. Ibid., 172.
60. Ibid., 172–73.
61. Ibid., 173.
62. Abigail Masham to Robert Harley, 10 Mar. 1710, in Portland, *Report on the Manuscripts of His Grace the Duke of Portland* (or HMC *Portland MSS*), 4:536.
63. Swift, *Memoirs Relating to that Change which Happened in the Queen's Ministry in the Year 1710,* 5:367.
64. Ibid., 375.
65. Delariver Manley to Robert Harley, 12 May 1710, reprinted in Herman, *The Business of a Woman,* 254.
66. Manley, *Memoirs of Europe,* in *Selected Works,* 3:142–43.
67. Ibid., 3:90.
68. Ibid., 3:8.
69. Ibid., 3:115.
70. Ibid., 3:115.
71. Luttrell, *Brief Historical Relation of State Affairs from September 1678 to April 1714,* 6:562.
72. Thos. to John Carte, Coleshill, 7 Apr. 1710, cited in Holmes, *The Trial of Doctor Sacheverell,* 233.
73. England, *Pray for the Peace of Jerusalem,* 25–6.
74. Manley, *Memoirs of Europe,* in *Selected Works* 3:104.
75. Burnet, *Bishop Burnet's History of His Own Time,* vol. 6: 7n.

76. Queen Anne to Godolphin, 13 June 1710, in Anne, *The Letters and Diplomatic Instructions of Queen Anne,* ed. Brown, 303.
77. Coxe, *Memoirs of the Duke of Marlborough,* 5:184.
78. Marlborough to Godolphin, 12 May 1710, in *The Marlborough-Godolphin Correspondence,* ed. Snyder, 3:1480.
79. Marlborough to Godolphin, 22 May 1710, in *The Marlborough-Godolphin Correspondence,* ed. Snyder, 3:1504.
80. Marlborough to Duchess, 19 May 1710, *Coxe, Memoirs of the Duke of Marlborough* 5:192.
81. Marlborough to Duchess, 29 May 1710, in *The Marlborough-Godolphin Correspondence,* ed. Snyder, 3:1510.
82. See, for example, BL Add. MS 61651, f. 227.
83. Somerset, *Queen Anne,* 416.
84. Marlborough to Queen Anne, [1710], BL Add. MS 61101 ff. 172.
85. Marlborough to Godolphin, [9/20 June 1710], in *The Marlborough Godolphin Correspondence,* ed. Snyder, 3:1522.
86. Queen Anne to Godolphin, 13 June 1710, in Anne, *The Letters and Diplomatic Instructions of Queen Anne,* ed. Brown, 303.
87. Boyer, *The History of the Reign of Queen Anne,* 9:230.
88. Marlborough to Godolphin, 20 June 1710, in *The Marlborough-Godolphin Correspondence,* ed. Snyder, 3:1522.

8. A Tory Victory Lap and Parliamentary Elections

1. Luttrell, *Brief Historical Relation of State Affairs from September 1678 to April 1714,* 6:562.
2. Boyer, *The History of the Reign of Queen Anne,* 8:335.
3. Bisset, *The Modern Fanatick,* 52.
4. Cunningham, *The History of Great Britain from the Revolution of 1688 to the Accession of George the First,* 2:300.
5. This set of playing cards is owned by the British Museum, online item number 1868,0808.3441; the image of Sacheverell is reproduced on page 8 of the illustrations gallery.
6. Cunningham, *The History of Great Britain from the Revolution of 1688 to the Accession of George the First,* 2:300.
7. Burnet, *Biship Burnet's History of His Own Time,* 5:437.
8. Holmes, *The Trial of Doctor Sachaverell,* 238.
9. [J. K.], *Dr Sacheverel's Progress from London to his Rectory in Salatin in Shropshire,* 4–6. At the time, this part of Wales (now in Denbighshire) was still part of Shropshire.

10. Holmes, *The Trial of Doctor Sacheverell,* 243.
11. Oldmixon, *The History of England, During the Reigns of King William and Queen Mary, Queen Ann King George I,* 448.
12. *Worcester Triumph* (1710); *Flying-Post No. 2254, July* (letter from Worcester, 17 July), both cited in Holmes, *The Trial of Doctor Sacheverell,* 244.
13. "A Letter from a Citizen of Worcester, in Answer to a Malicious Pamphlet," *Worcester Triumph, &c.* (1710), 1.
14. *The Banb—y Apes,* 3, 5.
15. Ibid., 5, 6, 8.
16. *Dr. Sacheverel's Progress,* 7.
17. Holmes, *The Trial of Doctor Sacheverell,* 247, 236.
18. Monson MSS 7/3/124: 1 July. King MSS 58, V, 205; 58, VI, 36, cited in Holmes, *The Trial of Doctor Sacheverell,* 248, 249.
19. *A Collection of the Addresses which have been presented to the Queen since the Impeachment of the Reverend Dr Henry Sacheverell,* 7–8.
20. Ibid., 8.
21. Holmes, *The Trial of Doctor Sacheverell,* 249
22. Hamilton, *Diary of Sir David Hamilton,* 17.
23. Holmes, *The Trial of Doctor Sacheverell,* 251.
24. Sundstrom, *Sidney Godolphin.* While Sundstrom details Godolphin's immense contributions, he also points out that Godolphin and Marlborough probably erred in making the credit markets too "dependent on his ability" and on the "domestic and military success" of Godolphin and Marlborough (254).
25. [Robert Harley] to Arthur Moore, 19 June 1710, in Portland, *Report on the Manuscripts of His Grace the Duke of Portland* (HMC Portland MSS), 4:545.
26. Lord Weymouth to [Robert Harley], 24 July 1710; Viscount Dupplin to Robert Harley, 26 June 1710, both ibid., 4:551–2.
27. Backscheider, *Daniel Defoe,* 282.
28. D[aniel De] F[oe] to [Robert Harley], 28 July 1710, in Portland, *Report on the Manuscripts of His Grace the Duke of Portland* (HMC *Portland MSS*), 4:553.
29. Hamilton, *Diary of Sir David Hamilton,* 17.
30. Godolphin to Marlborough, 18 July 1710, in *The Marlborough Godolphin Correspondence,* ed. Snyder, 3:1572.
31. Godolphin to Marlborough, 31 July 1710, in *The Marlborough Godolphin Correspondence,* ed. Snyder, 3:1584.
32. Sundstrom, *Sidney Godolphin,* 257.
33. Harley to Newcastle, 5 August 1710, in Portland, *Report on the Manuscripts of His Grace the Duke of Portland* (HMC *Portland MSS*), 2:213.

34. Coxe, *Memoirs of the Duke of Marlborough,* 5:321.
35. Queen Anne to Lord Godolphin [8 Aug. 1710]: BL Add. MS 61118, ff. 47–48.
36. Marlborough, *Memoirs of Sarah, Duchess of Markborough,* 235.
37. Godolphin to Queen Anne [8 Aug. 1710]: BL Add. MS 28055m ff. 432–33.
38. Burnet, *Bishop Burnet's History of His Own Time,* 6:143–4.
39. Marlborough to the Duchess, [14]/25 August 1710, in *The Marlborough-Godolphin Correspondence,* ed. Snyder, 3:1605.
40. Hamilton, *Diary of Sir David Hamilton,* 76 n50.
41. Boyer, *The History of the Reign of Queen Anne,* 9:231.
42. Burnet, *Bishop Burnet's History of His Own Time,* 6:10.
43. Churchill, *Marlborough,* 2:760.
44. Burnet, *Bishop Burnet's History of His Own Time,* 6:12.
45. Luttrell, *Brief Historical Relation of State Affairs from September 1678 to April 1714,* 6:634.
46. Churchill, *Marlborough,* 2:762–63.
47. Burnet, *Bishop Burnet's History of His Own Time,* 6:13–14.
48. Ibid., 6:13–14.
49. [Clement], *Faults on Both Sides: or an Essay upon the Original Cause, Progress, and Mischivous Consequences of Factions in this Nation* (London 1710), 4.
50. James Craggs to Marlborough, 13 Oct. 1710, cited in Churchill, *Marlborough,* 2:762.
51. Daniel Defoe, *A Weekly Review,* 7:333–37, cited in Churchill, *Marlborough,* 2:762.
52. Holmes, *The Trial of Doctor Sacheverell,* 253.
53. Hamilton, *Diary of Sir David Hamilton,* 14.
54. Manley, *Memoirs of Europe,* in *Selected Works,* 3:306–8.
55. Ibid., 3:309–10.
56. Swift, *Examiner* 16 (23 Nov. 1710), in Swift, *The Examiner and Other Pieces Written in 1710–11,* 23–24.
57. Duchess of Marlborough to David Hamilton, BL Add. MSS 61423 ff. 16–23.
58. Hamilton, *Diary of Sir David Hamilton,* 20.
59. Barber, "'It is not Easy What to Say of our Condition, Much less to Write it,'" 293–316.
60. Marlborough, *Memoirs of Sarah, Duchess of Marlborough,* 314.
61. Anne, *The Queen's Speech to both Houses of Parliament on Monday the 27th Day of November, 1710.*
62. Hamilton, *Diary of Sir David Hamilton,* 28.
63. Churchill, *Marlborough,* 2:797.
64. Somerset, *Queen Anne,* 437.

65. This is part of the set in the British Museum collection, online item number 1868,0808.3441.
66. The signed account statement is housed at the Blenheim Archive, Treasury XXIII.77.8.
67. Somerset, *Queen Anne,* 437.
68. Churchill, *Marlborough,* 2:880.
69. Manley, *The D. of M——h's Vindication: in Answer to a Pamphlet Lately Published, call'd Bouchain,* in *Selected Works,* 5:64–65.
70. Swift, *Journal to Stella,* 2:390.
71. Marlborough to Duchess, Oct. 1711, cited in Churchill, *Marlborough* 2:868.
72. Marlborough to Oxford, 19 Oct. 11; Oxford to Marlborough, 19/[30] Oct. 1711, both cited in Churchill, *Marlborough,* 2:869.
73. [Swift], *The Conduct of the Allies,* 32; in *The Prose Works of Jonathan Swift,* 5:99.
74. Cobbett, *Cobbett's Parliamentary History,* 6:1038.
75. Coxe, *Memoirs of the Duke of Marlborough,* 6:152.
76. Cobbett, *Cobbett's Parliamentary History,* 6:1077.
77. Cited in Churchill, *Marlborough,* 2:913.
78. Churchill, *Marlborough,* 2:963.
79. Churchill, *Marlborough,* 2:994, 995.
80. See Pincus, *1688,* for a discussion of the Whig "Financial Revolution" (399), and Raworth, *Doughnut Economics,* for the dangers to humanity and the planet of the insatiable desire for "growth."
81. Randall Lesaffer, "The Peace of Utrecht and the Balance of Power," *OUP Blog,* November 10, 2014, https://blog.oup.com/2014/11/utrecht-peace-treaty-balance-power-europe.
82. The last high-profile impeachment proceedings were launched in 1787 against Warren Hastings, Governor General of India, for a "miscellany of misbehaviors," including "disregard of instruction" from the East India Company's directors, a "mismanagement of regions under his administrative control," and other "high-handed or deceitful dealings with local ruler," and other corrupt acts while in office. Though Hastings was eventually acquitted by the House of Lords in 1795, the initial parliamentary vote against this administrator for misbehavior in carrying out his official duties in May 1787 would have been fresh in the thoughts of the American Founders as they convened that same month in Philadelphia to draft the U.S. Constitution. Bowman, *High Crimes and Misdemeanors,* 42.
83. Pincus, *1688,* 482. This practice of "occasional conformity" had been in use until 1711, when the Tory Parliament voted it out, but it was restored by a Whig Parliament in 1719. Although convenient to those Dissenters who

did not mind the hypocrisy of taking communion in a religion to which they did not adhere, it hardly constituted full civil rights.

84. Speck, *Stability and Strife,* 151, 147, 405.
85. Homes, *The Trial of Doctor Sacheverell,* 266.
86. Manley, *The Adventures of Rivella,* in *Selected Works,* 4:54.
87. See her begging letter of 3 June, her thank-you note of 14 June, and her follow-up with suggestions about future pamphlets of 30 August, in Herman, *The Business of a Woman,* 257–60.
88. Churchill, *Marlborough,* 2:795, 1:53.
89. Nevertheless, as Brian Cowan points out, the significance of the public response to his trial bears revisiting in light of recent critiques of Habermas's paradigm for the eighteenth-century public sphere ("Introduction," in *The State Trial of Dr. Henry Sacheverell,* 8).
90. Pincus, *1688,* 16.
91. As the economist Paul Krugman points out, a moderate Democrat like Joe Biden may be able to effect more social reform in American politics than the avowed socialist Bernie Sanders. See Krugman, "Bernie Sanders Is Going for Broke."

Epilogue

1. Pew Research Center, "Party Affiliation,"
2. See, for example, Mounk, "Brexit is a Cultural Revolution."
3. Elizabeth II, "The Queen's Broadcast to the UK and Commonwealth, April 5, 2020," royal.uk.
4. Tribe and Matz, *To End a Presidency,* ii, 6.
5. *New York Times* Editorial Board, "Why President Trump's Ukraine Scheme Matters."
6. Burnet, *Biship Burnet's History of His Own Time,* 5:437.
7. Grynbaum, "Trump Renews Pledge to 'Take a Strong Look' at Libel Laws."
8. Rauch, "Autocorrect: How Advances in Real-time Fact-Checking Might Improve Our Politics."
9. Egan, "How the Insufferably Woke Help Trump."
10. Witmer, *The Property Qualifications of Members of Parliament,* 40–45, 217–21.
11. Alderman, Eddy, Tsang "Migrant Farmworkers Whose Harvests Feed Europe are Blocked at Borders."
12. Miriam Jordan, "Farmworkers, Mostly Undocumented, Become 'Essential' During Pandemic," *New York Times,* April 2, 2020, online edition.

13. David Edgerton, “Boris Johnson Might Break Up the U.K.” *New York Times,* January 10, 2020.
14. John Jay, *The Federalist No. 5.*
15. Rich, *Losing Earth,* 200.
16. Elgot, “Semi-naked Climate Protestors Disrupt Brexit Debate.”
17. Klein, *Why We're Polarized,* 401.
18. Klein himself acknowledges the cliché of a “liberal Californian vegan” preaching mindfulness. Ibid., 494.
19. Sunstein, *How Change Happens,* 19.
20. Mills, Gage, and Khan, “Potential Influence of Climate Change on Vector-Borne and Zoonotic Diseases.”
21. Schmemann, “The Virus Comes for Democracy.”
22. John Ikenberry is cited by Simon Tisdall in “Power, Equalty, Nationalism.”

BIBLIOGRAPHY

Archival Sources

British Library—Additional Manuscripts
Blenheim Papers
Portland Papers
  Canterbury, Prerogative Court of Related Probate Jurisdictions,
    Will Registers
  Hampshire Archives and Local Studies
Hertfordshire Archives and Local Studies
Manuscript Archive of the Cowper Family of Panshanger
The National Archives (UK)
  State Papers Domestic, Anne

Published Collections of Letters and Family Papers

Anne, Queen of Great Britain. *The Letters and Diplomatic Instructions of Queen Anne.* Edited by Beatrice Curtis Brown. London: Cassell, 1935.

Bath, Marquis of. *Calendar of the Manuscripts of the Marquis of Bath,* 5 vols. Historical Manuscripts Commission. London: Eyre & Spottiswoode, 1904.

Buccleuch and Queensbury, Duke of. *Report on the Manuscripts of the Duke of Buccleuch and Queensberry, Preserved at Montagu House, Whitehall,* 3 vols. Historical Manuscripts Commission. London: Her Majesty's Stationery Office, 1899.

Clavering, James. *Correspondence of Sir James Clavering.* Edited by H. T. Dickinson. Publications of the Surtees Society. Gateshead: Northumberland Press, 1967.

Marlborough, Sarah, Duchess of. *Private Correspondence of Sarah, Duchess of Marlborough,* 2nd ed., 2 vols. London: Henry Colburn, 1838. New York: Kraus reprint, 1972.

Marlborough, John, Duke of. *The Letters and Dispatches of John Churchill, First Duke of Marlborough.* Edited by George Murray, 5 vols. London: John Murray, 1845.

Marlborough, John, Duke of, and Sidney Godolphin. *The Marlborough-Godolphin Correspondence.* Edited by Henry L. Snyder, 3 vols. Oxford, Clarendon 1975.

Montagu, Mary Wortley. *The Complete Letters of Lady Mary Wortley Montagu.* Edited by R. Halsbad, 3 vols. Oxford: Clarendon Press of Oxford University Press, 1965.

Portland, Duke of. *Report on the Manuscripts of His Grace the Duke of Portland,* 10 vols. Historical Manuscripts Commission. London: Eyre and Spottiswoode.

Rutland, Duke of. *Manuscripts of his Grace the Duke of Rutland,* 4. vols. Historical Manuscripts Commission. London: Eyre and Spottiswoode, 1888–1905.

Wentworth, Thomas, Lord Raby. *The Wentworth Papers, 1705–1739.* Edited by James Cartwright. London: Wyman, 1883.

Published Sources

Alderman, Liz, Melissa Eddy, and Amie Tsang. "Migrant Farmworkers Whose Harvests Feed Europe Are Blocked at Borders. *New York Times,* March 31, 2020. Online edition.

Anne, Queen of Great Britain. *The Queen's Speech to both Houses of Parliament on Monday the 27th Day of November, 1710.* Dublin: P. Dickson, 1710.

Anquetil, Louis-Pierre. *Histoire de France depuis les Gaulois jusqu'à la mort de Louis XVI.* 12 vols. Paris: Ledentu, 1836.

Avery, E. L., ed. *The London Stage, 1660–1800; A Calendar of Plays, The London Stage 1660–1800: A Calendar of Plays, Part 2: 1700–1729.* 2 vols. Carbondale: Southern Illinois University Press, 1960.

B., A. *A Letter to the Good People of Great Britain.* London: Abigail Baldwin, 1710.

Backscheider, Paula. *Daniel Defoe: His Life.* Baltimore, MD: Johns Hopkins University Press, 1989.

The Banb—y Apes: or, The Monkeys Chattering to the Magpye. London: R. Mawson, [1710].

Banks, John. *The Unhappy Favourite.* London: R. Wellington, 1704.

Barber, Alex. "'It is not Easy What to Say of our Condition, Much less to Write it': The Continued Importance of Scribal News in the Early 18th Century." *Parliamentary History* 32, no. 2 (2013): 293–316.

Bennett, G. V. *White Kennett, 1660–1728, Bishop of Peterborough.* London: Church Historical Society, 1957.

Bisset, William. *The Modern Fanatick. With a Large and True Account of the Life and Actions of the Life, Actions, Endowments, &c. of the Famous Dr. Sa*——l. London: A. Baldwin, 1710.

———. *Modern Fanatick: Part II.* London: A. Baldwin, 1710.

Bowman, Frank. *High Crimes and Misdemeanors: A History of Impeachment for the Age of Trump.* Cambridge: Cambridge University Press, 2019.

Boyer, Abel. *The History of the Reign of Queen Anne, Digested into Annals.* 11 vols. London: A. Roper, 1703–13.

Bradley, Simon, and Nikolaus Pevsner. *London 6 Westminster.* New Haven, CT: Yale University Press, 1994.

[Brémond, Sébastien]. *Hattige: or the Amours of the King of Tamaran. A Novel.* Translated by B. B. Amsterdam: Simon the African [Richard Bentley], 1680. Originally published as *Hattigé, ou les amours du Roy Tamaran,* 1676.

Burnet, Gilbert. *Bishop Burnet's History of His Own Time.* 6 vols. Oxford: Clarendon Press, 1823.

Butterfield, Herbert. *The Whig Interpretation of History.* London: G. Bell, 1963.

Caird, Jack Simson, *Impeachment: Briefing Paper CBP7612,* 6 June 2016. London House of Commons Library. https://researchbriefings.parliament.uk/ResearchBriefing/Summary/CBP-7612.

[Simon Clement]. *Faults on Both Sides: or an Essay upon the Original Cause, Progress, and Mischievous Consequences of Factions in this Nation.* London, 1710.

Carnell, Rachel. "Delarivier Manley and the Queen's Bench." *Notes & Queries* 63, no. 4 (2016): 582–84.

———. "The Lye of Queen Anne's Lesbianism," *Notes and Queries* (2019) 66 (4): 565–67.

———. *A Political Biography of Delarivier Manley.* London: Pickering & Chatto, 2008.

Churchill, Winston. *Marlborough: His Life and Times,* 2 books, consolidating 4 vols. London: George G. Harrap, 1947.

Clark, J. C. D. *English Society 1660–1832: Religion, Ideology, and Politics during the Ancien Regime.* Rev. ed. Cambridge: Cambridge University Press, 2000.

Cobbett, William. *Cobbett's Parliamentary History: From the Norman Conquest in 1066, to 1803.* 12 vols. London: R. Bagshaw and others, 1804–12.

A Collection of the Addresses Which Have Been Presented to the Queen Since the Impeachment of the Reverend Dr Henry Sacheverell. London: John Morphew, 1711.

Congreve, William. *The Tears of Amaryllis for Amyntas, A Pastoral.* London: Jacob Tonson, 1703.

Cowan, Brian, ed. *The State Trial of Doctor Henry Sacheverell.* Malden, MA: Wiley Blackwell for the Parliamentary History Yearbook Trust, 2012.

Coxe, William. *Memoirs of the Duke of Marlborough: With His Original Correspondence Collected from the Family Records at Blenheim.* 6 vols. London: Longman, 1920.

Cunningham, Alexander. *The History of Great Britain from the Revolution of 1688 to the Accession of George the First.* Translated by William Thomson from Cunningham's Latin manuscript. 2 vols. London: A. Strahan, T. Cadell, 1787.

[Defoe, Daniel]. *The Shortest way with the Dissenters: or Proposals for the Establishment of the Church.* London, 1702.

———. *A Tour through the Whole Island of Great Britain.* 2 vols. London: Everyman, 1927.

[———]. *The True Born Englishman: A Satyr.* [London], 1701.

Downie, J. A. *Robert Harley and the Press: Propaganda and Public Opinion in the Age of Swift and Defoe.* Cambridge: Cambridge University Press, 1979.

———. "'What If Delarivier Manley Did *Not* Write *The Secret History of Queen Zarah*?" *Library,* 7th ser., 5, no. 3 (September 2004): 247–64.

Dr. Sacheverel's Speech Upon His Impeachment: With REFLECTIONS thereupon Paragraph by Paragraph. London: B. Bragg, 1710.

Edgerton, David. "Boris Johnson Might Break Up the U.K. That's a Good Thing." *New York Times,* January 10, 2020.

Egan, Timothy. "How the Insufferably Woke Help Trump." *New York Times,* November 8, 2019. Online edition.

Elgot, Jessica. "Semi-naked Climate Protestors Disrupt Brexit Debate." *Guardian,* April 1, 2019.

Elizabeth II, Queen of the United Kingdom. "The Queen's Broadcast to the UK and Commonwealth, April 5, 2020." www.royal.uk.

England, John. *Pray for the Peace of Jerusalem.* London: John Clark; Sherborne: John Miller, 1710.

Evelyn, John. *The Diary of Sir John Evelyn.* Edited by E. De Beer. Oxford: Oxford University Press, 1959.

———. *The Life of Mrs. Godolphin.* Edited by Harriet Sampson. London: Oxford University Press, 1939.

Field, Ophelia. *The Favourite: Sarah, Duchess of Marlborough.* London: Hodder and Stoughton, Sceptre, 2002.

Freeman, Hadley. "Was the Queen Sending Coded Messages to Donald Trump via Her Brooches? Absolutely." *Guardian,* July 18, 2018.

Geary, Caroline ed. *Royal Friendships: The Story of Two Royal Friendships.* London: Digby & Long, 1898.

Gelfand, Michele. "Here's the Science behind the Brexit Vote and Trump's Rise." *Guardian,* September 17, 2018. Online version.

———. *Rule Makers, Rule Breakers: How Tight and Loose Cultures Wire Our World.* New York: Scribner, 2018.

Goodwin, Doris Kearns. Interview by Ellen Fried, "An Extraordinary President and His Remarkable Cabinet: An Interview with Doris Kearns Goodwin about Lincoln's *Team of Rivals.*" *Prologue Magazine* 38, no. 1 (Spring 2006). https://www.archives.gov/publications/prologue/2006/spring/interview.html.

———. *Leadership in Turbulent Times.* New York: Simon and Schuster, 2018.

Gregg, Edward. *Queen Anne.* New York: Routledge, Kegan, Paul, 1980.

Grobe, E. P. "Gabriel and Sébastien Brémond." *Romance Notes* 4, no. 2 (1963): 132–35.

Grynbaum, Michael M. "Trump Renews Pledge to 'Take a Strong Look' at Libel Laws." *New York Times,* January 10, 2018.

Hamburger, Philip. "The Development of the Law of Seditious Libel and the Control of the Press." *Stanford Law Review* 37 (1985): 661–755.

Hamilton, Anthony. *Memoirs of Count de Grammont: Containing the History of the English Court under Charles II.* Translated and edited by Sir Walter Scott. London: Swann Sonnenschein, 1911.

Hamilton, David. *Diary of Sir David Hamilton.* Edited by Philip Roberts. Oxford: Clarendon Press, 1975.

Harris, Frances. *A Passion for Government: The Life of Sarah, Duchess of Marlborough.* Oxford: Clarendon Press, 1991.

Hawkins, William. *A Treatise of the Pleas of the Crown: or a System of the Principal Matters Relating to that Subject.* 2 vols. London: J. Walthoe, 1716–21.

Hearne, Thomas. *Remarks and Collections.* Edited by C. E. Doble et al. 11 vols. Oxford: Clarendon Press, 1886.

Herman, Ruth. *The Business of a Woman: The Political Writings of Delarivier Manley.* Newark: University of Delaware Press, 2003.

Hoadly, Benjamin. *The Works of Benjamin Hoadly, D.D.* 3 vols. London: W. Boyer and J. Nichols, 1773.

Hoffer, Peter Charles, and N. E. H. Hull. *Impeachment in America, 1635–1805.* New Haven, CT: Yale University Press, 1984.

Holmes, Geoffrey. *British Politics in the Age of Anne.* New York: St. Martin's Press, 1967.

———. *The Trial of Doctor Sacheverell.* London: Eyre Methuen, 1973.

House of Commons. *Journal of the House of Commons: Vol. 16, 1708–1711.* London: Her Majesty's Stationer's Office, 1803.

House of Lords. *Journal of the House of Lords: Vol. 19, 1709–1714.* London: Her Majesty's Stationer's Office, 1767–1830.

Howell, T. B. *A Complete Collection of State Trials and Proceedings for High Treason and Other Misdemeanors.* 21 vols. London: T. C. Hansard, 1816.

An Impartial Account of What Pass'd most Remarkable in the Last Session of Parliament, Relating to the Case of Dr Henry Sacheverell. N.p., 1710. [Title page falsely lists Jacob Tonson as publisher.]

Johnson, Samuel. *Lives of the Most Eminent English Poets (1779–81).* Edited by Roger Lonsdale. 4 vols. Oxford: Oxford University Press, 2006.

Jordan, Miriam. "Farmworkers, Mostly Undocumented, Become 'Essential' during Pandemic." *New York Times,* April 2, 2020. Online edition.

K., J. *Dr Sacheverel's Progress from London to his Rectory in Salatin in Shropshire.* London: The Booksellers of London and Westminster, 1710.

[Kennett, White]. *A Visit to St Saviour's, Southwark, with Advice to Dr. Sachevrell's preachers there.* London: A. Baldwin, 1710.

[King, William]. *A Vindication of the Reverend Dr. Henry Sacheverell.* 2nd ed. London: H. Clements, 1711.

Klein, Ezra. *Why We're Polarized.* New York: Simon & Schuster, 2020. eBook.

Krugman, Paul. "Bernie Sanders Is Going for Broke: Is Maximalism the Best Political Strategy?" *New York Times,* March 5, 2020. Online edition.

Landler, Mark. "Brexit Turmoil Increases as Court Rebukes Boris Johnson." *New York Times,* September 24, 2019.

Latour, Bruno. *Down to Earth: Politics in the New Climatic Regime.* Cambridge: Polity, 2018.

Lesaffer, Randall. "The Peace of Utrecht and the Balance of Power," *OUPblog,* November 10, 2014. https://blog.oup.com/2014/11/utrecht-peace-treaty-balance-power-europe.

Life and Character of John Barber. London: T. Cooper, 1741.

Luttrell, Narcissus. *A Brief Historical Relation of State Affairs from September 1678 to April 1714.* 6 vols. Oxford: Clarendon Press, 1857.

M., W. *The Female Wits: or The Triumvirate of Poets at Rehearsal. A Comedy.* London, 1704. Edited by L. Hook. Augustan Reprint Society publication 124. Los Angeles: William Andrew Clark Memorial Library, 1967.

Machievelli, Niccolò. *The Works of the Famous Nicholas Machiavel.* London, 1680.

Madison, James, Alexander Hamilton, and John Jay. *The Federalist Papers,* ed. Isaac Kramnick. Harmondsworth, Middlesex: Penguin Books, 1987.

Manley, Delarivier. *Selected Works of Delarivier Manley.* Edited by Rachel Carnell and Ruth Herman. 5 vols. London: Pickering & Chatto, 2005.

Marlborough, Sarah, Duchess of. *Memoirs of Sarah, Duchess of Marlborough.* Edited by William King. London: George Routledge, 1930; New York: Kraus Reprint, 1969.

Marvell, Andrew. *An Account of the Growth of Popery.* Amsterdam, 1677.

[Maynwaring, Arthur]. *Four Letters to a Friend in North Briton, Upon the Publishing the Tryal of Dr. Sacheverell.* London, 1710.

Mills, James N., Kenneth L. Gage, and Ali S. Khan, "Potential Influence of Climate Change on Vector-Borne and Zoonotic Diseases: A Review and

Proposed Rresearch Plan." *Environmental Health Perspectives* 118, no. 11 (2010): 1507–14.

Mounk, Yascha. "Brexit Is a Cultural Revolution." *Atlantic,* October 24, 2019. Online edition.

New York Times Editorial Board. "Why President Trump's Ukraine Scheme Matters." *New York Times,* November 24, 2019, online edition.

Nye, Eric W. "Pounds Sterling to Dollars: Historical Conversion of Currency." https://www.uwyo.edu/numimage/currency.htm.

The Officers Address to the Ladies. London: A. Baldwin, 1710.

Oldmixon, John. *The History of England, During the Reigns of King William and Queen Mary, Queen Anne, King George I.* London: Thomas Cox, Richard Ford, and Richard Hett, 1735.

Otterness, Philip. *Becoming German: The 1709 Palatine Migration to New York.* Ithaca, NY: Cornell University Press, 2004.

Pew Research Center, "Party Affiliation," *Religious Landscape Study* (2014). https://www.pewforum.org/religious-landscape-study/party-affiliation/.

Pincus, Steve. *1688: The First Modern* Revolution. New Haven, CT: Yale University Press, 2009.

Pointon, Marcia. "Material Manouvres: Sarah Churchill, Duchess of Marlborough, and the Power of Artefacts." *Art History* 32, no. 3 (June 2009): 485–515.

Prokopios of Kaisareia. *The Secret History.* Edited by Anthony Kaldellis. Indianapolis: Hackett, 2010.

Rauch, Jonathan. "Autocorrect: How Advances in Real-time Fact-Checking Might Improve Our Politics." *Atlantic* 323, no. 5 (June 2019): 11–14.

Raven, James. *The Business of Books: Booksellers and the English Book Trade, 1450–1850.* New Haven, CT: Yale University Press, 2007.

Raworth, Kate. *Doughnut Economics: Seven Ways to Think Like a 21st-Century Economist.* London: Chelsea Green Publishing, 2017.

Rich, Nathaniel. *Losing Earth: A Recent History.* New York: Farrar, Straus and Giroux, 2019.

Sacheverell, Henry. *The Answer of Henry Sacheverll. D. D. to the Articles of Impeachment.* London, 1710.

———. *The Perils of False Brethren, in Church, and State: Set forth in a Sermon Preached before the Right Honourable the Lord-Mayor, Aldermen, and Citizens of London.* London: Henry Clements, 1709.

A Satyr against Love. London, 1703. [Title page falsely claims "Revised and Corrected by Mr. Congreve."]

Schmemann, Serge. "The Virus Comes for Democracy." *New York Times,* April 2, 2020. Online edition.

Siebert, Fredrick Seaton. *Freedom of the Press in England 1476–1776*. Urbana: University of Illinois Press, 1952.

Snyder, Henry. "The Duke of Marlborough's Request of His Captain-Generalcy for Life: A Reconsideration." *Journal for the Society of Army Historical Research* 45, no. 182 (1967): 67–83.

Society for the Diffusion of Useful Knowledge. *The Lives of Eminent Persons*. London: Baldwin and Craddock, 1833.

Somerset, Anne. *Queen Anne: The Politics of Passion*. New York: Knopf, 2013.

Speck, W. A. "James II and VII." *Oxford Dictionary of National Biography*, online edition, 2009. doi-org.winchester.idm.oclc.org/10.1093/ref:odnb/14593.

———. *Stability and Strife: England, 1714–1760*. Cambridge, MA: Harvard UniversityPress, 1977.

Starr, Kenneth W. *Communication from Kenneth W. Starr, Independent Counsel*. House Document 105–310. Washington, DC: US Government Printing Office, 1998.

Stewart, Katherine, and Caroline Fredrickson. "Bill Barr Thinks America Is Going to Hell." *New York Times*, December 29, 2019. Online edition.

Steele, Richard. *The Tatler*. Edited by Donald F. Bond. 3 vols. Oxford: Clarendon Press, 1987.

Sundstrom, Roy. "Sidney Godolphin." *Oxford Dictionary of National Biography*, online edition, 2004. https://doi-org.winchester.idm.oclc.org/10.1093/ref:odnb/10882.

———. *Sidney Godolphin: Servant of the* State. Newark: University of Delaware Press, 1992.

Sunstein, Cass R. *How Change Happens*. Cambridge, MA: MIT Press, 2019. eBook.

———. *Impeachment: A Citizen's Guide*. Cambridge, MA: Harvard University Press, 2017.

Swift, Jonathan. *The Conduct of the Allies*. In *The Prose Works of Jonathan Swift*. Edited by Temple Scott. 12 vols. Vol. 5, 55–124. London: George Bell, 1907; New York: AMS reprint, 1971.

———. *The Examiner and Other Pieces Written in 1710–1*. Edited by Herbert Davis. Oxford: Basil Blackwell, 1966.

———. *Journal to Stella*. Edited by Harold Williams. 2 vols. Oxford: Clarendon Press, 1963.

———. *Memoirs Relating to that Change which Happened in the Queen's Ministry in the Year 1710*. In *The Prose Works of Jonathan Swift*. Edited by Temple Scott. 12 vols. Vol. 5, 359–90. London: George Bell, 1907; New York: AMS reprint, 1971.

Tinniswood, Adrian. *His Invention So Fertile: A Life of Christopher Wren.* London: Pimlico, 2002.

Tisdall, Simon. "Power, Equalty, Nationalism: How the Pandemic Will Reshape the World." *Guardian Weekly,* April 3, 2000, 9.

[Toland, John]. *High Church Display'd: Being a Complete History of the Affair of Dr. Sacheverell.* London, 1711.

Trevelyan, George Macaulay. *England under Queen Anne: The Peace and the Protestant Succession.* London: Longman, 1936.

Tribe, Laurence, and Joshua Matz. *To End a Presidency: The Power of Impeachment.* New York: Basic Books, 2018.

A True Answer; or, Remarks upon Dr. Sacheverell's Speech, March 7th, 1710. London: B. Bragg, 1710.

The Tryal of Dr. Henry Sacheverell, Before the House of Peers. London: Jacob Tonson, 1710.

Walker, Amy "Most Voters Think Risk of Violence against MPs Is 'Price Worth Paying' over Brexit." *Guardian,* October 24, 2019.

Walpole, Horace, *The Works of Horace Walpole,* 5 vols. London: G. and J. Robinson, 1798.

[Ward, Edward]. *The Whigs Unmask'd: Being the Secret History of the Calf's-Head-Club.* London: J. Morphew, 1713.

Ward, F. R. "The Early Influence of John Locke's Political Thought in England, 1689–1720." Ph.D. diss., University of California, 1995.

Witmer, Helen E. *The Property Qualifiations of Members of Parliament.* New York: Columbia University Press, 1943.

Worsley, Lucy, and David Souden. *Hampton Court Palace: The Official Illustrated History.* London: Merrell, 2005.

INDEX

Illustrations are indicated by italicized illustration gallery page number.

Account of the Conduct of the Dowager Duchess of Marlborough, An, 81, 183–84, 218
Account of the Growth of Popery (Marvell), 18–19, 33
Addison, Joseph, 41–42, 98
Adventures of Rivella, The (Manley), 34, 37–38, 40, 55, 124, 130, 217
Althorp (Spencer family estate), 29, 135
Anekdota (Procopius), 44, 127
Anglican Church. *See* Church of England
Anglo-Dutch wars, 20
Anne, Queen of Great Britain: accusation of lesbianism, 9, 80–81; and cabinet ministers, xi, 33, 212; childhood and adolescence, 20–21; death of, 5, 215; depicted in Manley's secret histories, 45, 51–54, 78, 176, 186–87, 206–7; exile from William and Mary's court, 26, 30; friendships with women, 17, 21; and Glorious Revolution, 6, 24, 28, 140, 147, 228; and Sidney Godolphin, 22, 50, 199, 202–3; handwriting of, 109; and Robert Harley, 185, 201, 214; and immigration, 4, 121–22; lack of conversational skill, 3, 22, 29, 109, 154; leadership style, 109–11, 154, 184, 218–19, 225, 235n1; and Duchess of Marlborough, 7–8, 9, 21, 22, 71–74, 77–78, 82, 136, 181–84, 208, 210; and Duke of Marlborough, 12, 14, 85–85, 105–8, 110, 209; marriage of, 21; and Abigail Masham, 9–10, 73, 76, 80; memory of, 154; and Parliament, 173, 193, 200, 204; portrait of, *gallery 3;* and religion, 4, 114, 155; and Sacheverell's impeachment, 139–40, 145–46, 165–67, 169, 172, 188; and Earl of Sunderland, 189–91; and Tories, 113, 134, 193, 198, 210, 221; and Union with Scotland, 229–30; and War of Spanish Succession, 88, 134, 185; and Whigs, 72, 134, 221, 224
Apology for the Life of Colley Cibber, 93
Aumont, Louis duc d', 130

Backlash: The Undeclared War against Women (Faludi), 231
backlash, political (contemporary), 1, 220–21, 223, 230–33. *See also* Tory backlash of 1710
Bacon, Francis, 41, 127
Baldwin, Abigail, 120, 139
Banb—y Apes, The, 196–97
Barber, John (printer): and *Memoirs of Europe,* 175; and *New Atalantis,* 210; relationship with Manley, 32, 42–43, 45, 57, 125–26, 130, 137
Barrier Treaty, 86, 88
Barry, Elizabeth (actress), 41, 88
Bath-Albemarle lawsuit, 41–42, 74
Bentinck, William. *See* Portland, Earl of
Bishop Burnet's History of His Own Time, 93–94, 203–5
Blagge, Margaret. *See* Godolphin, Margaret
Blenheim, Battle of, 11–12, 14, 27, 97, 209; tapestries commemorating, 135

Blenheim Palace, 12; architect for, 87, 94, 138; construction of, 7, 27, 29, 187, 205, 216–17; costs of, 87; Manley's satire of, 47, 54, 135, 187, 211
Boleyn, Anne (wife of Henry VIII), 19
Bowman, Frank, 99–100, 259n82
Boyer, Abel, 157
Brexit, 1, 5, 222, 229–31, 245n42, 251n73, 253n29, 254n32, 255n50
Brief History of the Poor Palatine Refugees, A (Defoe), 123
Brown, Beatrice Curtis, 109
Browne, Joseph, 50, 68, 239n45
Burgess, Daniel (Presbyterian minister), 151–53, 157, 188
Burnet, Gilbert (bishop of Salisbury), 65, 121, 129, 139, 189, 205

Cadogan, William, 205
Cardonnel, Adam de, 13
Castlemaine, Countess of. *See* Cleveland, Duchess of
Cat, Christopher (tavern chef), 98
Catholicism: and Charles II, 20, 127; and Henry VIII, 19; and James II, 20–23, 56; and Glorious Revolution, 25, 98, 104; and Guy Fawkes Day, 58; perceived threat of, 2, 8, 11, 15–16, 18, 47, 196, 224
Cavendish, Georgianna. *See* Devonshire, Duchess of
Charles Edward Stuart (grandson of James II), 214
Charles II, King of England: death of, 22; illegitimate children and grandchildren of, 40, 48; and Manley's father, 36; and payments from Louis XIV, 11, 15, 19–20, 33, 224, 236n24; and relationship with Duchess of Cleveland, 15–16, 74; secret histories about, 32, 35, 44–45, 52, 127
Churchill, Arabella (sister to John), 15, 46
Churchill, John (son of John and Sarah), 50, 68, 72, 94–95
Churchill, John. *See* Marlborough, Duke of
Churchill, Sarah. *See* Marlborough, Duchess of
Churchill, Winston: comments on Marlborough, 10, 26, 86, 88, 105, 135, 213, 219; view of Manley, 6, 38, 219
Church of England, 8, 160; and Queen Anne, 4, 105, 140, 145, 163, 193, 207; and Glorious Revolution, 60; and Guy Fawkes Day, 58; and high church clergy, 84, 104; and latitudinarianism, 65; and Duke of Marlborough, 16, 22–23; and passive obedience, 172; perceived threats to, 4, 59, 65, 102, 140, 144, 149, 158, 193, 205, 216, 224; and pluralism, 194–95; and political resistance, 115. *See also* occasional conformity; Toleration Act of 1689
Clements, Henry (printer), 86, 166, 174, 217
Cleveland, Duchess of (Barbara Palmer; née Villiers): and Charles II, 15, 45, 127; and Manley, 38–40, 71; in Manley's works, 44; and Duke of Marlborough, 16–17, 46, 74
Compton, Henry (bishop of London), 24, 140, 149
Congreve, William, 129; *Love for Love*, 92, 98; portrait of, *gallery 12;* relationship with Henrietta Godolphin, 92, 95–96, 218; *Tears of Amaryllis*, 94
constitution, U.K., 5, 59, 100, 102, 130, 143, 150, 159
Constitution, U.S., 1, 223–24, 226, 259n82
Constitutional Convention (U.S.), 237n27
Copyright Act of 1710, 173

COVID-19, 222, 224, 229–30, 232
Cowper, Sarah, Lady (née Holled; diarist), 52, 69, 141
Cowper, Spencer (brother of William), 44, 148
Cowper, William (lord chancellor of Great Britain): in Manley's works, 44, 52, 69; and Sacheverell's impeachment, 98, 115, 141–42, 165, 171, 177, 204
Cunningham, Alexander (historian), 99–101, 104

Defoe, Daniel, 62, 63, 131, 137, 158, 185, 205; *A Brief History of the Poor Palatine Refugees,* 123; *An Essay on Projects,* 201; *An Essay on Publick Credit,* 200–201; *The Shortest Way with the Dissenters,* 63; *The True-Born Englishman,* 26–27
Devonshire, Duchess of (Georgianna Cavendish; née Spencer), 218
Devonshire, Duke of, 164, 204
Dissenters (Dissenting Protestants): and Queen Anne, 145, 189; cultural politics of, 59, 179, 221; and Daniel Defoe, 131, 201; and Robert Harley, 103, 198, 205; and occasional conformity, 59, 116, 216, 225; and Sacheverell's sermon, 59, 61, 63–64, 66; and Toleration Act, 143, 148–49; violence toward, 187–88, 192
Dolben, John, 101–2, 152
Dover, Secret Treat of, 18, 20, 33
Dryden, John, 128

elections of 1710, 172–73, 193–96, 198, 200–201, 203–7, 214–17, 228
Elizabeth I, Queen of England, 58, 91, 100, 109, 196
Elizabeth II, Queen of the United Kingdom, 222–23, 236n7
Essay on Projects, An (Defoe), 201
Essay on Public Credit, An (Defoe), 200–201
Essex, Earl of (favorite of Elizabeth I), 91
Essex, Earl of, Algernon Capell (lieutenant of the Tower of London), 105
Evelyn, John, 96
Examiner, The (Swift, Manley), 207, 210

fake news, 227, 232
Faludi, Susan, 231
Favourite, The (Field), 80
Favourite, The (film), 3, 235n1
Federalist Papers, The (Hamilton, Madison, Jay), 230
Female Wits, The (W. M.), 40
Field, Ophelia, 80
Four Letters to a Friend in North Briton (Maynwaring), 180

Garrard, Samuel (lord mayor of London), 60
Gazette. See *London Gazette*
Gelfand, Michele, 158, 251n73
George, Prince of Denmark (consort of Queen Anne), 9, 21, 24, 28
George I, King of Great Britain, 109, 213, 215–18, 232
Glorious Revolution (Revolution of 1688), 2, 23–25, 215, 219–23, 225–28; and Queen Anne, 28, 48, 105, 108–9, 140, 167, 172, 198; in histories of England, 5, 23, 102; and Benjamin Hoadly, 114; and John Locke, 97; Manley's satire of, 37, 44, 47, 51; and Duke of Marlborough, 11, 104; and Henry Sacheverell, 58–60, 102–3, 138–39; and Sacheverell's impeachment trial, 143–50, 180. *See also* Pincus, Steve; Revolution principles; Whig interpretation of history
Godolphin, Francis (son of Sidney), 68, 93–94, 96

Godolphin, Henrietta (née Churchill; Duchess of Marlborough *suo jure*), 68, 92–96, 136; portrait of, *gallery 12*
Godolphin, Margaret (née Blagge), 67, 96
Godolphin, Mary (daughter of Henrietta), 96, 218
Godolphin, Sidney, Earl of: character, 67–68; correspondence with Duke of Marlborough, 12, 14, 106, 159, 190–91, 203, 212; death of, 213; dismissal by Queen Anne, 199–202, 206; friendship with Duchess of Marlborough, 28, 72, 75, 77; and Robert Harley, 184; and impeachment of Sacheverell, 100, 119, 169, 171; marriage of, 67; mentoring of Queen Anne, 50, 109, 181; portrait of, *gallery 2;* satirized by Manley, 45, 49, 51, 53–54, 69, 108, 126–28, 207; satirized by Sacheverell, 66; and Toryism, 99; and Treasury, 67, 199, 203; and Whigs, 65, 69–70
Godolphin, William (son of Henrietta and Francis), 149
Godolphin House, 95
Grand Alliance, 3, 7, 86
Granville, George (Baron Lansdowne), 125
Grub Street, 27, 33, 126
Gunpowder Plot, 2, 58
Guy Fawkes Day, 2, 4, 24; Sacheverell's sermon on, 58, 64, 120, 144, 171, 192

Hamilton, David (Queen Anne's doctor), 81, 170, 208
Hampton Court Palace, 87, 109–11, 219
Harcourt, Simon, 159–60, 195
Harley, Robert: as chancellor of the exchequer, 204; coordination with Abigail Masham, 9, 11; and Daniel Defoe, 63, 158–59, 201; dismissal by Queen Anne, 214; and Sidney Godolphin, 200, 202–3; influence on Queen Anne, 3, 11, 76–77, 140, 154, 181, 184–85, 189; and Delarivier Manley, 53–54, 77–79, 206, 214; and Duke of Marlborough, 211, 213; as Earl of Oxford, 217; and political moderation, 198, 205; portrait of, *gallery 4;* removal from ministry in 1708, 108, 172; and Henry Sacheverell, 103, 170, 195; and Jonathan Swift, 207, 209–10
Hattige: or the Amours of the King of Tamaran (Brémond), 45, 236n17
Hearne, Thomas (diarist), 115, 131, 144, 156–57, 163
Hearst, Edward and Katherine (adoptive parents to Henry Sacheverell), 61
Henry VIII (king of England), 19, 100, 160, 229
Hill, Jack (brother of Abigail Masham), 105
Hoadly, Benjamin, 114, 197
Holmes, Geoffrey, 60, 117, 157–58
Holy Roman emperor, 8, 88, 113, 210, 213
Holy Roman Empire, 7–8
Holywell (Jenyns family manor house), 29, 213
Horsey, Captain (of Her Majesty's Foot Guards), 155
Howard, Stuarta Werburge (illegitimate granddaughter of Charles II), 48

immigration, 3, 122–23, 221, 229, 248n34. *See also* Palatine immigrants
impeachment: and Queen Anne's view of, 139, 166, 170, 172, 193; of Bill Clinton, 226; cultural divides over, 5; in English history, 19, 99–101, 165, 215, 245n40, 259n82; of Robert Harley, 217–18; of Richard Nixon, 226; and punishment for Sacheverell, 170–72; and riots during Sacheverell trial, 151–57; trial of Sacheverell, 2, 102, 113–18, 141–51, 161–79; of Donald Trump, 1, 224–25; in United States,

223, 245n40 ; and vote on Sacheverell impeachment, 168, 206; and Westminster Hall, 137; and Whigs, 4, 137, 157–58, 163, 173

James Francis Edward Stuart (son of James II, half-brother to Queen Anne), 8, 23, 47, 66, 150, 172–73, 206, 213–15, 224
James II, King of England (previously Duke of York): and Catholicism, 11, 21–22, 60; death of, 8, 125; and John Churchill, 46–47; depicted in Manley's *New Atalantis,* 5; and Glorious Revolution, 2, 11, 24–25, 147, 215, 222; second wife of, 35, 150; womanizing of, 74
Jay, John, 230
Jekyll, Joseph, 146–47
Jenyns, Richard (father to Sarah, Duchess of Marlborough), 35–36
Johnson, Boris, 1, 222, 245n42
Johnson, Samuel, 180
Junto, Whig. *See* Whig Junto

Kensington Palace, 8–9, 80, 82, 110, 136, 173, 182, 255n56
King, Peter, 148
Kit-Kat Club, 3, 91, 98–101, 112, 124, 129, 244n32

Landguard Fort, Suffolk, 126
latitudinarianism, 65
Latour, Bruno, 235
Lechmere, Nicholas (queen's counsel), 143–44, 156
Leopold I, Holy Roman Emperor, 8
lesbianism, accusations of, 3, 9, 76–77, 79–82, 108, 235n5
L'Estrange, Roger (royal licenser), 32
Letters Writen by Mrs. Manley, 125
libel, seditious: definition of, 32–33; and Defoe's *Shortest Way,* 63; and lapse of Licensing Act, 117; legal precedents for, 100; and Manley's arrest and trial, 112, 130–32, 142, 175–76; and Manley's *New Atalantis,* 2, 4, 32–33, 45, 55, 127–78; Duchess of Marlborough's views on, 208, 211, 227; and Sacheverell's sermon, 69, 89, 99–102, 127–28, 165, 223; Richard Steele's comments on, 91; and Earl of Sunderland prosecution of, 33, 90
Licensing Act, lapse of, 33, 117, 173, 179, 227
Locke, John, 97, 114
London Gazette, 42, 90
Louis XIV, King of France: and balance of power in Europe, 2, 6, 8; and Catholicism, 23, 121; and Charles II, 15–16, 18–19, 33, 127, 224, 236n24; and Duke of Marlborough, 20, 212; and peace negotiations, 11, 14, 207; and War of Spanish Succession, 3, 8, 82, 126, 185–86; and William III, 26–27
Love for Love (Congreve), 92, 98
Luttrell, Narcissus (diarist), 131, 156

Magdalen College, Oxford, ix, 57, 62–63, 66, 195
Maintenon, Marquise ("Madame") de (Françoise d'Aubigné), 78–79
Malplaquet, Battle of, xi, 7, 10–14, 29–30, 80, 87–88, 134, 176, 190, 235n1
Manley, Cornelia (sister of Delarivier), 37
Manley, Delarivier: *The Adventures of Rivella,* 34, 37–38, 55, 124, 130, 217, 238; arrest for libel, 31–32, 56–57; and John Barber (printer), 42–43, 45; and Bath-Albemarle lawsuit, 74; bigamous marriage of, 39; and Duchess of Cleveland, 39–40; death of, 218; depicted in *The Female Wits,* 40; *The Duke of Marlborough's Vindication,* 210–11; *The Examiner,* 210;

Manley, Delarivier (*continued*)
father (Roger), 26, 34–37; friendship with Jonathan Swift, 43, 55, 210–11; and Robert Harley, 159; interrogation by Sunderland; libel trial, 4, 56, 112–13, 124–32; maligned by Winston Churchill, 6, 38; *Memoirs of Europe,* 174–77, 185–89, 206–7; and Mary Pix, 40; relationship with John Tilly, 41; *The Royal Mistress,* 41; and Richard Steele, 41–42, 45, 90–91, 129, 186, 248n50; sues for habeas corpus, 56; and Catherine Trotter, 40. See also *New Atalantis*

Manley, John (cousin and bigamous husband of Delarivier), 37–39, 62, 159

Manley, Roger (father of Delarivier), 34–37

Marlborough, Duchess of (Henrietta Godolphin; née Churchill). *See* Godolphin, Henrietta

Marlborough, Duchess of (Sarah Churchill; née Jenyns), *Account of the Conduct of,* 81, 183, 202; correspondence with Queen Anne, 71, 75, 78–80, 82–83, 176; court positions of, 28; and death of son John, 94; depicted in Manley's secret histories, 51–52, 176, 186–87; dismissal by Queen Anne, 209; exile in Frankfurt, 212–13; father of, 35; friendship with Queen Anne, 17, 21–22, 26, 71–72, 81, 107, 181; friendship with Sidney Godolphin, 50, 69–70, 96; friendship with Arthur Maynwaring, 55, 74, 78; handwriting of, 109; and Henrietta (daughter), 95–96, 218; losing favor with Queen Anne, 29, 73, 85, 92, 133–34, 181–83, 189; as maid of honor, 17, 35–37; and Marlborough House, 135–38; marriage of, 18, 75, 93; and Abigail Masham, 8–11, 74–76, 82, 88, 107; portrait of, *gallery 2;* and privy purse accounts, 77, 110, 136, 208, 210–11; role in Glorious Revolution, 24; and Sacheverell trial, 141–42, 146, 160–62; and Earl of Sunderland, 28; and Jonathan Swift, 208; and threat of blackmail, 77, 210; and Robert Walpole, 218

Marlborough, Duke of (John Churchill), 6; and Queen Anne, 9, 106, 111, 211; arrest for treason, 26, 56; and Blenheim, Battle of, 11–12, 14, 27, 87; and Blenheim Palace, 87, 138, 205, 216–17; and Charles II, 15–16; and captain-generalcy, 27, 30, 85–86, 105; childhood, 15; and Duchess of Cleveland, 16–17; death of, 218; depicted in Manley's secret histories, 14, 16–17, 39, 44–47, 49, 54, 127, 186–88, 207, 210–11; defection to William of Orange, 23–24; dismissal by Queen, 212; European outlook of, 86, 113, 123; and George I, 215; and Glorious Revolution, 23–24, 104, 227; and Sidney Godolphin, 70; and James II, 20, 22–23; as "King John," 30, 88; and Malplaquet, Battle of, 7–8, 12–13, 89; and military appointments crisis, 105–8, 181; military genius of, 67, 219; and Oudenarde, Battle of, 10–11; portrait of, *gallery 1;* and princedom of Mindelheim, 88; and Ramillies, Battle of, 11; and Sacheverell impeachment, 99–100, 132; sister of (Arabella), 37; and Earl of Sunderland's dismissal, 191; and Toryism, 25, 98–99; and Whigs, 53, 100, 172; William III's distrust of, 26

Marlborough House, 135–38, 208–9

Marvell, Andrew, 18, 33

Mary I (Queen of England), 19

Mary II (Queen of England), 2, 20, 32, 110, 182, 219; death of, 27; and Glorious Revolution, 25, 48, 97, 109,

147, 222; and rift with sister Anne, 26, 30, 73
Masham, Abigail (née Hill): accusations of lesbianism, 78–81; brother of, 112; depicted in Manley's secret histories, 31, 33–34, 53–54, 108, 132, 175, 186, 207; favorite of Queen Anne, 8–10, 28, 73, 75, 139–40, 154, 235n1; keeper of the privy purse, 209; liaison for Robert Harley, 54, 76, 109, 181; and the Marlboroughs, 10, 75, 80, 88, 92, 105–6, 119; portrait of, *gallery 4*
Matz, Joshua, 19
Maynwaring, Arthur: death of, 213; *Four Letters to a Friend,* 180–81; and freedom of press, 84, 97, 211; friendship with Duchess of Marlborough, 9, 55, 74–79, 95; and Kit-Cat club, 98, 129; *The Medley,* 210; portrait of, *gallery 11;* relationship with Anne Oldfield, 74, 96; and *The Rival Dutchess,* 79; satirical writings of, 74, 79, 180, 210
meetinghouses (Dissenting place of worship): Thomas Bradbury's, 153; Daniel Burgess's, 151–52, 157, *gallery 9;* Jabez Earl's, 153; John England's, 188–89; Christopher Taylor's, 153; Samuel Wight's, 155
Memoirs and Manners of . . . the New Atalantis (Manley). See *New Atalantis, The*
Memoirs of Europe (Manley), 174–77, 185–89, 206–7; title page of, *gallery 10*
Mindleheim, princedom of, 88
Modena, Mary of (wife of James II), 17, 35, 150
Mons, siege of, 11, 14
Montagu, James (attorney general), 112, 142–44
Montagu, Ralph, Duke of, 42, 74, 93
Morgan, Delariviere (née Chomondeley), 36
Morphew, John (trade printer), 32, 45, 175, 178

Naturalization Act of 1709, 121–23
New Atalantis (Manley): depiction of Sidney Godolphin in, 45, 48, 51–53, 65, 128–29; depiction of Marlboroughs in, 13–17, 28, 45, 51–55, 71; depiction of Abigail Masham in, 108; depiction of Richard Steele in, 42, 45; first volume of, 52; frontispiece to, *gallery 5;* keys for, 45, 89; lesbianism in, 77–79; libel charge for, 32–34; libel trial for, 113, 124–32; mocked in *The Tatler* (Steele), 90–91; publication of, 44, 52; second volume of, 44, 89–90; as secret history, 44–45, 127–28; seizure of, 83, 89; summary of, 43–55; and Earl of Sunderland, 33–34, 55–56; title page of, *gallery 6;* as Varronian satire, 65, 127–28
New Atlantis, The (Bacon), 127
Newgate Prison, 131
Newington-Butts, church of, 102–3
Nichols, Mr. (grocer), 116
Nimrod, 110

occasional conformity, 59, 64, 216, 225, 259n83
Officers Address to the Ladies, The, 120–21
Oldfield, Anne (actress), 74, 78, 91, 96
Oldmixon, John, 195
Original and Institution of Civil Government Discussed, The (Hoadly), 114
Oudenarde, Battle of, 11, 82
Oxford, Earl of. *See* Harley, Robert

Palatine immigrants, 4, 121–23, 157–58, 229
Parker, Thomas, 149–50, 162–63, 166, 178
Parliament, prorogation of, 1, 173, 182, 193, 225, 245n42, 254n32

Parliamentary elections. 173, 193–96, 200–201, 203–7, 214–16. *See also* elections of 1710; Septennial Act; Triennial Act
Perils of False Brethren (Sacheverell's published sermon): burning of, 192; delivered as a sermon, 59-60, 64–66; publication of, 83–84, 89, 98. *See also* impeachment; Sacheverell, Henry
Petre, Father Edward (Jesuit priest), 20
Pierrepont, Lady Mary, 44, 89–90
Pile, Seymour (Sir), 118
Pincus, Steve, 23, 219, 235n2, 237n35, 259n80
Pix, Mary, 40
Portland, Earl of (William Bentinck), 48–49
Procopius of Caesarea, 44, 127
Protestantism, England's conversion to, 19

Queen's Bench, Court of the, 45, 56, 99, 112–13, 116; and Manley's libel trial, 32, 124, 128–31

racehorses, Godolphin Arabian line, 94, 244n22
Ramillies, Battle of, 11, 209
religious toleration, 5, 23, 187, 223, 225. *See also* Toleration Act of 1689
Revolution principles, 2, 53, 97, 99, 116, 180. *See also* Glorious Revolution
Riley (glover in Oxford), 63
Rival Dutchess, The, 79
Royal Mistress, The (Manley), 41

Sacheverell, Benjamin (uncle of Henry), 61
Sacheverell, Henry: adoption of, 61; *Answer* (to impeachment articles), 113–15; death of, 218; depicted in Manley's secret histories, 132, 176–77, 185, 187; education of, 62; as electioneering tool, 204, 206, 217; impeachment of, 4–5, 101–5; impeachment trial of, 134, 139–69, *gallery 7;* legacy of, 219; and Magdalen College, 62–62, 195; mezzotint engraving of, 119–21, *gallery 6;* mobs supporting, 123, 188, 204; and passive obedience, 60; popularity of, 84, 121; portrait of, 57, 247n27, *gallery 6;* Selattyn (Wales), living of and journey to, 194–97; sentencing of, 169–72, 182; sermon preached on Guy Fawkes Day, 58–70, 83, 89. *See also* impeachment; *Perils of False Brethren;* Toleration Act of 1689
Santlow, Hester, 98
satire: Juvenilian, 44; and libel, 90–91; Varronian, 65, 127–28. *See also* Licensing Act, lapse of; secret history
Satyr against Love, A, 95, 98
secret history (genre), 25, 44–45, 69, 127, 158. See also *Anekdota; New Atalantis; Secret History of . . . Queen Zarah*
Secret History of Queen Zarah and the Zarazians, The (Browne), 50, 68, 239n45
Secret Memoirs and Manners of . . . the New Atalantis. See *New Atalantis*
Secret Treaty of Dover, 18, 20, 33
seditious libel. *See* libel
Selattyn, Wales, 195, 197
Septennial Act, 172, 216, 228
shared governance, 6, 230
Shortest Way with the Dissenters, The (Defoe), 63
Somers, John, 53, 100, 108
Somerset, Anne, 80–81
Somerset: Duchess of (Catherine Seymour; née Wyndham), 146, 182, 184, 209; Duke of (Charles Seymour), 167–69, 182, 184, 204

Southwark Cathedral. *See* St. Saviour's Church
Spanish Succession, War of. *See* War of Spanish Succession
Spectator, The (Addison and Steele), 41
Spencer, Charles. *See* Sunderland, third Earl of
Spencer, Diana (granddaughter of Sarah Churchill), 218
Spencer, Diana Francis (wife of Prince Charles), 218
St. Bride's Church, London, 140
Steele, Richard: depicted in Manley's secret histories, 42, 45, 129, 186; editor of *London Gazette,* 42, 90; friendship with Addison, 41–42; friendship with Manley, 41–42; and Kit-Cat club, 98; portrait of, *gallery 10;* and *Tatler,* 90–91
St. James's Palace, 10, 17, 66, 85, 106, 110, 113, 136, 145–46, 154
St. Margaret's Church, Lothbury, 84
St. Paul's Cathedral: military thanksgiving services in, 10, 88; rebuilding of, 57; Sacheverell preaching in, 57–58, 65–66, 217. *See also* Wren, Christopher
St. Saviour's Church, Southwark, 63–64, 102–3, 217
Sunderland, Countess of (Anne Spencer; née Churchill), 13, 29, 93, 136, 184, 209, 216
Sunderland, third Earl of (Charles Spencer), 28–29, 31–35; dismissal of, 189–92, 199; and Manley's libel charge, 54–55, 124–26, 129–30, 175; and Palatine immigrants, 121–23; portrait of, *gallery 2;* and the press, 158–59; and Sacheverell's impeachment,100, 116, 153–55; and Whig principles, 90, 97
Sunstein, Cass, 232
Swift, Jonathan: Queen Anne's view of, 79; comments on Queen Anne, 184–85; *The Conduct of the Allies,* 210; *The Examiner,* 207; and Robert Harley, 159, 210; and Delarivier Manley, 43, 55, 211; Duchess of Marlborough's view of, 208, 227; portrait of, *gallery 11; A Tale of a Tub,* 70
Syon House, 26

Tatler, The (Steele), 41, 90–91, 129, 186
Tears of Amaryllis (Congreve), 94–95
Tenison, Thomas (archbishop of Canterbury), 64
Thompson, William, 149
Tilly, John (governor of Fleet Prison), 41–42, 55
Toleration Act of 1689, 2, 4, 187, 219, 223; Sacheverell's repudiation of, 59, 65, 84, 102, 116, 158; Whig defense of, 143–44, 146, 148–49
Tonson, Jacob (printer), 173–75, 177–80
Tory backlash of 1710, 3–5, 169, 193, 206, 210, 215–16, 219–26, 229, 232
Tribe, Laurence, 19
Triennial Act, 172, 214, 216
Trotter, Catherine, 40, 79
True-Born Englishman, The (Defoe), 26, 131
Tryal of Doctor Henry Sacheverell, 177, 180, 187, 226
Two Treatises of Government (Locke), 97, 114

Unhappy Favourite, The, 91–92
Union of 1707 (with Scotland), 2, 149, 159, 199, 229–30
Utrecht, Treaty of, 213–15, 225

Vanbrugh, John, 87, 94
Varronian satire, 65, 127–28. *See also* satire

Villars, Duke of (Charles-Louis-Hector), 1, 12
Villiers, Barbara. *See* Cleveland, Duchess of

Walpole, Robert, 109, 119, 147–48, 208, 216, 218–21
War of Spanish Succession, 2–3, 8–9; costs of, 11, 49, 89, 199, 209, 213–14; and Robert Harley, 184; and an "honourable peace," 14, 129; and Duke of Marlborough, 30, 44, 54, 76, 82, 86, 89, 190, 224; and "No Peace without Spain," 186; Parliamentary funding for, 33, 65, 71; Tory view of, 126, 134, 204, 207, 210; winter breaks from, 70. *See also* Utrecht, Treaty of; *and under names of individual battles:* Blenheim; Malplaquet; Oudenarde; Ramillies
Wentworth, Thomas (Lord Raby), 136, 170
Westby, Mr. (of the Six Clerks' Office), 116
Westminster Hall, 112; and Manley's trial, 113, 124, 131; and Sacheverell's trial, 32, 112–13, 115, 118, 124, 130–33, 139, 141, 150–52, 167, 171. *See also* Wren, Christopher
Whig interpretation of history, 5, 102, 219, 235n3
Whig Junto, 53, 56, 86, 93, 108, 118, 170
Whitehall Palace, 21, 24, 51, 87, 101, 140, 153, 211
Whole Duty of Man, The (Allestree), 76, 93
Why We're Polarized (Klein), 231
William III, King of England and Prince of Orange: death of, 27; depicted in *New Atalantis,* 47–49, 51; and Glorious Revolution, 2, 20–24, 97, 109, 143, 147; and Louis XIV, 8, 27; and Duke of Marlborough, 20–24, 26, 27. *See also* William and Mary, reign of
William and Mary, reign of, 2, 30, 32, 49, 73, 125; and Hampton Court, 109–11, 219
Windsor Castle, 29, 85
Windsor Lodge, 29, 85, 106, 112–12, 135–36, 142
Woodstock, Oxfordshire, 29, 204
Woodward, John (trade printer), 32, 45, 175
Wortley Montagu, Lady Mary. *See* Pierrepont, Lady Mary
Wren, Christopher, 57, 110, 118, 132–33, 135, 137–38